Hippy Dinners

www.**transworldbooks**.co.uk

Hippy Dinners

A memoir of a rural childhood

Abbie Ross

Doubleday

LONDON · TORONTO · SYDNEY · AUCKLAND · JOHANNESBURG

TRANSWORLD PUBLISHERS
61–63 Uxbridge Road, London W5 5SA
A Random House Group Company
www.transworldbooks.co.uk

First published in Great Britain
in 2014 by Doubleday
an imprint of Transworld Publishers

A CIP catalogue record for this book
is available from the British Library.

ISBN 9780857522290

Addresses for Random House Group Ltd companies outside the UK
can be found at: www.randomhouse.co.uk
The Random House Group Ltd Reg. No. 954009

The Random House Group Limited supports the Forest Stewardship
Council® (FSC®), the leading international forest-certification organisation. Our
books carrying the FSC label are printed on FSC®-certified paper. FSC is the only
forest-certification scheme supported by the leading environmental organisations,
including Greenpeace. Our paper procurement policy can be found at
www.randomhouse.co.uk/environment

Typeset in 10.5/15 pt Scala by Falcon Oast Graphic Art Ltd
Printed and bound by CPI Group
(UK) Ltd, Croydon, CR0 4YY

2 4 6 8 10 9 7 5 3 1

To my dearly beloved Mum and Dad

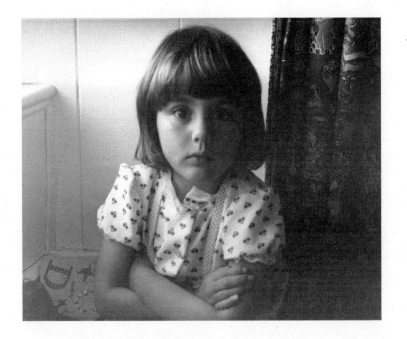

Preface

They wanted something more, that's what my parents say when I ask them about it now. They'd had me, and my sister was on her way, and London didn't seem to matter quite so much. They wanted a different, simpler kind of life. They left behind their small house in Islington, a secure job in advertising for my father, their friends, the parties – all that London had to offer a hip young couple in 1972 – for a farmhouse in the middle of rural, Welsh-speaking North Wales. Some friends were envious, others baffled. My father's parents in particular thought they'd lost their minds.

They could have gone anywhere, but it was the house that decided it, according to my mother. She *just knew* when she first saw the photograph. It was an instant attraction, a visceral kind of pull that she felt to its whiteness, its absolute plainness; the fact that it was high up on a hill.

It was March when we first went to see it. I was nearly two years old. My father drove our battered Volvo up the lane when the blackthorn was out and the hedgerows were a mass of fuzzy white. Everything looked so bright, as if the colour had been turned up on the TV.

It was the bubbling, plaintive call of the curlews they noticed first as they lifted me out of the car. The sheep-filled fields spread out wide and flat ahead, and the Berwyn Mountains rose colossal in the distance, against an empty, endless sky. They just looked at each other and grinned.

'We're going to get it, aren't we?' said my father.

'Didn't I tell you?' my mother said, before they'd even looked inside.

Part One

1

Peach mohair

There's a family snapshot of us taken in 1977, when I was seven. In the photo we are all standing outside our house in North Wales: my parents, my sister, and me. It looks like a late-summer afternoon. The light is soft pink, and it's a little hazy, or perhaps the photo is slightly out of focus, which meant my nana most probably took it. That's the sort of thing they did, my nana and poppa. They made us line up outside the front gate before they left: all scrubbed up, with our hair especially brushed for the record.

In the photo my mother is leaning against our front gate. She has long blonde hair in a middle parting, and she's waving to camera, eyes squeezed shut with a smile. She was relieved: my grandparents were just about to leave. My father is leaning into her, laughing – delightedly relieved – with his arm around her shoulders. His beard was at its longest then, curly and a bit wild and woolly, like his hair: the kind of hair a hostage might have, say, after a long stretch in captivity. He is wearing vast sunglasses with thick black frames. The glass in them is not quite tinted enough, so they look like normal glasses that just need a good clean. I hated those glasses. I thought they made him look like a serial killer.

My father's other arm is resting on my head, and I'm looking down, with one foot perched on top of the other. At a glance, you could easily mistake me for a boy, for which I blame my scissor-happy mother. I'm sporting the only hairstyle that she could actually manage: a short, lop-fringed, wonky version of a pudding basin. The style had nothing to recommend it, other than being free. In other words it was 'a bag of cach', as is shortly to be pointed out to me in the playground by Sara Fiddick, whose own hair, to be frank, wasn't a lot to shout about. My younger sister, Katherine, is next to me. She is clearly a girl, with proper girl's hair: long and blonde like my mother's but curly like my father's. She's grinning unselfconsciously at the camera and scrunching her eyes shut into the sun. Even squinting, she is, like my mother, beautiful.

My father, sister and I are all dressed in shades of autumn. I'm wearing my least favourite item of clothing of that time – which may be the reason why I'm not smiling – a pair of rust-coloured, flared dungarees, with a strip of dark brown fabric sewn around the bottom of each leg – a trouser-leg extension. I'd been wearing them since I was five, so I'd had a lot of time to grow to hate those trousers. My sister is wearing the matching, untampered-with version in plum. They had my mother's inter-pretation of oak leaves embroidered on the knees. Both of us have plimsolls on our feet, though only half of mine are intact: their ends cut off by my ever-resourceful mother, turned into 'sandals' as they were imaginatively called, to give my feet more space to grow. I'd had a growth spurt that summer.

My father is dressed top to toe in rich conker brown. He is wearing a fitted, V-neck T-shirt with his chest hair frothing out over the top, and his trousers thankfully have no bib, though they're high-waisted and painfully tight-looking at the top, flaring out from the knee like a carthorse's legs. My mother stands out, the evergreen amongst us, in her Biba bottle-green maxi-dress with a matching dark green ribbon tied around her forehead: typically seventies – or Tudor; the look is interchangeable.

Looking at that photo, I can see what you might think of us, but you'd actually be quite wrong. In fact, if you were looking for a way to insult me then, '*cachu mochyn*' might have made my eyes prick with tears, but 'hippy' would have made me cry with shame; I'd have rather been called pig shit than mistaken for a hippy any day. You might not think it to look at us, but my mother couldn't stand the smell of patchouli oil; we had electricity – a dishwasher even – and my father had a job, which had nothing to do with healing, or yoga, or plaiting anything; and it was just us who lived in our house – we didn't share it with anyone but our couple of cats, which meant we definitely didn't live in a commune. Not like some.

My parents were leading an 'alternative lifestyle', that's what my nana said – whispering out the words as if she was swearing – and 'alternative' meant hippy to me. I could think of nothing worse than communal living. I had a vivid enough imagination, but still, it was beyond its realms for me to picture a more unappealing way to live. I was seven, so the thought of sharing anything – a bag of sweets, if I was lucky enough to have them, let alone my parents and my bedroom – made me sweat with panic. Our family could never survive a commune; *I* would never survive one, I knew that for sure. We'd be lost for ever, 'doomed to a life on the margins of society' like Nana said. I wasn't interested in margins; I didn't even know what they were. I didn't want to be different. Why be different? As Nana said: 'What on earth's the point in that?'

It was always a big event when my nana and poppa came to stay; at least it felt like that to me. In the days before they were due a sense of expectation hung in the air, ramping up day by day, altering us all, making my sister and me louder and more excitable, and my parents notably quieter. At seven I took my parents' altered state, their quiet, tense way of being before these visits, as an adult's peculiar way of showing excitement, a kind of nervous anticipation. Nana and Poppa were family, and family were to be loved, so there was no other way to interpret it but that.

My nana and poppa would be with us any minute now. We were practically wetting ourselves with excitement – my sister was even crossing her legs just in case – as we both sat waiting for them on the lichen-covered wall outside our kitchen window. How long had it been since we'd seen them? Six months? They might not recognize me. I'd gone up a shoe size and grown an inch and a half.

We sat and bickered and squashed the minuscule red spiders that swivelled over the stone slabs, and held up our forefingers every now and again to examine their remains: tiny bright red pinpricks on our skin, like the dot left by the mark of a pen. We bounced our feet against the springy cushions of wallflowers that grew from the gaps in the stone, comparing fingers, counting the dots, ears trained all the while for that distant sound, the promising hum of their car engine.

Phillip Brown, our unnaturally white-skinned next-door neighbour, was waiting too, peering out, eyes bulging, from the rhododendron bushes in front of farmer Colwyn's field. His mother Olive had sent him, bribed him with a bag of sweets to be her eyes and ears; that's what she did whenever she got wind of any visitors at ours. He wouldn't have been my first choice of spy, I'll admit: he stood out too much with his bright orange hair and his nervous blinking; and he was easily distracted, especially by sugary treats. I watched him sitting there, cross-legged in his tiny nylon racing shorts and slightly too small brown vest, steadily working his way through a packet of pineapple chunks, jaw rotating, pausing to stick his finger into his mouth to retrieve a sticky bit lodged at the back. He looked up and smiled.

'Do you want this bit then, Ab?' he said, holding it aloft. He knew about my parents and their funny London ways: their alien dislike of too much sugar. 'If you do, you got to come over and get it, mind; I'm not coming out, no way!' he said, swiping a line of drool from his chin. We had so few sweets, my sister and me, that for a second I actually contemplated it.

'No, but I'll have a whole one,' I shouted back.

'Sorry, Ab, I've only got . . .' and he paused as he counted the contents of the bag, 'yeah, thought so, only *twelve* left in there, just the twelve. Sorry about that then,' he said, holding one up to the sky and examining it like a jeweller inspecting a rare and precious gem, before popping it into his mouth and sitting back down in his hidey-hole with a happy-sounding sigh.

They weren't here yet. We shoved and pushed each other and sang relays of 'London's Burning', with Phillip chiming in whenever we got to 'pour on water', out of time and in a different tune, ruining it altogether. Inside the house our parents were going through the ritual of digging out grandparental gifts of old from the cellar. A collection of glass, fruit-bordered chopping boards, coated with dust, would be wiped down and placed in a prominent position on our kitchen sideboard. A china figurine, a lady in a bonnet, all in white, with improbably small and pointy feet, would be put on the end of the shelf in the kitchen, where she stood leaning against her parasol, demure and elegant next to a battered copy of Elizabeth David. I still believed my father then, when he told me they put them away for safekeeping: they were too precious to keep out all the time, he said. I accepted that, of course, because I *agreed*. Anything given to us by my nana, anything selected by her magical eye, was a precious, superior thing to me – superior certainly to any of our belongings, specifically anything chosen by my parents. Then there was the sign, they couldn't forget the sign: a slice of varnished wood, with the name of the house painted in swirly black writing, almost overlooked, grabbed last minute from behind a box of wine. My father secured it to the wall by the gate, with a nail shoved into a hole in the render and strict instructions not to touch.

'What's that you're doing there then, Ba?' asked Phillip from the bushes.

'Shh,' said my father, 'you didn't see a thing.'

Their red car arrived at last, screeching up our road, sending the sheep in the neighbouring field scattering and Phillip shrinking back into the bushes. Phillip was 'introverted', that's what his mother Olive said, which my sister told me meant his winkle was inside out. My mother swiftly put me right: *it meant shy*, she said, and I wondered about that now: shy didn't really seem to cover it, as he sat there in the bushes panting with panic, while Poppa turned their car around, Nana waving frantically from the passenger side.

'They're here! Mum, Dad, come on, they've arrived!' we shouted above the frantic beeping of their horn. Nana was the first out, disembarking before the handbrake was on to fall upon us and claim us as her own.

'Darlings! Aah, my darlings! Come to Nana!' she said, even though she already had us, clamped tight into her chest, encased in scented peach mohair as she laughed and cried at the same time just like they did in films.

'Let me look at you,' she said at last, grabbing our cheeks, squeezing them tight like she was checking for ripeness, as we stood there for inspection in our dungarees and checked shirts – my sister's blue, mine brown. 'Look at your outfits!' she said. 'They match the colour of your eyes. Ah! How dinky! Beautiful, beautiful, both of you: you look just like your daddy, you lucky things,' she said. It was a well-meant, if bemusing, compliment, as my father appeared from the house, six foot two and bearded, with his generous Jewish nose.

'Mum, Dad, you're here,' he said, arms outstretched to Nana, and she leapt on him with the same astonished-sounding proclamations she greeted us all with, as if she hadn't expected us to be there, in our own house, and seeing us was a lovely, unexpected surprise.

Across the road the rhododendron bush shuddered as Phillip recovered himself just enough to crane forward to get a better view. He looked scared, terrified still, but he couldn't help himself; he stared open-mouthed, mashed-up pineapple chunks on full, glistening display. How could he not? My grandparents looked like film stars.

Nana was standing by the car, one hand on hip as she patted down her hair with the other. She wore an outfit that was super-skin-tight as always: black trousers and a fitted jumper with a belt around it, and high-heeled patent-leather boots that shone like freshly licked liquorice. Everything had to fit where it touched with my nana, and if it didn't, she belted it, tied it or tucked it in until it did. It was her hair, though; you just really needed to see that hair: big and bouffy like candyfloss and a delicate shade of pastel peach, like the mane of an orange My Little Pony.

Poppa lit a cigarette with a gold lighter, one hand up to shelter the flame. He was nut brown, like my nana, and his clothes were similarly slim-fitting: a pale blue polo shirt, monogrammed, always – so he wouldn't ever lose them, I presumed – and beige fitted slacks belted high on the waist. Everything about him was slick. His shoes shone and he wore his hair Brylcreemed back like a gangster. He looked like someone important, like he knew people – *and he was related to me*; when I reminded myself of that I felt myself go hot all over, boiling up, sizzling with pride.

'I've made you your favourite chopped liver, girls, and that lemon drizzle cake that you like,' said Nana, as Poppa handed her one of her special cigarettes, ready lit: pale green with a gold-coloured filter. 'We've brought you some really *super* clothes this time, haven't we, Les?' she said. Her voice was deep, surprisingly so for someone so tiny, and it crackled like an un-tuned radio. She took a deep, urgent-looking suck of her cigarette and blew the smoke out slowly from the side of her mouth, in a way that I tried to emulate for months after in the bathroom mirror. Side-blowing of cigarette smoke – even from the pretend sweet ones like we had – was one of those life skills that was essential to me then, like making a part of you look double-jointed, or being able to turn your eyelids inside out.

There was the distant hum of an engine, and the sheep in the opposite field raised their heads and gave startled-sounding, expectant bleats as they trotted on their twiggy legs towards the fence. Colwyn, our neighbouring farmer, appeared then in his Land Rover from around the corner, from the road that carried on up the hill.

'Hello!' my father shouted, as Colwyn reversed without even looking behind, backing up towards the gate of his field, a sea of sheep now gathered, pushing their black muddy faces through the fence.

'All right there,' said Colwyn from somewhere under his

peaked cap, head bent down to avoid eye contact, and he jumped down on to the gravel, steel caps of his boots flashing silver through the worn-away leather. He gave my nana a cursory wave, and she pulled her head back, surprised, and turned her back to him, affronted, as if he'd flicked her the Vs instead.

'What have you got in here then, Dad?' asked my father, pulling their suitcase out from the back seat with a grimace. 'I thought you were just coming for the weekend.'

'That'll be your mother – two new pairs of boots and she insisted on packing them both,' said my poppa, blowing a swirl of smoke upwards into the clear blue sky and slicking down his hair, which the wind had disturbed into upright greasy spikes like the plume of one of our Silkie hens. 'You look smart, son,' he said, stepping back to take my father in, in his entirety. 'Ed, take a look at Baz – doesn't he scrub up when he wants to?'

'So handsome, Barry!' said Nana, who didn't call him Baz herself. She didn't believe in shortening names, that's what she told me once: *a woman should never shorten*. My poppa could call my father Baz, that was okay because he was a *man*, and it was a *masculine* thing to do, she said, like slapping another man on the back, or reversing a car with your arm around the passenger seat. I nodded gravely and pretended to understand, while I wondered how I'd manage it, how I'd ever work out the complications – limitless as they then seemed – of being a grown-up.

'That's what happens when you wear a shirt, Barry. You look all lovely and smart and make your mamma proud,' she said, smoothing down his collar. My father just made a blowing noise through his nostrils by way of reply, a snort of acknowledgement.

'Smart' was the gold standard as far as my grandparents were concerned, relative though it was. I could see that my father looked smarter than normal for a weekend, but not slick, or sporty-looking or anything that would have genuinely passed muster with them. His hair looked as wild as ever, though he'd trimmed his beard and he was co-ordinated at least, but in colours that didn't look fatherly to me. Fathers wore pale browns and any shade of blue, and he was dressed in fruits of the forest: dark purple cords and a shirt the colour of blackberry mousse.

'Looking good, son, looking good,' said Poppa, nevertheless, as he joined my father in unburdening the boot of their car of its first layer of gifts: the edible ones at the top, faded pastel Tupperware stacked one on top of each other, and plates and bowls covered in foil and cling film. The smallest one was handed to my sister, who took it gingerly, as if it was made of fine porcelain, and walked carefully, arms outstretched, and headed through the gate to the door.

'I'll take that one, Les,' said Nana, scooping up a bowl with cling film stretched over it tight as a drum. 'Aah,' she sighed, gazing down at her beloved chopped liver, her special secret recipe passed on from her mother, and hugging it tight, as if it was a newborn baby.

'Well. The house is coming on, I must say,' she said, leaning back to look at it, spanning out the fingers of her free hand and waving it in front of her in a jazz-hand salute of approval. She said that every time, ever hopeful, I think now, that it would come on and come on until it became something she could recognize.

'The front door's been painted – look, Les! Yellow. That's an interesting choice. Very bright, very modern,' Nana said, as my mother came flying out of it, horribly un-nipped in by comparison: all billowing cheesecloth and flowing long blonde hair.

'You're here!' she exclaimed, in a high-pitched voice, sounding surprised, as if she'd only just realized they'd arrived.

It wasn't enough; it really wasn't enough for them. My

grandparents should have arrived by helicopter, like Hollywood royalty, to be met by a crowd of adoring fans, flashbulbs popping as they strode down the red carpet to our front door. As it was, they were greeted by a few disconsolate-looking sheep peering over the fence at them, a scared-looking boy lurking in the bushes, and a family dressed predominantly in corduroy who all needed to give their hair a really good brush. I could understand why they might feel disappointed.

We'd been about to take the suitcase upstairs. I'd followed my father and Poppa, scuttled behind them excitedly, because I loved this bit: the ritual of showing them up to their room, where there were towels folded on their bed and flowers on the chest of drawers: primroses in an egg cup, picked by me. We'd been way-laid, though, by my poppa's urgent need of a television: there were pressing golf results to see. 'I can't relax,' he said, 'until I know how he's done. You know how it is.' I wished that I did. I wanted us to be people who could say things like that, who could understand what he meant. Who was *he*?

The suitcase had been abandoned at the foot of the stairs, and the three of us were in our study, as it was optimistically named: a small, dark yellow room with a wall of bookshelves and Indian miniature paintings, with heavy red cord curtains at the windows. Our television was in the corner – the actual reason we used this room – perched on a wooden stool.

'You can sit down there, Poppa, if you like,' I said, pointing to our new beanbag, as I laid myself across the entirety of our small, dark brown velvet sofa, stretching out on it from head to foot. *Do unto others as thou would do unto thineself* – that had been the theme in assembly on Friday, and there was not a chance that I, mineself, would sit on this hard, bony sofa out of choice if there was a beanbag free on the floor.

Poppa gave me a stretchy-mouthed smile, hitched up his trouser legs, squatted down and released his weight on to it, and tipped violently to one side.

'Goodness, what *is* this thing?' he said, flashes of mahogany ankle revealed above his silky-looking socks as he splayed out his legs to steady himself.

'Are you okay there, Dad?' enquired my father, fiddling with the aerial of our television. A snowstorm of no reception filled the screen, and he growled with frustration and said 'bullshit' quietly, under his breath, and 'Jesus, please, Christ, JESUS!' as he flung the aerial left and right. 'Come on, you bastard! Come on!'

'Is this your new television, son?' asked Poppa. 'Dinky,' he added eventually and my father muttered 'Fuck!' by way of reply.

'They come bigger than this, don't they?' said Poppa, rotating his bottom around and around to gain purchase before settling, upright, in the middle of the beanbag, like a hen about to lay an egg. 'I thought. Don't they, Baz?' he asked, fiddling about in his pocket now for his cigarettes. 'These portables? Come quite big nowadays?'

The screen fuzzed and crackled as my father gritted his teeth, head down.

'No rush, we've a minute or so to go,' Poppa said, unlit cigarette now gripped between his fingers, held up in front of him in a victory V salute. 'You've got a VHS player now,' he added, nodding towards it where it sat under the stool, surrounded by a tangle of wires. 'Not tempted by Betamax then, Barry? We've no complaints about ours, no complaints at all.'

'Good, that's good,' said my father vaguely, moving the television back and forth.

'*Business* going well?' asked Poppa, eyes trained on my father, one eyebrow raised, as he rifled in his pockets for a lighter. 'Is it then, son? The *business*? Advertising? Going well?'

'Business' was a hallowed word to my poppa, to be mentioned only in a hushed, reverential tone of voice.

'It's okay,' said my father. 'I'm working on a couple of new accounts, but I'm enjoying writing my book more than running the business if I'm—'

'No one got rich from writing a book, did they?' said my poppa, cutting in. 'Stick to what you know, stick to writing adverts, if you want my advice. That's what you want to do, *get yourself back to London*,' he said, addressing my father's pinky-purply back now as he bent down to the socket and pulled a lead out and pushed it back into the wall.

'But it's not what I want to do, not really, that's the thing,' replied my father, staggering up, red-faced with the effort, and he gave a sharp little laugh, like a hiccup. 'I've been thinking about taking on less work, so I can spend a bit more time at home, writing.'

This made my poppa look just like my sister did when she swallowed a giant gobstopper down in one by accident – startled and indignant and eyes all watery with shock. '*Be responsible, son.*' He whispered this, and leant in closer to my father, legs spread wide for balance, but I could hear it all the same; he had a whisper that amplified rather than reduced his voice, the dramatic kind like they use in pantomimes. 'You've got a family to think of,' he said. 'That's the country air: I was saying this to your mother in the car; I think it's getting to you,' and he was looking at my father's feet as he said this, at his brown sandals, handmade by his friend Hippy Wiggy. 'It's not good for people in business, the countryside. *Move back to London*, that's what you need to do,' he urged, an elbow now propped on each knee. 'And as for all this commuting up and down, well, you just ask your mother what she thinks of that.' Poppa was forgetting even to try to whisper now, as he aimed his cigarette at my father, holding it between forefinger and thumb as if it was a dart he was about to throw. 'You'll end up like your Uncle Larry. Remember what happened to him?' he said. 'It was the travelling, that's what made his heart go dicky. You need to be careful, or you'll be dead as a doorknob, like him.' He half turned and saw me sitting behind him, and dropped his cross expression in an instant.

'Hello, darling,' he said, 'lovely, lovely girl, ahh,' then he turned and leant in further towards my father. 'It's not right, son,' he pretend-whispered again, 'that's all I'm saying. This set-up, it's not a right way to live,' and I lay behind him, springs digging into my hipbone, feeling faintly sick: *we didn't live right,* and I watched my poppa give a slow, wise-looking nod to confirm it, making it official and absolute.

'Good to see you too, Dad, welcome, welcome,' my father muttered, but not loud enough for my slightly deaf poppa to hear. He bashed the top of the television, and the screen sprang instantly to life.

'That's it, there we are. Turn it up now, son, would you?' said my poppa, leaning back, settling in, as my nana appeared at the study door, her arms stacked high with the proper gifts, the gifts I'd been waiting for: plastic bags packed tight with clothes.

Back in the sixties, in between running nightclubs in Liverpool, my grandparents had briefly owned a clothes shop in the city centre. A decade or so later we were still the recipients of the seemingly limitless supply of unsold stock that took up half of their garage. It was the garage that just kept on giving: polyester denim-look playsuits, geometric-knit jumpers in mustard and brown, enormously collared orange rayon blouses with oversized yellow plastic buttons . . . all of my favourite clothes had come from that garage. Katherine and I were just grateful for any man-made fibres that came our way. This was city clothing. Just touching it made us feel worldly and sophisticated. Any garment we were given would be ferreted away to the back of our wardrobe before our natural-fibre-loving mother got her hands on it and made it magically disappear.

Even then I could tell that my grandparents, for all their generosity, saw these sartorial gifts first and foremost as a necessity. We lived in the countryside, and they thought that we needed smartening up, and they knew all about smart – they lived in the city. In a semi in the suburbs of Liverpool, to be exact, but they looked as if they lived on a yacht in Monte Carlo.

We heard my mother coming down the stairs before we saw her: the zipping swish of nylon as her flared trouser legs màde contact with each other on every step of her descent. When she got to the middle landing she paused, taken aback by the sight of her expectant audience: a neat row of five, packed in tight, gazing up at her from the hallway. My nana gasped and raised her clasped hands in front of her in a gesture of prayer. She was briefly silent – unusual for her – and I wondered then if she was in fact praying, giving gratitude to God for helping her to find those spectacular trousers.

'Oh, Anna!' she said at last, pressing both hands to her neck to steady herself. Her fingernails were just like my father's: large and domed, but painted, as always, a beautiful, shimmering pale pink, like the inside of a seashell. 'They look *super* on you,' she said, as my mother stood with one foot in front of the other and stared above our heads without expression, like a model in one of Olive Brown's clothing catalogues.

The trousers were Nana's gift to my mother: high-waisted, stay-press slacks in a modern greeny-brown, the colour an avocado goes when it's been sliced open and left out on a plate for a while.

'*Try them on*,' my nana had said.

'Go on!' we'd chorused, my sister and I, dressed now in our new orange dresses: dresses that made us grin until our faces ached, with collars shaped like huge petals, made out of fabric as thick as cardboard, so the skirt stuck out like an A.

'I just *knew* when I saw them that I had to give them to you,' said Nana. 'Didn't I say, Leslie? I said: Anna is *made* for those trousers! They had your name written all over them,' and her eyes glazed with tears. 'I said, didn't I? I said: I bet Anna has got a smashing figure hiding somewhere under that great big dress, and there it is! Look at that waist! Oh doesn't she look super, Les?'

My poppa nodded. 'You really do, Anna. Knockout. Oh yes,' he said, his voice cracking at the end of the sentence. I didn't need to look; his eyes would be filled with tears too. When it came to family, it didn't take much to set my nana and poppa off, but nothing moved them more than the sight of one of us in an actual, proper outfit, handpicked by Nana. She 'had an eye', according to my poppa – though they both looked the same to me, even under her magnifying lenses: big and a watery kind of blue and ever so slightly protruding.

'You really do,' he said again. 'Yes. Oh yes. Very good choice, Edna. Well done.'

'Such a good colour for the spring, that green,' said my nana. 'They'd look lovely with a primrose-coloured blouse. Do you ever wear primrose, Anna? It would suit you, it really would – very good colour for blondes.'

'Thank you, Edna,' said my mother, as if she was reading out lines, 'they're lovely. You really shouldn't have been so generous.'

For a grown-up, she possessed an alarming, almost childlike lack of conviction when it came to lying. I was too young still to pick up on the more subtle nuances of adult interaction, but it was obvious, even to me then, that she didn't like them. Luckily it wasn't to Nana, who was still fixing her with her wavering coral-coloured smile, oblivious, blinking like a barn owl through her huge, tinted Sunnie Mann bifocals.

My mother took a deep breath in, held her head high and swished down to the foot of the stairs, building up the static with every step, and I gasped at the sound of her. Audible clothing was the apex, the absolute pinnacle of sophistication to me, and here she was: the proof of it.

'Right, I'd really better get on with the lunch,' she said, *still not smiling*. I willed her to love those trousers, encouraged her all the way as she sashayed across the terracotta-and-black chequered tiles in the hall. 'Beautiful,' I whispered as she crackled elegantly past, looking just like an American soap star, I thought, but without any make-up on, and definitely before she'd had her hair done. I imagined her picking me up from school in those trousers, her face covered all over in sparkling make-up, eye-shadow up to her eyebrows, shiny pink lipstick and hair that had been done by a hairdresser – hair that went up instead of down – my friends' faces slack-jawed with wonder as she shimmied through the gates; and I basked in that joyous image as we followed her through to the kitchen.

'Avon are doing some lovely eye-shadows at the moment, a whole palette full of shades of green, Anna,' said my nana, as if I'd said my thoughts out loud. 'I nearly bought you that too to go with your trousers, didn't I, Les?' she said, swiping her hand along the wooden sideboard before leaning up against it. 'But you're not one for make-up, really, are you? You favour the *au naturel* look, don't you?' and when she said this I noticed that she was staring straight at my mother's T-shirt, directly at her chest. I looked back at my nana's, and it looked different from my mother's: rock solid and pointy and proudly sticky-out, like a Sindy doll's.

'I'm glad you didn't. You've been generous enough with these trousers, Edna,' said my mother, chopping up cucumber fast and loud – attacking it – with an oversized kitchen knife.

'Hmm,' said Nana, distracted now by her reflection in the window, smiling delightedly at the sight of herself: as if she'd just bumped into a much-loved friend. She leant closer into the glass, to primp her hair, while I pulled myself up on to our wooden sideboard so I could be right next to her, immersed in her musky, sweet-smelling perfume. Outside I could see Phillip Brown, in our garden now, attempting to climb up on a wooden chair. I watched him wobbling about on it, leaning on our birdhouse for support. He straightened up, craning to look into our kitchen window, and his little white moon-face must have cut through my nana's reflection then, because she squealed and slapped one hand on her upper chest – I loved it when she did that; such a dramatic and feminine gesture – and shouted 'Shoo!', flicking her hands at him. 'Off!' But there was no need. He was gone, chair tipped up, bag of sweets hurled into the herbaceous border as he stumbled away down our garden, howling for his mam. I made a mental note of where his bag had gone, so I could retrieve it after lunch.

'Well. I wouldn't stand for *that*,' said Nana. 'Locals, trespassing in my garden.'

'That's Phillip,' said my mother, lighting a gas ring with a match. 'You've met him, Edna, several times.'

'Never seen him before in my life,' said Nana. 'You could always get lace curtains, did you ever think of that, Anna?' she asked, and behind her my mother caught my father's eye and bashed her forehead with the palm of her hand, and he smiled and nodded as he pulled the drawer out next to her to get the corkscrew.

I thought of Lisa Evans' pretty, frilly house. She had lace curtains everywhere, proper Welsh lace; even her doll's house had lace curtains. Our house could do with some frills; I knew my nana would be thinking that as she gazed around the kitchen. Nana stared in an obvious way, like a child younger than me might, like my sister might; staring, without even trying to hide it, at the scuffed-up pine table, and the big plain brown floor tiles, and the wooden blinds that hung above the window instead of curtains, held in place by a hook on the side of the window with a great big knot of string.

'We don't live in a town, Edna,' said my mother, 'and anyway, why would we want to hide that view?' she asked. She nodded towards Colwyn's fields spreading out towards the marshland, and the mountains beyond, vast and empty and humming bright, *buzzing* with new yellow-green grass. Dragons lived in those mountains; that's what I thought back then.

My nana held her hand out and shrugged: her way of saying 'so what?', because views didn't wash with her, unless perhaps they were of a golf club green or a casino floor, or maybe a nice clean beach in Marbella.

'Ah well,' she said, which she used often when speaking to my parents: her way of rounding off a subject. *What can I do?* she meant. *I've tried my best.*

'Now then, Anna,' she said, glancing up at our kitchen clock, 'I can't help but notice the time. What can I do to help?' and she zoomed in on my mother, rubbing her hands together with intent.

'Nothing!' replied my mother, shouting it out, even though Nana was right next to her, leaning in, chin jutting in over her shoulder. 'It's fine, Edna. I'm fine. Thank you,' she said, in a lighter voice, and she wiped her forehead with the back of her hand as she turned on the Roberts radio, twiddling the knob until Radio Four came blasting through, loud and clear, drowning out the sheep outside, all of them bleating now, gathered in a bedraggled mass by the gate as Colwyn lugged a sack full of feed from the back.

'Why don't you read the papers for a while, Edna? It'll be fifteen minutes or so until lunch,' said my mother, accepting a glass of wine from my father with a grateful-looking nod.

My nana didn't read though; how could my mother forget that? Not books, or magazines, and especially not newspapers; she didn't like the bother and the noise and the mess of them, the way the ink dirtied her hands, that's what she said.

'Leave her be, Ed,' said my poppa, unfolding the sports section of the paper. 'Let her get on and work that culinary magic of hers, will you? It's gone two o' clock already,' he added, shooting my nana an anxious-looking grimace, as he made for the armchair by the Jotul stove, hitching a trouser leg up as he sat down.

'Here, have a seat, Mum, will you?' said my father, pulling out the opposite chair for her as if he were a waiter – an oddly formal gesture for him – and she shrugged, and tipped her head to one side.

'Well, if I really can't be of any use . . .' she said, balancing daintily on the edge of the chair and casting her eyes around the room with a sigh. She fixed them eventually on the cover of the newspaper supplement: a photograph of Liberace in a cream fur coat, with jewels on every finger.

'Liberace: now there's an entertainer for you,' she said, and she sighed. 'He's got such flair and style, that man. I'll never understand why he hasn't got himself a wife. Didn't I say, Les? All that talent, and no one to share it with. Such a shame.'

'It doesn't make sense, Edna, I know. It just doesn't make sense,' Poppa said, in the flat monotone he used when he was required to talk while reading the paper, tracking the football results with a gnarled forefinger.

Nana loved Liberace. My grandparents lived in a small semi in the suburbs of Liverpool, but no matter: she'd kitted it out like a baroque palace in homage to her favourite man. 'I don't mind being your number two, Ed,' my poppa would say. 'I might not play the piano, darling, but I know I'd thrash him at golf.' There were ornate gilt mirrors and vast crystal chandeliers and nests of coffee tables everywhere – glass- and marble-topped – and stemmed bowls filled with foil-wrapped chocolates in every room, even the downstairs loo. There was no room for a white grand piano, but Nana would measure up in the sitting room every once in a while, just in case, convinced she could squeeze one in by the mahogany-trimmed mini-bar. There was space, she said; there had to be plenty of space for that. I knew what she meant. Their house seemed palatial to me too, its astonishing, otherworldly glamour magnifying it somehow, extending it to mansion-like proportions. I'd never encountered anything that touched it – not even Eleanor Williams' mum's house, which had a big white fur rug in the sitting room and a standard lamp with a shelf on it to put your glass of wine. It was hard to believe, their house, like something you would only ever see on television. It hummed with possibilities and promise: glamour and fabulousness is open to all, it said. You don't have to be an American soap star, you just need to live like this, to be important: to be a part of that big buzzing world.

'Girls, come over here and sit with me,' said Nana to my sister and me, standing shyly back, watching on, as we leant up against our vast, cream-coloured lozenge of a fridge. I liked to rest my ear on it and listen to its constant, comforting hum, like blood rushing around a body. 'Squeeze on and give your Nanni a cuddle,' and we climbed up on to the chair, fitted ourselves against her as she wrapped a mohair arm around each one of us. 'I wonder why don't you grow your hair longer, darling?' she said. 'You'd look cute with pigtails and ribbons, wouldn't she, Les? Les! Wouldn't Abbie look darling if she grew her hair?'

'Lovely, Ed, hmm,' said my poppa from somewhere inside the paper, a small cloud of cigarette smoke rising up around him, defining his space.

Nana got her comb out now and dragged it through my hair, eyes darting around the kitchen as she did so. 'What an *unusual* picture,' she said, looking at the abstract painting that hung above the stove: slashes of fat brushstrokes of pink and grey paint. 'Isn't that an unusual painting, Les? So different,' and I felt my cheeks flush hot with embarrassment as I realized then what she meant: that 'unusual', like 'different' – words she used often when she came to our house – were euphemisms to her for 'crap'.

'Do me a favour, Anna, before you get stuck in,' said my nana, plumping up her hair on one side and then the other, bouff, bouff, my sister and I ducking down to avoid her elbows. 'Put an apron on, will you? I couldn't bear to see you get anything on those trousers,' and I thought then that my mother mustn't have heard her, because she said nothing, just carried on chopping – tomatoes now – on one of Nana's glass, fruit-bordered chopping boards, and the noise of it, scraping and grating and loud, echoed around the kitchen,

'Yes, don't dirty them, whatever you do,' said my father. 'You look so super in them, Anna,' and I looked at him, because 'super' wasn't a word he used, and he was looking at my mother, surveying her with his arms crossed and his face set tight like he was holding back a laugh. I didn't understand. I thought that my mother looked like a goddess in those trousers.

2

Orange cheese

'Do you know what?' said Phillip Brown. I turned towards him, and saw that his face had changed colour. Last time I'd looked it was pink and a bit sweaty, like my sister's; but now, despite the baking heat of our den, it had turned a waxy pale blue. I looked at Katherine and sighed. We did know what. That was it, then. Playtime was over: Phillip Brown was having one of his turns.

'You just need some air,' I said, shoving back a roof blanket, and then him, out on to our sitting-room floor, where he lay, arms and legs flung wide in the middle of the Indian rug, as if he were offering himself up to the gods.

'Too late for air,' said Katherine, who wanted to be a nurse. 'Look at the eyes.'

I didn't much like to. I'd seen a run-over tabby cat at the bottom of our lane, his body flattened to a scrap of blood-encrusted fur. Phillip Brown's eyes looked just like that cat's, bulging out unnaturally far, and pointy like a pair of rugby balls. His tongue, too, was lolling out – embarrassing – though his was fat and slick with spit, and the cat's had gone all dark and shrivelled from the sun, and looked exactly like a tinned anchovy. Exactly. Right down to the tiny hairs.

'What I want,' he said, panting in and out, 'is my MAM!' and he wailed, his voice wavering high and then low, like it was breaking.

'She can't help you now,' said Katherine, in her special nurturing voice, spitting on to a tissue, spreading her saliva out, dispersing it corner to corner, before laying it with great care across his forehead.

'This will cool you down. There there, now, there there,' she said, pressing her thumb on the inside of his wrist and wincing. 'No heartbeat,' she mouthed to me above his head.

'What's that you said?' His mouth sagged down to one side. 'What you saying, Kath? Am I *dying,* is that it?' He struggled to sit up, and my sister placed her palm across his forehead and pushed him, firmly, decisively, back on to the rug.

'Hush now, don't fuss or Mum will hear,' she said. 'Just breathe now. Relax.'

'No, I don't want to breathe! I want to go home. Get my MAM for us, will you? *Get her*!' he cried, his voice all high and girly-sounding, like one of the Fiddick boys from across the fields when they tried to imitate their sister.

Phillip Brown lived just below us in a foreign-looking, modern house. It was wood-fronted and pebble-dashed, with a steep pointy roof, more of a chalet, really, than a cottage. Where we lived, houses and people were thin on the ground, so we were lucky to have Phillip right there. We knew that. There were other children in walking distance: Olwenna – wispy-looking and painfully shy – at the bottom of the hill, and the Fiddicks – a noisy rabble of four – a twenty-minute walk away, but that was it. Phillip, though, was instant, a ready-made playmate, available in thirty seconds. He liked to pop in; he popped in and popped out several times a day. Fleeting visits were his specialty: in through the back, via the short-cut up our garden, splatting a sticky hand against the sitting-room window to signal his arrival. 'Ab! Kath! I'm here, aren't I?' he'd say above the booming shudder of glass, too timid, always, to step inside until he'd caught sight of one of us; shrinking down into the flowerbed at the first glimpse of a parent. We were familiar to him – a daily occurrence – but even so, alone, without his mam, Olive, for longer than ten minutes, he was inclined to panic. 'That's Phillip: a sensitive little soul, God bless him,' Olive would say proudly, once in a while, when his sensitivity wasn't making her pink-faced and growly with frustration.

It was a hot, airless day – the height of summer now – and the place to be on a day like this was outside, immersed in water. There was a river down through the fields in front, and I thought of the shady spot under the alders, where it bent around a corner, spilling out wide and still like a pond. We could paddle there, sweat-free and happy, slipping over cool stones in search of stickle-backs. When we tired of that we could force up a breeze on the swing: the nerve-racking swing that hung from a bent-down tree, over the deepest part, where the rocks were covered up and the water was navy blue. The Fiddicks' dad, Dave, had made it last summer, a knobbled stick knotted to a frayed piece of sheep's twine, and it had never quite worked as he'd intended. It went spiralling, seat-tipping, across the river and back to the bank again, crashing you into the trunk of the tree, unless you leapt off, last minute, into the water. That would cool us down.

Instead here we were: in our sitting room, crammed in behind the sofa, playing house in a windowless den made from Donegal tweed blankets. Underneath we were squashed in tight in semi-darkness, hunched around the floor cushion that was our dining-room table, arguing about whose turn it was to go out to work at the corner shop – the leather pouffe counter by the bookcase. Phillip was a hard worker when it came to play. He considered his role of shopkeeper with impressive seriousness, lending him a certain – if rather joyless – gravitas. He liked the shop to be neat at all times and he fretted about how it was managed. 'What? Only two more tins of Spam left now? I don't believe it. I stocked up yesterday, didn't I?'

He worried about the pricing, counting out the cardboard money in the till again and again, making sure he had enough to take home when he shut up shop. At closing time he returned, weary and downtrodden, back to our den. 'What a blimmin' day I've had. What a day,' he'd say, pallid palm to brow. 'Is anyone going to make me a cup of tea then?' Both of us would fuss around him, fighting over whose turn it was to peel his sweaty socks off or spoonfeed him tepid water from our rusty tin cup: whatever it took to make him happy. Briefly he'd become an entirely believable grown-up, not the kind that we'd ever come across, but it didn't matter. It was a miraculous, almost humbling transformation given the very particular childish kind of child he was, and entirely worthy of our slightly-too-close-for-comfort, clammy adoration.

Once in a while we'd hear my mother's muffled shouts from outside: 'Kids, for goodness' sake! What are you *doing* in there? Get out, get some fresh air. Enjoy the sunshine!' There was a poss-ibility – likelihood, even – that she was saying this without her top on, even without her bra; perhaps, God help me, just in her knickers and gardening gloves. The thought of it – that reputa-tion-destroying image – made me think, for once, that I was at one with Phillip: happy to stay put and inside, all day long. Phillip wasn't keen on outdoors, especially in the heat; it was safer to be inside, he said. It was the flies that were the problem; he'd had a terror of them ever since last summer, when he'd swallowed a bluebottle, whole, on the bottom lawn. It was still living inside him, he told us, buzzing around his stomach, so loud sometimes it kept him awake all night. If he swallowed another, he explained, they could mate and have maggots, and then there would be wriggling to contend with as well.

Lunch was ready. My mother announced it through the lambswool walls. She'd leave it outside, she said, by the den's front door; eat it all up and there might be ice cream. When I was sure she was gone, when I heard her barefoot padding towards the kitchen on her definitely naked feet, I lifted up the corner of a rug and threw it back, sending dust motes swirling to the ceiling as sunshine and cool air rushed in. We gasped with relief, all of us, breathing in great gulps of oxygen as though we'd just surfaced from the depths of the sea. Outside, through the window, there was nothing but cloudless sky, blinding bright against the dark brown walls of the sitting room. I watched as a house martin swooped down from the eaves to loop the loop across the limitless blue. In front of us, on the red-lacquer coffee table, was a wooden tray piled high with a teetering tower of cheese and lettuce sandwiches. The bread was brown and lumpy-looking and cut into thick, jaggedy slabs. It was homemade – undeniably; anyone could tell. So Phillip wouldn't like it. That was definite. He only ate proper bread – my mother knew that – soft and white and from a packet, the kind that was already sliced to save time. As a family, behind closed doors, we ate homemade food most of the time, but to give it to guests, to *force* it on them, to my mind was plain rude. My mother told us, always, to be considerate, but where was the consideration here? Where was it? That's what I wanted to know, that's what I would ask her later, and she would probably break down and say sorry, you are right, *so* right, what on earth was I thinking? Never again, she'd say; it's white sliced all the way from now on. Or perhaps she wouldn't. Even I found it hard to picture my mother loving white sliced bread, and my imagination was vivid enough: I still believed in dragons then. I knew they existed because I'd seen one, through my mother's birdwatching binoculars: a distant, lumbering green mass disappearing around the side of the mountain with a lazy flick of its tail.

Phillip leapt from the den and did a floppy-limbed circuit of the room, swiping the air for non-existent flies, before he huffed down on to the rug, cross-legged, to give his lunch proffering a full and thorough examination. He picked off a sunflower seed from the crust, like a monkey picking off nits, and held it up to the light for scrutiny.

'What's that then?' he asked.

'Just taste it,' said my sister.

'Never,' he said, shoulders quivering. He lifted an unyielding corner of a sandwich and poked at a piece of lettuce. 'Hey! That looks like *weeds* to me, looks like something that comes from the garden,' and he looked at me through narrowed eyes, like there was a plan afoot to poison him. The lettuce *was* from the garden; all our vegetables were. At least the cheese had been bought, that's what I thought; my mother hadn't made that, I was sure. I'd seen her taking it out of the packet.

Greed overtook my shame, and I grabbed a sandwich, my sister too, and we shovelled them into our mouths as fast as we could.

Phillip, still poking, let out a shriek. 'It's YELLOW cheese! I hate yellow cheese,' he wailed. 'I never touch that, not ever!'

It was true. He did hate yellow cheese. He hated yellow food, in fact, preferring in general to eat food that was orange. My mother knew this, but she held little truck with fussy eating, so she persisted in foisting Cheddar on him regardless. That was it.

The sandwiches were the tipping point. The sudden jolt of the unfamiliar was all that it took for the delicate equilibrium to be shattered, and for Phillip to be desperate to return home to his mam. We knew that he would leave, and even though there was nothing we could do to stop him, we always relished the fuss, loved all the commotion of having a really good go.

Olive always said that, bless him, Phillip wore his heart on his sleeve – an unwelcome, disturbingly gory image in my mind. If he did, though, if he actually wore his heart strapped on to the arm of his dark brown nylon jumper – say, with his blue stripy S-belt – then I was sure that we would see it beating at bionic speed, ten to the dozen, because for Phillip panic was ever present. It bubbled away under the surface, pressure building like a geyser, until eventually, inevitably, it had to erupt. As a child who tried to keep my fears contained, I found his sudden lack of constraint, this giving in to absolute abandon, exhilarating to witness – a thrill by proxy – like watching someone skydiving from a plane from the safety of a cabin window.

'Stay!' we yelled, grabbing at his flailing arms. The more he resisted, the more desperate we were to keep him. There was a back door – wide open – but he propelled himself head first out of the sitting-room window instead. 'Don't go!' we said to his small, pale white bottom poking out of his too big trousers. We grabbed at his ankles, but they slithered eel-like from our grasp, and he was out and in the flowerbed and then up and running down the lawn, transformed by fear into someone who looked, from a distance, at a push, almost athletic.

We loved Phillip coming to play, but the ever-present worry that he might just up and go in an instant tinged our playtime and made it bittersweet, like a just-tuned-into episode of *Starsky and Hutch* that could end at any second. Each time that he stayed was a small triumph: proof that we had managed to have such a distractingly good time that all thoughts of his house and his beloved mam had been temporarily forgotten, and it was down to us, of course, all down to us.

Phillip's parents, Olive and Mike, made for an odd-looking pair; not that I thought that then. Compared with my parents – and I compared everyone with my parents then – I thought that they looked ordinary, run of the mill, which was a compliment coming from me. Mike was tall – massively so – with gangly, overgrown limbs that crashed into things left and right, as if he hadn't quite worked out how to use them yet. His work overalls were XXL, but even so, you could see a good few inches of white sock hugging his skinny ankles above his colossal, boat-like feet. He was so tall that he had to concertina his body down whenever he walked through one of their doors, with one hand hovering protectively over his head each time, to guard against a possible knock. Olive, though, was tiny, about half his height, or less. Mike had to pick her up to give her a kiss, balancing her sometimes on the breakfast bar, squeezing her in between the mug tree and the deep-fat fryer. Despite this, they looked like they belonged together. When Mike changed out of his overalls they dressed identically in a regulation uniform of navy sweatshirts, ironed jeans and bright white trainers, like team leaders at a summer camp. This way of dressing was called *unisex* – according to Eleanor Williams' mother – an alarmingly rude-sounding word for something that turned out not to be at all.

Olive's unisexiness was countered by her enormous bosoms, hoisted up high in a pointy bra to just below her chin, and to which Mike made constant, delighted references. 'Page Three, eat your heart out!' he'd say, grabbing at them with both hands as Olive batted him off and squealed in mock outrage; and I'd laugh along too. The *Sun* newspaper was fun – *this was fun*; there was no fun at all to be had with my parents' paper, the *Guardian*, no topless ladies to laugh about in that.

Olive's second-best feature was her hair, which was shiny dark red and perfectly bowl-shaped, like hair from a Lego character. She fiddled with it constantly, double-checking it in the mirror to sighs of admiration and headshakes of disbelief. It was its bowliness she loved, and she helped it on its way to shiny-smooth perfection by washing it and Sellotaping it down to her forehead and around the sides of her face until it dried. In the winter, when her hair was slower to dry, in the safety of her own home she was to be found Sellotaped most of the time.

I channelled an uncritical focus on the Browns, fuelled by a covetous kind of jealousy. I loved to visit their house, as everyone did, I think. Olive delighted in people, and most people responded to that: loved to be delighted in. She cherished all her visitors, every one of them, greeting all with the same effusive welcome: 'Ooh! Well . . .' – whispering the 'well' and pausing to stand back and admire – '. . . Would. You. Look. At. You!' Never mind that she may have been looking at you just yesterday. She was always more than happy to be looking at anyone all over again, any excuse to marvel. She was probably making up in part for Mike, who was as taciturn as she was effusive. A welcome from Mike was a mumbled 'All right' – a statement, never a question – and a panicky flash of eye white revealed over the top of his copy of the *Sun*, before he retreated back behind it to study Page Three through his smeared, bottle-top, black-rimmed glasses. Phillip, I think, was a mixture of them both.

There were three of them living there then (baby sister Kerry was to come along later), but somehow the front door belonged to Olive, and though it was always closed to keep out the flies, figuratively it was always open to all. She appeared to know and love everyone, and everyone I knew loved Olive in return. She set out to like and accept all people, no matter what, believing, probably correctly, that she could find something in common with anyone. If you dropped by unannounced to Olive's house, it was rare not to find a guest perched on a bar stool at the breakfast bar, and it could be anyone. You were just as likely to find Hippy Maya from Commerce House commune sitting there plotting Olive's astrological star chart as you were to find Colwyn, the farmer from down the road, taking the weight off his feet before he went back to the lambing, all traces of shyness vanished as he basked in the glow of Olive. 'Best tea this side of the river, cariad,' he'd say, giving her bottom a slap as he picked up his greasy cap and headed out.

On the surface Olive appeared to be completely straightforward, which was just how I saw her then, but there was something contradictory about her all the same. For someone so open to everything and everyone, she managed to remain oddly impenetrable even so. Whoever she spent time with, no matter which part of the social spectrum they were from, she still remained resolutely, reassuringly Olive. Maya gave her a tasselled Indian skirt for her birthday one year, and Olive wore it once, probably out of politeness, with her navy sweatshirt and white trainers, and because she was Olive, she didn't suddenly look like she'd stepped off a love bus in Haight Ashbury – as my mother might have done; she just looked the same, like herself. I loved that. It felt safe. I thought that she possessed some kind of astonishing superpower: everything that she touched turned to normal, and that hopefully included me.

It was always balmy round at Phillip's – tropical – even in the winter. Olive was a big fan of central heating and she loved a nice cosy gas fire, so it was on all year round, no matter what, with the windows always firmly shut in case of flies. Phillip preferred to be without his trousers and Y-fronts, to keep himself cool. It made him feel free and relaxed, he said, and he *looked* relaxed, draped, half naked, in exaggerated repose over the back of the beige leather sofa. We'd find him there, or cross-legged on the sitting-room windowsill. That was his preferred dining spot, because tables, he said, made him nervous. Just sitting at them, he explained, made him want to wet his pants – another reason not to wear any. At home he could eat whenever he wanted, calling out to Olive when he got a bit peckish, 'Mam, get us a tray of something, will you?' His preference for orange food meant that he mainly lived off Red Leicester on Jacob's crackers, baked beans and segments of orange, brought to him by Olive on a smoked-glass plate, accompanied by a smoked-glass mug of Fanta, and most often a sweet or two on the side.

When Phillip played at our house he was biddable enough, happy to play whomever we suggested: the shopkeeper, the younger brother, even once or twice the baby when pushed; but in his house he always had to play the daddy. He seemed to have a very real need to go to work, though the pleasure it gave him wasn't obvious to the untrained eye. We'd wave him off, my sister and I, as he sighed heavily, shoving papers into an old battered burgundy leather briefcase before he left for the office behind his dad's chair. 'Another day at the millstone, then – wish me luck.' Once, briefly coming out of character as his put-upon, surrendered wife, I suggested that a father would definitely not go to work without trousers or pants – ours never did; but Phillip assured me that I didn't know what I was on about, did I? Of course he would, he said, if it was really hot. Something that I hoped, really prayed, he was wrong about.

*

There were hippies in our garden this morning, two of them. Maya and Wiggy, a couple from Commerce House, the big house on the High Street with the messily painted purple front door. They lived there with about twenty other people: the town hippies, as they were called. The country hippies lived upriver from the Fiddicks, in a house called The Mill. I watched Wiggy and Maya from the top of our slide, studying them from a safe distance, as I buffed up the metal until it shone with a pulled-down bit of my sleeve. They were bent down, both of them; hunched over, with their backs to me, one either side of my mother. My mother was in a hippy sandwich in the fruit cage. What would my nana think of that?

The slide was warm from the sunshine, and I wondered how it felt for Wiggy and Maya to be outside in the heat, out in fresh air, out in *thin* air, not like the thick, soupy air of their commune, weighed down with sweet incense and smoke. They didn't have a garden in Commerce House, no outside space at all. I'd got lost the first time I visited; there were so many rooms, one leading on to another and all looking the same to me. Throws hung from every window, blocking out the day outside, so it was dark, and crowded too, with mattresses and people. There were people wherever you looked.

I'd been in Commerce House just the day before with my mother. She'd picked me up from my ballet lesson at the chapel in town, and as we were getting into the car I had a sudden desperate need for the loo. Can't it wait, she asked, until we get home? And when I said no, I didn't think it could, she grabbed my hand and said not to worry, and led me back up the street. I knew where she was taking me. I wanted to wail out in protest, but I couldn't: it was either that or go right there in the middle of the High Street.

Minutes later we were standing in the half-light of the smoke-filled main sitting room of Commerce House. My eyes were still adjusting from the brightness outside, but I could see that it was crowded, crammed full of people, all lying around on cushions on the floor. A man in the corner was playing his guitar, strumming 'Mr Tambourine Man' – my mother's favourite. He was half singing, half mumbly-humming along and the lady next to him was clapping and yelping, which was over the top, I thought, given that he couldn't remember the words. Guitar playing seemed like an evening kind of thing to me, but then it *looked* like evening, with the candles and all the incense sticks burning, and everyone slumped around like they were exhausted at the end of a long hard day. Maya leapt up when she saw us, booming out our names; and she hugged us – my mother first, then me – and I thought she'd be clamped on to me like that for ever, silver rings pressing into my shoulders as she squeezed me tight, as if I was a tube of toothpaste and she was trying to get the little last bit out of the bottom. Seconds pass much more slowly when you're trying not to wet yourself, I realized then, as she pressed against my bladder; time slows down by at least half, like it does when you hold your breath.

I was glad of the semi-darkness when my mother explained our visit, and I felt my cheeks prick red with shame.

'Sasha, can you show Abbie where the loo is?' said Maya, and an older child emerged up through the smoky fug from the floor. He was a boy, but he had hair that was longer than mine; it was a dark kind of blonde, the colour of the wet sand on Rhyl beach, with a spattering of matching-coloured freckles on his nose.

'This way,' he said, without looking at me or smiling; he just walked out ahead of me, his bare feet slapping across the floorboards. My mother was always telling me to look people in the eye, but Sasha didn't have to if he didn't want to. I'd met Maya's daughter, Nell, a few times now, and she'd told me once that there were no rules for commune kids. She hadn't bragged about it, just said it flatly as a matter of fact: they had no school, no bedtime and they could eat their breakfast at suppertime if they wanted; and I couldn't help but feel a bit jealous, even if they never really got to eat sweets or watch telly.

Sasha led me down some stairs and then up some stairs and the door was at the top. I knew it was the loo before he told me, because I could see it even though the door was closed. There was one panel missing on the bottom right-hand side, and there was the loo, just like that, for everyone to see, bold as brass, as Olive would say. It was about as rude as you could get – obscene, in my mind – to have a loo on permanent, full display.

'Please would it be okay if I use the downstairs loo?' I asked.

'We don't *have* a downstairs loo,' Sasha replied, addressing a poster advertising the tour dates of the Grateful Dead. He looked like a lion, with his mass of hair and matching sandy-coloured shirt, which was more of a blouse really, with big bouffy sleeves and no collar.

'Okay then, sorry; *another* loo, I meant,' I said, trying to keep my voice sounding normal and not squeaky high and desperate-for-a-wee-sounding. I'd let just a tiny bit out – just a drop – but that didn't work for long, and all I could think of now, the only thing on my mind, was that scene in *Superman* where the dam burst.

'We don't have another one. This, right here, this is our one and only loo,' he said, spanning out his hands like he was presenting it to me as a prize.

'Okay, that's fine,' I said. 'You can go, thanks,' I added, stepping through the panel to save time.

'Don't you want me to wait?' he asked.

'No!' I shouted, panicked by the thought of that hellish scenario. *I bet he'd be looking at me then.* He shrugged and left me to it.

'The flush doesn't work,' he called back to me, 'so you have to use the bucket.'

My horror was diverted briefly by the sight of a rusty, ancient-looking Quality Street tin on the top of the loo without its lid on. I peered in, hoping for jewel-like, foil-wrapped chocolates; but no. Instead it was filled to the brim with water, and in it was a huge rainbow trout – beautiful, dappled with brown spots and a flash of pale pink, its body curved to the shape of the tin.

I had a sudden pang to be at my nana's house. She had actual chocolates in her bathroom, on the windowsill in a cut-glass bowl so you could help yourself when you'd washed your hands. The top of her loo was where she kept her spare loo roll, which was peach-coloured, always, and covered in a knitted doll. There was no spare loo roll here, no loo roll at all that I could see, just a stack of newspaper – was that what I was supposed to use? – next to the bucket-instead-of-a-flush. There was a damp towel on the floor, and I tried to hang it on the wobbling doorknob to cover the missing panel, but it slipped off again and again.

'Abs?' My mother was calling me. 'All right up there? Have you fallen in?'

'Fine!' I shouted. 'Nearly done!'

There was no loo seat – not attached to the loo at least; it was on the floor next to the sink with a potted spider plant in the middle of it, so I had to hover above the loo then, thighs shaking with the effort of it. The inside of the loo was stained a dark brown, as though a teabag had been left in overnight, and there were coins at the bottom of the bowl, coppers mainly: pennies and halfpenny pieces and one gleaming tenpence piece. Was it a wishing loo? Please, loo, I wished, as I did the longest, noisiest wee I'd ever done, if you have any magical powers don't let anyone come out and see me this way, I beg you. I tilted sideways, directing the stream against the porcelain to try to silence the echoey drumming.

When I was done, I struggled with the taps, forcing the cold one anti-clockwise until it screeched out a trickle of rust-coloured water. I half filled the bucket and upturned its contents in the direction of the toilet bowl, but it missed and went everywhere but. I heard a door open then, and the soft padding of bare feet outside, and panicked. I chucked the damp towel over the sodden pile of *Guardian*s-meant-for-wiping-bottoms and scrambled back out through the hole. Wiggy was emerging, stretching and sleepy-looking, from a bedroom, and I ran past him, head down along the corridor, doing up my flies as I went.

Downstairs in the sitting room, Maya was admiring my mother's jewellery.

'It's beautiful, Anna,' she said, holding up what I thought was her worst piece, a knuckle-duster double ring, which locked two fingers together side by side, making it uncomfortable as well as ugly. 'Did you make this one too?'

Yes, my mother said, she did.

'Well . . .' Maya rolled her eyes as if she was concocting a plan, '. . . we've got Wiggy the artist and John the sculptor living here, and Jenny who makes pots. I'm the weaver . . . All we need now is a jeweller!' she said. 'And Barry's a writer, isn't he?' She clapped her hands. 'Between us all, what do you reckon? We could make Commerce House into a centre for the arts! I think we need you to de-camp and move in with us!'

I wanted to punch Maya when she said that. I wanted to

knock that thought out of her: swing her a left hook, send her flying up to the ceiling and back down to the floor, where she'd lie slumped in a corner, crosses for eyes, with birds circling and tweeting above her.

I tried to think of a worse scenario: us living in the bus shelter opposite Gwalia shop – the one that smelled of wee – or in the dank, dripping cave beyond the marshes where the sheep went to die, or perhaps in Mike Brown's rusty, corrugated-iron shed where I'd seen a rat once with a fat, pink tail.

My mother was actually laughing. She looked delighted by Maya's crazy, rude suggestion.

Maya came with us down to the street to say goodbye. She stood on the pavement in her bare feet and gave my mother another hug.

'You have to come over and pick some of our raspberries,' said my mother. 'We've got an absolute glut, we need help! Come tomorrow!' she said, in a loud and embarrassingly friendly-sounding voice, right in the middle of the High Street.

Eleanor Williams' mum walked past just as she said it, in her cork wedge sandals, with her hair all flicky, pulling a checked shopping trolley behind her, and I cringed, and tried to hide my face in my mother's back. Eleanor's mum would tell Eleanor, she would tell *everyone*; telling was her favourite thing. The Rosses are friends with the hippies, don't you know? That's what she'd say, flashing her eyes wide open as she said it – *believe me*, that meant, *I'm just as surprised about that as you are.*

I didn't speak as my mother drove us back home. The back windows were wound down as far as they would go and the air juddered through the car, buffeting my face as I pictured my whole family sharing a bedroom in Commerce House: all of us, including the cats, squeezed on to a double mattress on the floor, surrounded by spider plants. My father would be writing by candlelight, sitting cross-legged, probably in just his pants; my mother would be welding with a blowtorch, with my sister and me squished in between. 'This is fun!' my sister would say, because she was like that: the sort of child who could easily see fun.

We were on the last stretch now, where the road narrowed and the fields dropped down steeply to the valley below.

'Are you okay back there?' my mother asked, turning to look at me, making us veer across the road as a car heading towards us beeped its horn. 'Honestly! I was nowhere near!' she said, shaking her hand in the mirror at the now empty again road. 'I'm not used to traffic, that's the thing.'

'I hate going to Commerce House,' I said, as a vast articulated lorry bore down on us. '*Don't look at me!*' I said, and this time she didn't. She pulled the car into the viewing point on the side of the road, where the occasional tourist – en route to Barmouth beach, or Dolgellau mines – would stop off and eat their packed lunch.

'Bloody lorries,' she said, wheels popping over plastic drink cartons, and turned round now to look at me safely. 'Hate is a very strong word.'

She didn't *sound* cross – it wasn't often that she did, but her cheeks had flushed pink, so she was. 'Not everyone chooses to live the same way,' she said, blowing a strand of hair from her face, 'and a good thing too. Wouldn't life be boring if they did?'

I thought of that. I pictured everyone living in a house like my nana and poppa's, with the same big telly, and chocolates in every room; and I didn't think that it would.

'They're lovely, Maya and Wiggy, they just live differently, that's all. They don't want to be hemmed in by life,' she said, swerving back on to the road. 'I like them for that.'

I looked out through the fingerprint-smeared back window. In the valley below, the river curved through fields, glittering silver like a giant slow-worm. I'd found one once in the compost heap and it looked like it was made of molten metal.

'Can I tell you something?' I said, the words coming out weighted and slow.

'Of course, honey bun, what is it?'

'I don't want us to move in with them.'

My mother laughed. She threw her head back like I'd said the funniest thing in the world, as I slumped in the back seat and she drove me up our hill to our house; and I felt the helplessness of being seven then – sheer and absolute – of life being out of my hands.

My mother didn't care what I thought; my feelings were not her concern. That's why Wiggy and Maya were in our garden now, greedily taking my mother up on her offer and picking all our raspberries. Wiggy had long hair like Sasha's. It was parted down the middle and straight, long enough to plait if he wanted to; ladies' hair, like my mother's. I watched him now, flicking it out of the way, over his shoulders, as he worked his way along the row of bushes, and imagined what my father's hair would look like if it were long like Wiggy's. It would grow up and out, in a great curly cloud of hair like Crystal Tipps, and it made my scalp prickle to think of it.

Maya was eating the raspberries as she went along, bell sleeves flapping, one in her mouth, one in the basket, as she sang something unrecognizable and folksy, hey nonny-nonnying while she filled up her basket, *our* basket, with fruit – fruit that belonged to me. They'd been invited, I knew that, but I was angry even so: it still felt like they were stealing. My father leant out of his office window, from the stable block behind them where he was supposed to be working, and shouted out to ask if anyone would like a cup of tea. 'Yes!' they chorused. 'Yes, please!' I wondered if they'd be invited to stay for supper as well, as I examined my distorted face looming back at me from the shiny metal: a surprising and dismaying sight. Was it just the angle? My hair clung to my face, cupping my upper cheeks, and stopping then, right there, just over the top of my ears. Nana was right again, right about those pigtails, I thought, as I made my breath go all hot and steamed over my reflection until it disappeared, until it was thankfully lost under a cover of condensation.

Wiggy and Maya were outside the netting now, on the bank with my mother, relaxing in the sunshine above the steps to the middle lawn. They were sitting in between the box bushes, the bushes that had been destroyed by my mother when she'd had a go at topiary last summer. 'I've made a chair. Sit on it!' she'd said, garden shears still in hand. 'Go on, have a go, it looks comfy!' and I'd done it, just to please her – she'd been chopping away all day – but was swallowed into the bush, tipped backwards into the spiky branches. 'It just needs a bit more work,' she said, reaching in to pull me out, and she carried on attacking it, on and on, because nothing seemed to stop her when she had scissors in her hand. Even now, a summer on, the bushes were half the size they used to be, with huge holes gouged out of their middles as if they'd been hit by a giant cannon ball.

As I slid down the slide, I heard a jangle of bangles, and I looked up to see my mother, arms raised above her head as she made to *take off her blouse*. I closed my eyes and stayed put right there, on the feet-scraped bare bit of earth, and prayed – there was nothing to do but pray – *please, please, please let there be some-thing underneath*, and when I opened my eyes I could breathe again because she wasn't naked, she was in a pea-green bikini top. She waved at me, and lay down, in just that and a very large necklace and small, short denim shorts, and took a lit cigarette from Wiggy and smoked it lying face up, staring at the sky.

My father was coming from the sunroom with a tray of tea and I was about to join them, in case there would be biscuits, but I stayed where I was, because now Maya was taking her blouse off and Wiggy was giving her a hand, *helping her to be naked in front of my father*. I knew this time there would be breasts – no point in praying – and I was right; there they were, revealed from behind a curtain of cheesecloth: small and shiny white like a couple of iced cherry buns. 'Ah, Barry!' she said, as she took a mug of tea. 'Just what I fancied,' as if it was completely normal to be naked from the top down in our garden, and my father handed out the mugs, and flopped down next to her; and I looked for signs of embarrassment or upset from my mother or my father, but there were none.

They were all laughing and chatting now, passing each other homemade cigarettes. Wiggy was saying nice things about our house; Maya said how lovely the garden was; she was compli-menting my mother on her gardening and my mother was soaking it all in and loving it, I could see. I knew what they were doing. This is just what Eleanor Williams did to Lisa Evans at school. She kept telling her she loved her shoes, she loved her coat; *I love you*, she meant, *I want to be your friend*. Wiggy and Maya were going to flatter my parents into loving them; and then they'd get us all to move into their stinking commune. Well, they could flatter away – good luck to them, as Olive would say. My parents weren't blind, they weren't stupid either; and I heard my heart thudding in my ears when I thought that, like the music in an exciting bit in a film, because it wasn't true. My parents *were* stupid once in a while, I thought, as I looked at my father in his tiny, tight shorts, which were the colour of mustard, the bright kind that goes on a hotdog.

I sat there, seething, and kept my eyes away from Maya's chest, fixed them instead on the two baskets filled to the brim at their feet. *They were our raspberries*; they should leave them here with us. I could eat them all in one sitting if only my mother would let me. My sister had tried to do just that the summer she was two. She'd worked her way through the whole fruit cage, shuffling along in her nappy, squashing the berries into her mouth in handfuls, until she was coated all over – her face, her hands, her taut white melon belly – with dribbled-out seeds and pink juice and mashed-up, pulpy fruit. There was no proof of it, no doctor would back her up, but my mother was convinced that was how my sister got peritonitis: a raspberry pip stuck in her appendix. My sister nearly died that summer. I had no idea how close she was to dying, even though she was gone, in hospital, for months, because my parents hid what was happening from me. This might explain why my mother didn't like us gorging on raspberries, and perhaps made sense of my sister's obsession: her absolute fixation with nursing.

I could see my sister now, on tiptoes outside the sunroom by our pond, in her new nurse's outfit, admiring her reflection in the glass, smoothing down the creases, adjusting her pin-on watch, fiddling about with her hat. She loved that outfit because it wasn't homemade, like most of our fancy dress, but a proper one, bought from an actual shop, given to her for her fifth birthday. When she'd unwrapped it she'd sighed and nodded her head very slowly. She had prayed for this, she said, and God had heard her; of course he had, because healing was her destiny. Katherine was always self-assured, but in that uniform her quiet confidence was elevated even further. Dressed as a nurse she had a collected, authoritative manner and imparted what appeared to be genuine medical advice. Phillip was in awe, and our games together had recently taken on a medical bent. Drawn as he was to hard work, his daddy character kept having to take days off so that my sister could tenderly nurse him back to health.

'Don't you look professional?' said Maya to my sister, who was striding past the fruit cage now, nurse's bag in hand, heading down the lawn.

'I'm off now!' she said, giving them a cheery wave, oblivious, it seemed, to the nudity. 'Just doing my work – see you soon,' she added, checking her plastic pin-on watch.

'Okay then, not too long!' called my mother as my sister batted away the tall grass that grew wild and unchecked at the stony bottom part of the lawn and made her way past our tree house towards the adjoining gate and the Browns' house on the other side of the fence.

It was me who usually led the way, me who decided what we did and where, so it was unnerving to see my sister taking off without me, without even a backwards glance. I got up – relieved now to have a purpose to leave – and followed after, trailing her down the lawn. She vaulted the gate as I crouched in amongst the laurel and watched from our side of the fence as she ran down the bank to their yard and knocked on the Browns' front door. I heard Olive 'Ooh' at her and tell her that Phillip was in his bedroom, and she nodded without smiling, disappeared into their house and up the stairs.

By the time I got to his bedroom door, a trouserless Phillip was lying face down on his Superman bedspread, legs, arms and fingers all outstretched, eyes scrunched shut in joyful embarrassment.

'You're sick, really sick. Did you know that?' said my sister.

'Yeh, thought I was,' he replied, grinning, his pink cheeks shining in a hearty, happy vision of health.

'It's not funny,' she said, placing her hand on his shoulder. 'Stay still now while I get the injection ready, Phillip. This is the only way to save you.' The grin dropped from his face.

She took our toy spud gun, gleaming red and barely used, and a battered-looking sprouting potato from her nurse's bag. I watched as she plunged the gun into the potato with a vigorous-sounding grunt, crunching it wetly through the potato's flesh. I could have stopped her then – just a cough to alert her to my presence would have done it – but I didn't want to. There was something thrilling about watching her so confidently, defiantly, breaking the rules. She didn't care. She'd pole-vaulted over the line.

'Open up your bottom,' she said, in her calm nurse's voice. Phillip obediently parted his cheeks. She took aim with the ease of a Charlie's Angel: gave her hair a quick flick, put one leg in front of the other, bent her knees, both hands on the gun, and pulled the trigger. There was that shriek again, but this time it got higher and higher until the sound just disappeared into nowhere. Phillip thrashed around, mouth open, looking like he ought to be shouting, but not, like the sound had been turned down on the television. My sister was usually able to keep her emotions enviably in check, but she looked a bit flustered now, as she tried to steady him. The springs squeaked out in protest as he jerked around on the bed, then he found his voice again and the room shook with the full force of Olive hurtling up the stairs.

That was the one and only time that we saw Olive truly furious. She had Sellotape stuck all around her face, contorting her skin as she shouted, but it didn't stop her looking terrifying. I was too shocked to say a word – even to think about pointing the finger at my sister – that's how shocked I was.

We stood on the stairs, halfway down, and listened to Olive ringing the doctor. Opposite us, on a shelf above the stairs, her collection of Toby jugs stared back at us, chests puffed out, smugly pleased. She looked up as she slammed the receiver down, swiped a tear from her face with the back of her sleeve and yelled at us to get out, softening it slightly then to could we please go home? Her voice also went frighteningly high when she was upset, so it must have been genetic.

I looked down at my sister, sitting now two steps down from me, chin propped on her hands. It was hard to believe it was her – so blonde and little and sweet – and one small piece of potato that had caused such an upset. It wasn't Phillip that concerned me – children hurt each other all the time – but Olive's reaction that had shocked me, that my sister had the power to upset her. I didn't know children could affect adults like that, adults who weren't their parents, and it gave me an uncomfortable glimpse of us being less different, less separate somehow, the young and the old, than I'd safely assumed that we were. I would be an adult too one day; I'd grow up and become one of them. I'd known that but never believed it.

We couldn't bring ourselves to leave completely, so we sat and waited on the dock-leaf-covered bank outside their house. Behind us, in front of the sprouts that grew tall and strong at the edge of their vegetable patch, was our half-built Olympic swimming pool, lined with binbags, ready and waiting to be filled. We'd dug it last weekend, right in the middle of their lawn, while

Olive sat in her deckchair drinking dandelion and burdock, giving us the thumbs-up as we churned the lawn up into a mud bath. She was generous like that. The plan was to fill it up from the river, three fields down, dig a channel through farmer Colwyn's fields. 'Lovely idea,' she'd said. 'You do that, kids. I'll be here, ready and waiting with my swimsuit.'

'Do you think we'll ever get to finish it now?' asked my sister.

'I doubt it,' I said, picturing our desired end result: a vast azure-blue pool sparkling in the sunlight, the three-tiered diving board at the far end; and in front of it the red-and-white striped changing hut, which would go right in the middle, instead of the sprouts.

What havoc had my sister caused? We'd have no swimming pool now, no popping in and out with Phillip. We'd have next-door neighbours who'd hate us, for ever; things could go like that sometimes, I knew. Sara Fiddick's mum, Eirian, and her sister, Megan, hadn't spoken for years, and no one knew why but them. They ignored each other if they walked past each other on the High Street, just looked in the other direction or busied themselves in their bags. I ripped up clump after clump of grass as I pictured us walking past Phillip's kitchen window, waving to Olive as usual, and she staring coldly back then turning the other way. What would become of us without the Browns? Commerce House would become of us. Wiggy and Maya would become of us instead.

The front door burst open and we watched Olive carry a still-frenzied Phillip out to their Ford Cortina. His blue-white bare bottom, a common-and-garden sight to us, looked new to me in the broad daylight; free from the confines of his cosy sitting room, all familiarity lost, it looked unexpectedly, nauseatingly rude. As Olive attempted to settle Phillip down on the back seat, with soothing tut tuts and bless yous, Sara Fiddick, from over the fields, appeared on the road below, her pointy little face craning up over the railings. A shiny liquorice stick hung wetly from her mouth. She pointed to it triumphantly, thin lips pursed possessively around it as she surveyed the scene, and dipped it then in a scrumpled paper bag of sherbet, sucking it clean again with lipsqueaking relish.

'Oi, bitches!' she shouted, when her work was done, waving her liquorice wand towards the wailing car. 'What's all this then? What's going on?' she said, swiping the dark brown juice that stained her chin with the back of a chewed-up-looking sleeve. Too miserable even to kow-tow to Sara, we stared at the ground, the two of us, hoping she'd move on. I knew she wouldn't; I could see her nostrils flaring with excitement, like a horse approaching a jump. She wasn't called Sticky Beak Sara for nothing.

'Eh? Did you hear me or what?'

'Nothing,' said my sister, head hung low as she ripped up clumps of grass from the bank.

'Lying cow,' said Sara, her voice squeakily indignant. 'Stuck-up English cows, the both of you. Like I give a shit what you spazzes are up to anyway,' she said, stepping back on to the road. 'Oh, watch out when you leave here, will you? There's some dog shit by here. Don't tread in it, mind – looks like it's your mam,' and she threw her head back to give an exaggerated, uncomfortable-looking laugh, revealing her tiny, sharp, pale-brown goo-coated teeth. For a small, skinny child she had a surprising mouth: disproportionately massive, all the better for shouting with. 'Come over later if you want to play, will you?' she said, and I wished I already had my Sindy doll, promised to me by my nana: mine when they next came to stay. I was counting the days: three weeks and I'd be one up on Sara. I imagined waving my Sindy doll in her face, as I watched her strutting off down the lane, hop-scotching in and out of the potholes as she went.

When Sara had gone, Katherine, still in character, and certainly in denial, stood up, bag in hand, and cleared her throat to ask Olive politely if she please might come along to assist the doctor. Olive, grappling with the driver's door – which jammed shut unless you gave it a good kick – looked up to her for a moment to shout in a voice that had now gone deep like a man's that, no, she buggering well could not.

3

Food for free

It was autumn now, according to my mother, but the leaves still looked green to me and it was warm enough to wear a T-shirt, so I wasn't sure if I believed her. My mother was always hurrying things along; she was just fast-forwarding to her favourite season, that's what I thought: impatient for it to begin. She *liked* the changes, she said, welcomed the bracken turning rusty on the hillside, the daylight softening, tinted orangey-pink. Not me. I liked things to stay just as they were. Who could ever want the summer to finish? Why would you ever wish for that?

We were out when Nana and Poppa arrived this time. We would have been there, my sister and I, waiting for them on the wall outside from first thing, if my mother hadn't spotted mushrooms in the field in front of our house from the upstairs window of the blue room. The sight of them revived her in an instant, stirred her from her silent, trance-like preparations.

'Quick! Come on, let's get them, before they're trampled on by cows,' she called out to my father, who was heading to the old stable, sunken-shouldered, with a wheelbarrow to stock up with logs.

She folded the flappy legs of her jeans into her wellies and grabbed the wicker baskets from the bench in the porch, and she was off, striding down the lane, shouting over her shoulder at us all to hurry on up, the wind catching her voice and lifting it up and away. My father yelled back at her to wait, cursing when she didn't. 'Jesus! Bullshit, Anna!' and he lifted us then into the wheelbarrow, where we sat in amongst the flakes of bark and remnants of wood, soft and wormhole-ridden pieces that clung to our cords, coating them all over. He tipped the wheelbarrow from side to side, lurching from left to right, around the potholes that peppered the road, pushing us after her, while we held on as tight as we could, shouting out, our voices squeaky-high with glee, as we rolled down the road towards the field in front of Olive's kitchen window.

We were allowed to play together now, Katherine and Phillip and I. Olive didn't have it in her to stay cross for long, that's what she'd said when my mother had marched my sister round there to apologize, with a homemade card saying sorry and a big bag of sherbet pips from the Gwalia shop, which made me prickle with the injustice of it, *as if he didn't have enough sweets already.*

'Not to worry, no! Please don't worry, any of you, it's all right as rain up there now, isn't it, Phil? All hunkydory,' she said, eyes wide and trained on Phillip, waiting for him to agree.

'It never hurt in the first place, Mam, *I told you,*' he said, rubbing his neck with the palm of his hand, like he did when he got embarrassed.

'Any which way, water under the bridge, that's what I say,' Olive said, waving one hand over her shoulder then reaching for the Vimto. 'Let's have it hot, shall we? For a treat,' as my sister grinned with relief, and my shoulders dropped back to where they should have been all along and my breath came back in a rush. The world wasn't going to end after all. Things could carry on; *we could carry on* just as we were, and I felt a surge of lightness, just as when my sister climbed off my back after I'd piggybacked her across the whole of the bottom lawn; and I wondered what water and bridges had to do with Phillip's injured bottom, pictured the water under the humpbacked bridge in the village, dark and cold and filled with slimy stones. We paddled there sometimes after school, searching for sticklebacks, my sister, Sara and I, but Phillip had never been with us, you'd never get him to go in there. 'No chance, not me!' he'd say whenever we asked him to come.

'Why don't you all go on outside and have a play?' Olive suggested, taking two cups from the mug tree by the toaster. 'Anna and I can sit down and have a chinwag,' and we rushed into their hallway, with framed family photographs on one side of the radiator and love spoons on the other, and above it a picture, printed on metal, of a horse's head – a beautiful horse with a flowing mane who looked just like Black Beauty.

'Well, Anna,' said Olive, settling on the bar stool as we scrabbled for our plimsolls by the door, 'you are never going to believe this. Would you guess what I've just heard?' and the lilt of her voice, soothing and familiar, bubbled over me as I gazed out through the open door to the field, which looked empty, wide and inviting.

'There's treasure in that field,' said Phillip, loosening up his laces, 'I know there is. I'll show you where it is and all.'

So we'd climbed the gate and gone searching there together, Phillip glancing anxiously every now and again towards his kitchen window, checking Olive was watching. 'Mam!' and she'd wave, and nod, and give him a thumbs-up, and then she'd lean back in towards my mother, elbows on the Formica worktop, to tell her more news; there was always important news.

Phillip swore on his mother's life – crossed his heart and hoped to die – that he'd seen a robber in the field that very morning; a man in a stripy top with a shovel and a swagbag bursting with gold teapots covered all over in rubies. He'd spied on him from the rhododendron bushes, he said, and watched him as he buried it in the middle of the field. Then Olive had called him in for brekkie; his mam had ruined it, he said, but that was that, he couldn't be late for his brekkie.

We'd searched the whole field then, from the bramble bushes around the top fence, right down to the alders by the river that marked the end of farmer Colwyn's land. We scanned the ground, kicking at every molehill, but we found nothing, only the skeleton of a shrew, slightly stinking, with a small patch of velvety brown fur still attached, which my sister gently placed in the front pocket of her dungarees so she could take it home and dry out the smell in the airing cupboard.

Now, though, the ground was dappled with mushrooms that had popped up from nowhere: dazzling white and perfectly round, bulging out from the long grass that grew around the cow-pats. We pulled them from the ground, one by one, with a hollow-sounding rip. Their tops were slippery cool in our hands, their undersides delicate pale pink umbrellas. Soil, black with damp, clung stubbornly to their stalks. Only when the last one had been picked did we head for home, swinging our weighty baskets, singing 'Green Grow the Rushes, O' as we marched up the hill.

We clambered back into the wheelbarrow, my sister and I, thoughts now turned to Nana and Poppa, and the presents they would bring. I was busy elevating myself to a better kind of child, the sort that owns a brand-new Sindy doll, and possibly even a Barbie too – wondering what exactly Sara would think of me then – when I saw their red car in our drive, alone, doors ajar, horn already sounded.

'Shit!' said my father, wellies clunking as he sped up the pace, lurching us down the road.

'Damn it. They're early, aren't they?' said my mother, patting down her hair. She took a rumpled tissue from her jeans pocket, spat on it and leant down to give my face and my sister's a rough wipe, as we wailed out in futile protest, batting her hand away.

'House sign!' My father gave an exaggerated, wavering wail, like Tarzan. 'I've forgotten to put up the bleeding house sign,' he said. 'We're all doomed!' and my mother spluttered with laughter behind him.

I could see Nana and Poppa now, sitting on the bench by the front gate, fur coats draped around their shoulders, Nana's white and Poppa's dark brown: two bears, a polar and a grizzly, sheltering from the mild breeze. They were hunched over, cigarettes in hand, arms and legs crossed to protect against the Welsh elements, considered by my nana to be unusually harsh, always, even when the sun shone bright like today. My sister's wind-frizzed curls were whipping at my face, obscuring my vision, but still, I could tell Nana and Poppa were livid.

As we got closer the scene revealed itself in full. My grandparents were not alone. There was another couple standing by our front gate, actually *conversing* with them, the taller of the two gesticulating wildly, gangly arms flailing all over the place. That should have been fine – welcome even – except my nana and poppa didn't like meeting people; they mostly *hated* to, in fact, reserving a very particular, ill-disguised loathing for 'the locals', as they called everyone they ever met through my parents.

We drew closer still and the last joyous thoughts of Sindy drained away, like toothpaste juice gurgling down the plughole, as I realized who they were with. It was Wiggy and Maya, unmistakable now, horribly impossible to miss in their home-dyed colour-clashing clothes. My father gave a long, low, primal-sounding groan, like a sheep in the throes of a difficult labour. 'God no, please no, not now,' he said as he waved to them all, and shouted out 'Hello there!' in a strangulated, pretend jolly voice.

In the opposite field an audience of shabby-looking sheep were back again for more; they stood squished up together in a row, their fat, twitching bodies matted with twigs and leaves, as they studied everyone with bemusement through the barbed-wire fence. My father dropped the handles of the wheelbarrow next to them, thudding us to the ground, and we stayed put like that for a second and just stared. My perfectly coiffed grandparents were sitting rigidly side by side, wordlessly surveying our visitors. Twin plumes of cigarette smoke curled above them as they shivered in their heavy coats – with cold rather than distaste, that's how I saw it then. Wiggy and Maya were standing, animatedly chatting and laughing away to them, apparently oblivious to the discomfort emanating from the bench. Maya was jumping up and down with excitement like a child, and she looked like a child too, like Pippi Longstocking in her stripy black-and-white tights, her henna-ed red hair in two sticky-out plaits. Wiggy wafted about behind her, head thrown back, hair and clothes flowing as he waved a carved wooden staff around like a wizard performing a spell. Against the backdrop of the stark, purple mountain-face, the two of them looked made up: like a couple of actors in fancy dress performing to an unimpressed audience of two.

Wiggy saw us first and gave a whoop that echoed to us once, and then again.

'*There* you are,' crackled my nana from the bench, as Wiggy strode towards us, legs billowing in bright red clown trousers, his long hair drifting out behind him.

'The Ross Family returns!' he said, a homemade cigarette

dangling, crooked, from the corner of his mouth. 'Good to see you,' he said, as he wrapped my father in a hug, and I cringed because it was so familiar, so definitely friendly, there was no getting away from that.

'We were just wondering what had happened to you all, weren't we, Ed?' said my poppa, standing up and giving his slacks a good tug downwards, swiping his hair flat to his head above each ear. My sister and I jumped from the wheelbarrow and ran towards them, past Wiggy and Maya, towards our nana's kisses, woodchips flying from our turn-ups, as Poppa held his hand high in his signature stationary gesture of welcome.

'I'm so sorry we're late, Edna,' said my mother, as my nana offered up her cheek, slanting her head sideways so my mother could kiss it.

'Not to worry, darling,' said Nana, in a quiet, broken-sounding voice which seemed to be saying the opposite, air-kissing my mother back, coral lips pursed to one side, her eyes darting to Wiggy and back again.

'I presume you've all met?' said my father, rubbing his hands together. 'Maya, Wiggy, my parents: Leslie and Edna,' introducing them as if he were in a business meeting and everyone was in suits, not shoeless like Maya and Wiggy, or bra-less like Maya, which was definite; I could see her nipples, semi-covered now at least, through her Indian cotton blouse.

'We've already met!' Wiggy flashed his even-toothed grin. 'We've been enjoying getting to know your folks,' he said to my father, and he meant it, I knew. Wiggy liked people and always expected them to like him back. If they didn't, he never seemed to notice, or was it care? Either way, it was hard to tell. 'Never judge' was one of his mantras; 'let people be' – a philosophy I can see now was entirely lost on my nana and poppa, who loved nothing better than to judge, and harshly too, or what would be the point?

'Yes, we've all had a nice chat, haven't we?' said Maya, smiling up at my grandparents. 'We had a bit of a discussion about the fur coats.' She reached out to stroke my nana's elbow. 'Poor, poor bears,' she murmured, making a pretend sad face, pushing out her bottom lip in the direction of Nana, who had her back to her and kept it that way.

'We've got good news, though, haven't we, Edna?' said Wiggy. 'Your mother has *healing hands*,' and he actually touched one of them then, making Nana's whole body stiffen as if she was playing musical statues. I studied Nana's hands, scrunched into balls now, knuckles poking out white through her thin, yellowing skin. They looked more like gnarled chicken's feet to me, but then you never did know. Sometimes I felt my scalp prickle when she brushed my hair.

'There you go, Mum, if you're not golf captain this year, you could set up a healing business,' said my father, properly smiling for the first time all day.

'Don't be daft, Barry,' said my nana, spitting out the words towards the ground.

Wiggy let out a big, comfortable bellow of a laugh, the sort that made you join in without thinking. Good humour bubbled out of him non-stop, and it was infectious, his happiness; I couldn't deny him that. Usually I found myself grinning back, despite myself, faintly uncomfortable even so. Now I think that it was a kind of jealousy I felt. Uncontainable joy was the remit of children, unencumbered as we were by mortgages and mortality, and here he was, a fully grown adult, muscling in, treading on our patch with his great big bare hairy-toed feet.

He was bending down now, picking up a large, flat brown

parcel, propped against the wall by the front gate. My grand-parents' eyes were fixed on it, eyebrows raised in expectation, which made me anxious, and I willed them to drop their eye-brows right back down, because I knew what was in it, and I knew they would hate it too. It was a painting, one of Wiggy's paintings, bought by my parents at an art exhibition at Commerce House.

I wanted Wiggy to leave it wrapped, but he was already lifting it out of the paper, holding it out in front of him for all of us to see. I would have felt less embarrassed, truly, if he'd held out his willy for us to look at instead. The painting he revealed was hideous to me: a vast, abstract purple-and-pink-tinted universe of planets and stars; its ugliness made all the more so to me by my nana and poppa's identical slack-jawed look of utter incom-prehension. To my shame, my father said he loved it, and you could tell, absolutely, that he did.

Maya hugged my nana goodbye and hummed with pleasure, and I knew Nana wouldn't like that; I could see it in the way she was standing, straight, bolt upright, not fitting into Maya at all, as she squeezed my nana's body tight.

'We'll meet again, I hope,' said Wiggy, addressing my poppa with outstretched arms, fixing him with his light-sabre eyes. They were the palest blue eyes I'd ever seen – paler even than a sheepdog's eyes, see-through almost, as if they were made out of water. He could hypnotize you in a second if he wanted to, that's what my sister said, and it was true: he did it to my father often enough, made him go to parties at Commerce House just with the power of his magical stare.

We stood there and watched them both heading down our road, and even though we were outside the air felt heavy, as though we were all crammed together in a slightly too small lift.

'Well, what can I say?' said Poppa when they were barely out of earshot.

'Barry, tell me, who were they exactly?' asked Nana.

'They're just friends of ours,' said my father, examining his painting with his head cocked to one side. 'Friends from town,' he added.

My nana breathed in deep and stood up extra straight. 'You need to be careful with people like that. Very careful indeed,' she said slowly, and the tone of her voice, flat and very sure, like an official warning from the government, made my breath come out shallow and fast. What did she mean? I looked up at her for more, but she left it at that and drew me to her, hugging me extra tight.

'Look, Nana, do you want to see our mushrooms now?' asked my sister, holding up her brimming basket towards her.

'Oh Anna!' said Nana to my mother. 'My darling, why didn't you *tell* us you needed mushrooms?' She gazed up at my mother with watery eyes, scanning her face for the answer.

'Well, we didn't exactly *need* them,' said my mother, 'they were just there.'

'But if you wanted some, we could have *brought* you some from Liverpool, couldn't we, Les?' said Nana, turning to Poppa for back-up.

Poppa nodded. 'Of course we could, of course. You only had to ask,' he said, placing a hand on my mother's shoulder.

'These are free,' said my father, who had picked up my nana's white leather vanity case and was heading for the door.

'Yes, but it really wouldn't have been a problem for us to *buy* them for you,' said Nana, stubbing out her cigarette with the heel of her patent-leather boot.

They stood there in the porch, surveying us for a moment,

their faces slack with disappointment. It would never be said – not in earshot of my parents at least – but I knew what they were thinking: taking food for free was what beggars did. Nana had said that to me once when I picked a blackberry for her, slapping it from my hand as if it were deadly poison. They were appalled, you could tell, just from the way they'd forgotten to close their mouths. I had to look away, my cheeks burning with the shameful acknowledgement of it.

I found my grandparents' fear contagious. I couldn't help it; when they were worried, so was I. Their views were so delineated, so black and white, that I found it reassuring. In my nana and poppa's straightforward, ordered world there was simply right and wrong, and nothing else, no murky grey in between. They had such a sure sense of themselves and the world they inhabited that for a child as yet with neither, it was a great relief, a simple, easy-to-follow way of thinking, nervous as I was of anything in between.

I had no idea then, but their fears had a context, a grounding, I think, in their Jewish history, which explained the anxieties they felt and their uneasiness with anything new or different. They had an absolute need to be seen to be respectable, as I did too. Intentionally or not, my father, their errant son, had done much to sabotage that over the years, though it took another ten years or so for me to work that out. Back then, I being a happily narcissistic seven-year-old, my father existed only in relation to me. He had no past that I could picture. Life before I was in it didn't occur to me if I could help it, so I blithely questioned nothing, hooked into their way of thinking. Why? Because they said so.

'Oh, and Anna, you left the front door unlocked,' said Poppa, as he picked up his packet of cigarettes and shoved them into the inner pocket of the sports jacket under his bearskin.

'We don't ever lock it,' said my mother, shaking off her wellies. 'No thieves around here!'

'Well I hate to tell you, Anna, but that's not true,' said Poppa, smiling grimly as he directed his cigarette to the space on the wall where the house sign was meant to be. 'Unless I'm very much mistaken,' he went on, 'there was a beautifully crafted sign – handmade in Liverpool – right there last time I looked.'

My mother made her eyes go wide and looked pretend surprised.

'Stolen! I've said it before, haven't I, Edna?' he said, noisily clearing his throat.

'Yes, you have, my darling, many times,' said Nana.

'I say to you, don't I, Ed? I say: it's safer in Liverpool than it is out here in the countryside.'

'You do, Les,' confirmed Nana, placing a supportive hand on his furry back.

'You'd be better off there, you really would, if you ask me,' he said, but quietly this time, as he brushed his loafers vigorously back and forth on the doormat, before lifting up each sole to check for any remnants of mud.

Nana picked up a holdall and swung it over her shoulder. Two identical yellow-and-see-through plastic packages were sticking out of the open zip, and my stomach flipped when I saw their precious contents: two Sindy dolls, just their heads visible, one brunette, one blonde; unmistakable, incredible and ours. I felt a raw, uncomfortable rush of pleasure then, as I pictured Sara Fiddick's face horribly contorted with rage. She was going to scratch my eyes out when she saw them, or have a good go at least.

4

Born shouting

Phillip Brown wanted to come along too when he saw where I was heading, just as he always did. He was there as I turned the corner to the lane, slouching over the railings outside his chalet, with Olive safely behind him at the kitchen window, 'keeping an eye' as she did the washing-up.

'Hey! Are you going to the Fiddicks' then, Ab?' he asked, tentatively stepping on to the grass as if it might be booby-trapped, and shuffling down the grassy bank on his bottom. I nodded, picking up the pace, as I clutched my ballerina Sindy doll tight around her non-existent waist.

'That's good, that is,' he said, calling after me. 'I'm coming too, I am,' he said, louder now, already pink-faced with exertion as he struggled to catch up. I rolled my eyes and marched a little faster. He would never make it to the Fiddicks', and I knew that for certain. *Anyone* could tell you that – apart from Phillip himself, that is. He had a boundless optimism, you had to give him that, a magical ability to reinvent, to forget momentarily his true, timid self. He was eternally attached to Olive, you see, for ever and ever amen, bound by an invisible elastic that stretched for fifty yards maximum, before pinging him back to the safety of her warm, navy, sweatshirt-covered bosom.

Phillip stopped at the same place as he always did, the end

of the lane, just as the big oak tree loomed into view and the fields spread out wide and flat before us. It was the enormity of the space before him and the sheer scale of that tree that did it, I think. *Here it is: the big wide world stretching out, come and get it.* He couldn't. Phillip had a need to be contained, indoors ideally, in his own front room. He was safe there, on his windowsill, with four walls to protect him and his view comfortingly restricted by sprouts and runner beans and the back of the garden shed. It was his choice entirely, a self-imposed constraint, but it seemed temporary to me, even then: this stunted, cosy way of being – ever so slightly enticing though it was. He'd grow out of it, that's what I thought; he'd have to, wouldn't he? Life wouldn't allow him to live like that for ever. Sara Fiddick wouldn't either.

He paused in the shadows of the oak tree for a second, glanced towards the fields where we were heading, and turned back, swivelling on one heel. The crunching rip of gravel underfoot, like the jarring scratch of a record needle, signified the end of his brief elevation.

'I got to go back now, I have,' he said, adding no further explanation – none needed with me, he knew. He peeled off then, breaking away, like the fuel tank of a rocket heading back to earth, and I started running, fast and free away from him, the space shuttle heading for the moon.

It took me twenty minutes to get to the Fiddicks' house from there. Two paths, four fields and then this last creepy bit: the winding, stone-dashed track down to their valley, where the overgrown blackthorn blotted out the sunlight, and the stream that ran alongside it spilt out as it reached the bottom, coating the ground in a shiny black slick of water. I ran down it as fast as I could, zigzagging from side to side so I wouldn't slip, only slowing as I turned the last corner where the stream disappeared, bubbling underground to join the river, and the path widened, opening out into the morning sun. Below me, I could see the roof of their cottage, tucked back in the shadows of a row of pine trees that towered protectively behind it like a giant windbreak, and in front of it the river cutting through their garden, dissecting it clean in two.

I stopped there on the brow of the hill and listened out for signs of life. The three big ones would be outside by now – baby Evan most probably too – in the orchard most likely, or up at the back of the house by the old well where they had their bonfires. I was rewarded finally with a shout – cross and hoarse-sounding, typically Fiddick – rising up above the rush of the river, and then another.

'Oi! Get off, you bugger! Leave me alone!'

'That's it, I'm telling Mam!'

'Get down off of there and go and feed the blimmin' pigeons like she said, will you?'

'Mam! Tell him! Maaaam!'

I ran down to the front of the house, through the side gate falling off its hinges, and into their orchard on the edge of the river, where I found the two eldest boys, Neville and Aled, standing, sweaty-faced, underneath a vibrating plum tree. A pale, stringy-looking leg dangled down from its branches, blue-white and bruised all over, with a too-big slipper hanging from its foot.

'All right, Ab,' shouted Aled, as Neville raised a thumb to me in welcome.

'Hiya,' I said, navigating my way through the tall grass, damp and slick with morning dew.

'What's that you said?' shouted Aled, as he took a run at the tree and gave its trunk a good kick.

'I said: HIYA!' I shouted back this time through a half-cupped hand.

A gargled sounding 'Aaargh' came from towards the house, and there was baby Evan, sitting under the garden wall, propped up either side with a sofa cushion. He waved a sticky-looking hand at me and with the other pushed a plum into his mouth as if it was a blender; rivers of pink juice ran down his stomach and pooled at the top of his nappy.

Above us, Sara Fiddick's beaky face appeared from between the leaves, her hair still messy and big from bed, backcombed up at the back like a half-done beehive.

'Look,' I said, holding my Sindy aloft with ceremonial gravitas: the torch to my Statue of Liberty.

'Which one's that then?' asked Sara, wrinkling her nose and sticking her neck out for closer inspection. 'Ballerina, is it? Bollocks, that is,' she said, relegating me with a flippant wave of her hand. 'It's the riding one you want, that's the best one, that is. That's the one I got.'

Sara didn't have a Riding Sindy. She didn't have any – not Ball-gown Sindy, not Beach Sindy, not one. But what did it matter? She acted like she owned the entire set; and when it came down to it, *that* was what I wanted, not a small, bendy-limbed doll in fishnet tights, but the confidence, audacious and unwavering, of someone who knew they were destined to rule the world.

'Oi! Ab! Get a look at this then, will you?' she said, and she leant forward to reveal the contents of her upturned nightie: a pile of plums, pink and brown and overripe.

'It's my ammunition. I'm running out, mind. Get us some more, will you?' she said, pointing to the riverbank, where they were scattered, wasp-filled and sticky with sap, and dotted white with mould.

'Don't bother, Ab, we're going to kill her now, aren't we, Nev?' said Aled. 'Mind out the way now, will you?' He was shoving back the sleeves of his pyjamas. I stepped aside, and he roared through the gooseberry bushes and flung himself up on to the lower branch of the tree. He grabbed at Sara's legs, and she kicked him away as the plums rained down, skins splitting open to reveal soft yellow flesh, coating him with their boozy-smelling juice. Eventually, predictably, he was forced into retreat, to the sound of Sara's victorious laughter and baby Evan's laboured claps, as the last of the plums thudded to the ground.

Sara had a surprising laugh. It was the deep, knowing cackle of a world-weary woman who had been around the block a few times. She was eight years old, and skinny and small for her age; she had barely left her valley apart from to go to school, so I have no idea why she laughed like that, but it made me frightened and deeply in her thrall, just the way she liked it. She had the laugh of a leader and it was complicit between us from the start that I was there to follow.

'Blimmin' bitch, you are, Sara!' shouted Aled, bent over double, from the safety of the kitchen door.

There was a screech as the top window of the house was flung back and their mother, Eirian, poked her head out, like a cuckoo popping out of a clock.

'Oi!' she shouted, addressing the air in front of her with the authority of someone used to being listened to. 'What did I tell you just now, eh? Sara and Aled: pigeons. Neville, sort those ferrets.'

She was tiny, Eirian, thinner than Sara, with small, child-sized hands, which made the cigarette she held look ridiculous, vast, like an oversized prop.

'I was just going to, wasn't I?' said Neville. 'But that one there wouldn't blimmin' let me, would she?' he said, flicking the

Vs up at his sister, who swung herself down from the bottom branch and leapt to the ground with a gymnastic flourish as the window slammed shut above her.

Baby Evan stretched out his arms towards Sara and she hoiked him up to her hip with a weary sigh. 'Come on then,' she said, as he batted her cheek and let out an ear-splitting squeal of delight.

Neville gave a parting scowl, and kicked a clod of earth towards the river. It plopped into the khaki water, and he raised a triumphant fist and whispered, 'Yesss! Yesss! Goal!' Champion status safely reasserted, he strutted, hands in pockets, over the humpbacked bridge to the muddy bank on the other side of the river. Sheep paths cut across it, skinny and straight, and in between them, dotted up the hillside, a homemade shanty town of makeshift dwellings built from hardboard, chickenwire and wonkily nailed-in planks of wood. They were homes for their out-door pets, *country* pets: Neville's ferrets, Sara's mangy-looking rabbit, with one good eye and one milky, and their dad Dave's beloved racing pigeons.

Neville opened his ferrets' hutch and bent down to whisper to them, cocking his head to one side like he was waiting for an answer. He took a couple of them out and sat down with them, rubbing each one behind its ears, stroking them in turn as they whirled around in circles on his knee. They looked happy together, Neville and his ferrets, and they suited each other too; he looked a little like a ferret himself, with his pointy face and sharp little teeth and tiny brown eyes like raisins.

A large stone, thrown by Aled, flew past his ear and hit the pigeon coop behind, bouncing off the chickenwire, sending Dave's pigeons fluttering and Neville ducking for cover. He sat back up, sighed and shook his head, and returned his ferrets to their hutches. That was it. His precious time alone was up; protesting was futile.

'Nev, do the pigeons for us and all while you're there, will you?' shouted Sara, and baby Evan shouted along with her: flipped his head back and let out a roaring burble of half-formed words.

'Do it *yourself*, you lazy bitch,' Neville shouted back – or tried to – but his voice gave out, and it came out as a hoarse whisper, so he resorted then to the universal language of sign, sticking up his middle finger as he cleared the fence in front of him and vanished into the woods.

The Fiddick children were defined by their shouting; I still think of them now, necks outstretched, veins bulging, yelling their hearts out with fury or delight. Outside, they shouted nonstop. They had to, to make themselves heard above the rush of the river, and the still noisier roar of each other. Baby Evan had clocked on to that, choosing shouting over learning to speak. Eirian said they were born shouters, the lot of them; they came into the world screaming, she said, every one. So it was a combination of the two, I think: necessity as well as design. When you were with them you had to join in, shout too, or risk being thumped out of the way; worse still, ignored. They were different, though, as soon as they went inside. Through the door and they dropped their husky voices to a virtual whisper, as if there was someone sleeping who mustn't be disturbed. It helped that there was no river to compete with, reduced in there to a background murmur, but it was the ever-present Eirian that made the difference, I think, watchful and beady-eyed as she poked her head round from the kitchen, eager to pounce at the first sign of discord. When my ears could take the onslaught no longer, I would always find an excuse to go inside so we could sit down and murmur for a while.

At the riverbank Aled and Sara had turned to wrestling now, growling like a couple of angry tigers as they tried with all their wiry strength to tip each other one in the river. I sat on a tree trunk, next to baby Evan, who busied himself by patting the wet mud that surrounded him on to his stomach: swirling it all over in brown. We were a safe distance from the water – from them – and I pretended to referee, calling out 'Foul!' every now and again as I ate around the bruised bits of a plum.

'Kids!' Eirian's voice echoed down from the back door. 'Get up by here, will you, and give your dad a hand.' Sara and Aled groaned, but I was off. I hauled baby Evan inexpertly up, facing his muddy belly outwards with my arms under his slippery armpits, and we were first up the path and through the yard to the kitchen door, as the others scuttled behind me, yanking and grabbing and clutching at each other as they went.

The Fiddicks' dad, Dave, was leaning against the doorframe, mug of tea in hand, oil-slick wave of a quiff teased into a perfect point. He was small, like Eirian, though she was skinny and he was stockily built: unbreakable-looking, like a Tonka toy. From a distance, if you'd never met him, you'd think he was dark-skinned, but close up he was carpeted wall to wall with hair, springing thick and curly from his forearms, neck and knuckles, padding him out all over with an extra layer.

'All right there, Ab?' he asked. 'Chuck that babs in the kitchen, will you now then? You can give me a hand with Bevin then, can't you?'

'Course I will,' I said, and I grinned, because I didn't mind, it was just a bit of fun to me.

'Thank God for that,' said Sara, mud-smeared, like Aled, by the door. 'She likes doing it and all, the crazy bitch.'

'Language!' shouted Dave, tea slooshing over the edge of his cup, down the front of his factory overalls, splatting on to the lino.

'Dave! What did I say?' demanded Eirian. She had a voice like a crow, that's what I thought: imagine a crow talking and it would sound just like Eirian. 'I just did it! I said, didn't I? I said mind you don't dirty my floor!' and I wondered about that, why she always called it hers, why it was just her that owned their kitchen floor.

No one else I knew lived like the Fiddicks. They had no running water or electricity and no central heating either. 'Bevin' was a grey plastic dustbin which sat, filled with water, in the Fiddicks' tiny kitchen, next to the Belfast sink, so that Eirian – and it was always Eirian – could fill up the sink, and once a day the tin bath in the sitting room, and the bucket on the floor in the outside loo, which acted as a flush. It was a daily chore for one of the kids – and a hateful one at that – to go with Dave and Bevin the bin and fill it up from the river. I'd seen them do it a few times now, and Dave was guaranteed to lose his rag, as he yelled at them for *Chrissakes* not to spill, or *for the love of God* to watch what they were doing, and always, to *mind, mind, MIND!*

With me though, he curbed his tongue. 'Steady as you go, Ab,' he said, as we scooped the bin into the river, dragging it bumping over the stones. 'That's it, there we go, there we are.' We lugged it back through the orchard, past the redcurrants, blackcurrants and the rhubarb, ice-cold water sloshing on to my sandals as we made our laboured progress. 'Mind that rock by there, Ab, that's it!' And we rolled it then, tipping slightly to one side, up the garden path, past the family of ornamental rabbits, lop-eared and doe-eyed under the bird table, and carried it up the last bit, to the back door and the kitchen.

'That's lovely,' said Eirian, 'ta, Ab, just there, right by there,' she said, jutting her chin towards the sink, her hands taken up with the tray; and my heart soared at the sight of that tray with its plaited wickerwork around the edge and a photographically exact picture of flowers in a basket in the middle. The flowers were hidden now, covered up with a plate, and a large plate too, stacked with special biscuits, *assorted* biscuits: pink wafers, bourbons and custard creams, all the best ones, the ones with added extras.

'Let's take it through, shall we?' she said. 'Get you cosy by the fire.'

Their sitting room was the darkest room of the house. It had a window, just one, tiny and low down, the daylight filtered through the trees on the opposite side of the river. The room was lit by a couple of oil lamps, and a constant fire, which marinated the whole house, and everyone in it too, in a sweet and piny flavour. Next to the fire was the small, battered tin bath, propped up ready for bathtime. All three children crammed in it together, I'd seen them do it; watched them shoving and whacking each other out of the way, jostling for sitting space as the water sluiced over the sides and soaked the carpet, and made the fire spit and sizzle and hiss.

We sat down on the sofa, me in between Aled and Sara, and grabbed two biscuits each from the proffered tray, one for now and the other for two seconds' time.

'Nev's ran away, Mam,' said Sara through a mouthful of custard cream, crumbs spraying out on her lap.

'Ah well, he'll be back I should think,' said Eirian, filling up our glasses with neon orange squash. 'No point running against the wind, is there?'

'No, don't reckon this time,' said Sara. 'Bloody glad, I tell you, bloody glad to see the back of him, I am.'

'Do I get his ferrets, Mam,' asked Aled, draining his glass in one, 'if he's not coming back? Are they mine?'

The Fiddicks' house was familiar to me, every wood-smoked nook and cranny of it, and I weighed it up – like I did now with all the houses I knew – rated it in a chart in my head on my homemade scale of hippyness, where Commerce House scored a rounded ten out of ten, and Nana and Poppa's house was safely at the other end of the scale with a reassuring zero. I'd rated Olive's house a one (a hippy point added for the dreamcatcher hanging in the spare-room window), and I gave the Fiddicks' house a still very respectable two (they had an abstract oil painting of Wiggy's hanging incongruously in the kitchen next to Eirian's Cliff Richard calendar; possibly given to them by my parents – both points were added for that). I didn't mind the lack of space or running water at the Fiddicks' house. So what? There was a consistency that reassured me. I saw the way that they lived, naively, as some kind of deep resistance to change on their part – *I didn't like change either*. I was wrong about that: it was poverty, pure and simple, that kept them as they were.

Dave and Eirian were not alone. In rural Clwyd in the 1970s there were few with money to spare. Farming and factory work demanded hard graft for scant reward, and this had to contribute to the general contempt directed towards the hippies, I think; most of them middle class and helped along nicely by trust funds. The hippy philosophy rejected luxury, and yet hippies had the biggest luxury of all, which was time. 'Time to faff about doing bugger all,' as Dave would say, 'painting bollocks, and alternate nostril breathing.' Hippies didn't have to worry how to earn a living, how to afford to put the lentils on the table at the end of the day. Tensions simmered gently as the commune dwellers carried on merrily just as they were, and why wouldn't they? 'Live and let live' was just what they'd have to say to that.

'Mam, we're done now,' said Sara, 'we're going to play

upstairs, Ab and me,' and she turned to Aled. 'Sorry, girls only, I'm afraid: no bastards allowed,' she said, leaning over me to give his wrist a pinch with her sharp little fingers.

'COW!' he shouted, and then clamped his hand over his mouth and looked anxiously towards the kitchen door, but it was too late. Eirian flew through, teeth bared, like a ninja, grabbing both of them by their hair and knocking their heads together with a blunt, painful-sounding clunk.

'Better?' she said. 'Seen sense now? Now go!' she said. 'Get out and be off, the lot of you,' and Aled was off through the front door, and I grabbed my Sindy doll, almost forgotten – lying prone on the brown leather pouffe – and Sara and I ran up the stairs, panting up the brown and yellow carpet to the landing.

The Fiddicks' house was just one up and two down. Upstairs there was only a wide landing leading to the bedroom, where the children all shared a double bed, Sara and baby Evan at one end and the two boys at the other. Dave and Eirian had to make do with the landing, which was just about wide enough to house their ancient, broken double bed. Sara hitched herself up on to it now, on to its caved-in mattress, lumpy with springs all straining to be released, all grinding as her knees dug in.

'Ab, you're not going to believe this, you're not,' she said, delving down on the far side. 'You wait for this,' she shouted to me, upside down, 'wait by there, will you? Wait till I show you this,' and there was something about her keenness that made me feel ill at ease; she was one for keeping keenness of any kind at bay, containing it with enviable control – it was a weakness, that's how she saw it. I worried that she was going to pull out the big blue-and-white chipped chamber pot, which served as their indoor loo. Jokes were played with that pot; I'd seen its contents emptied on Aled, and Neville too when they were playing silly buggers – as Sara had said – taunting her from outside: 'Sara, Sara, wants to wear a bra-rer!' they shouted up to her from under the upstairs window, again and again, faster and faster, until she silenced them in a second with a stinking wet surprise. What else could she do? she had pleaded in her defence, as Dave whacked her with a rolled-up newspaper. They had it coming, she wailed, the both of them.

What was under that bed? I'd been under there with Sara before, and all I could picture was dusty shoes and dolls with chopped-off hair, scribbled all over with biro.

'I got them, here they are then,' she said, chucking a pile of magazines on to my lap. 'Take a look,' she urged. 'They're my dad's, they are – see what you think of them.' And she stared at me, her expression blank: frustratingly clear, as she waited, head cocked for my response.

I flicked through *Razzle* first, then *Big Boobs Monthly*, and *Knave*, I think it was called. I looked at page after page of naked women, and I laughed: that was all I could think to do; my way of showing Sara that it was all fine by me, just dandy; though it was horror that I actually felt, I think, or something like it.

'What do you reckon, Ab?' asked Sara now, her face so close I could feel her cool breath on my cheek.

'They're funny,' I said, and I could feel my heart beating in what felt like my throat.

'I know, they really are, aren't they? Brilliant,' she said.

I think Sara felt it too, I'm sure she did: a quiet, private kind of dread. *We didn't know it all, after all.* The world that I knew shifted on its axis then, revealed itself to be more like Phillip Brown already saw it: bigger, less contained, without fences.

5

Another planet

'Mark my words, kids. Don't ever forget what I am about to say to you.'

We waited with bated breath for the announcement. Mr Davies paused and breathed out, noisily, like an impatient pony, from under the thick tuffet of his strawberry-blond moustache. He turned to face the blackboard, where he'd drawn a picture of the earth, with the word *cartref* – which meant 'home' – written above it.

'It's not good news, I'm afraid,' he said, shaking his head, 'it's not good news at all.' And he took a small white stub of chalk and drew a cross through it, with an exaggerated flourish as if he were fencing, one line and then the other, his fitted jacket riding up as he did so, revealing a flash of red underpants and a ridge of white, freckled flesh above his belt. When he was done, he spun around to face us again, and stood there, grim-faced, as he dusted off the chalk from his hands.

'When you kids are my age, you will all be living on another planet.'

The class was silent while we attempted to assimilate the bombshell.

'Well?' he said. 'What do you think of that?'

No one spoke. His eyes darted round the room, back and

forth, searching for a show of hands, but there weren't any.

'I've just told you something very IMPORTANT! What do you THINK?'

Sianny Wyn Wyn half raised her hand.

'But . . . Mr Davies, what it is . . . I *like* living here,' she said, voice wavering. 'I don't think I want to move to another planet, to be honest,' she said, her good eye blinking at him extra fast from behind her smeared pink National Health glasses.

'Number one: you should SPEAK UP, Sian Roberts, and number two: you'd better get used to the idea! You'll have no CHOICE. Very soon we will run out of space to build houses!' he said, blue veins bulging on his temples. 'I'm telling you now, when you have children they will not be born on earth. There will be no ROOM! Mark my words, all of you. Have you marked them?'

We nodded frantically.

'Good! You may leave.'

We leapt up, our chairs screeching in unison on the parquet floor, and rushed out of the classroom as fast as we could, tumbling down the corridor to the playground.

Mr Davies was a supply teacher, though lately he'd been coming to teach regularly: once a week or so at least. Mr Roberts, our headmaster, should have been teaching us today, but he was out of school again, away on one of his conferences. Eleanor Williams said that her mam reckoned that Mr Roberts' conferences were always on the days when there were international rugby matches, and that, she said, seemed like a damned funny coincidence to her. Mr Roberts had a lot of out-of-school commitments, many business meetings to attend, and Eleanor's mam swore that that was code for 'popping down The Miner's for a swift one'; although how she knew that was anyone's guess.

Phillip Brown was unusually brave for him, keeping his tears in for a good minute or so at least. I watched him, lips quivering and tightly shut, as he gamely tried to stem the flow; until he leant over, defeated, and let it all out in one deep, primal sob – expelling it, almost – on to the floor, as if he were being sick.

'Get my mam, will you?' he said. 'I *hate* space. I'm not leaving! I want my mam!' A cluster of children gathered round him, where he sat clutching his belly on the bench. Sianny Wyn Wyn pushed through and put her skinny, white little arm around his shoulders. 'Don't cry, Phillip. It's just Mr Davies putting the shits up us, you know what he's like. There, there, darlin',' she said, patting his hand.

'What are you on about, Sianny?' said Rhys Prichard. 'I saw you! You nearly peed your pants when he said it, you did!' and everyone laughed as she glared at him as best she could with a plaster over one eye.

'Duw, I tell you, I don't know why you're all het up and all,' said Rhys. 'I'd *like* to live in space, I would – bloody *love* it there, I reckon – first one on the rocket, me!'

How could we be running out of room? I believed Mr Davies, of course I did, but I couldn't understand it even so. *Room* was all there was around here: barbed-wire fences and tumbled-down drystone walls, framing nothing at all but grass – field after empty field. If anything, we had too much space, that's what I thought; we could have done with a few more houses.

I was prone to nightmares as it was, and now I had a fresh addition to the roster – another sinister imagining to send me bolt upright in bed. My regular horrors of yetis and Loch Ness monsters made way now for visions of our overcrowded future, of homeless hippies knocking on the windows of our house, like zombies, begging to be let in.

*

There were three teachers who taught me at my time at that village school. They were notable, all of them, in their different ways, but most notable compared with each other. Neither one affirmed the others' way of doing things, each one contradicting the others; not that we noticed it then. I think now of the guileless way we accepted them all, took each one's way as the right way of doing things then: the truth as it was at the time.

You could tell that Mr Roberts was our headmaster because he looked like one. He had the confident, upright posture of someone who was comfortable with power. His thin, ginger hair had a natural wave to it and he wore it slightly long, to detract from the extravagant width of his face, I think, as well as the slight sticky-outiness of his ears. The length of his hair, and the style of it too – the way it curled under, peculiarly, at the bottom – along with the certainty with which he wore his weight, sticking his stomach proudly out before him; all of this combined to make him look oddly out of time, like a Victorian squire, or a Toby jug come to life.

When he was in school the air felt different. He was never there long enough for us really to know him, so he remained unfamiliar, mythological almost, which was just the way he wanted it, I'd think. A reverential hush descended as he strutted purposefully, silently around the corridors, hunting out trouble in his rubber-soled shoes. It was in assembly, though, where he really came into his own. He needed an audience; he became an even bigger version of himself – literally – puffing his chest out as he stood, legs apart, on the stage. He sang in a male voice choir and relished any chance to show off his fine baritone voice, enunciating every word and rolling his Rs with obvious delight: 'Rrrright everrrybody, and how arrre we today then?' he'd say, clapping his hands together, sounding as if he was about to break into song at any minute; and often he would, launching into an impromptu version of the Welsh National Anthem. '*Gwlad! Gwlad! Pleidiol wyf i'm gwlad!*' he'd sing, raising his hands to the ceiling – imploring us to join him – eyes brimming with tears as he hurled the words out in a voice tremulous with pride. Reluctantly, we'd accompany him, voices reedy high and weak with embarrassment; our lack of passion glaringly apparent in comparison, all of us appalled by his spontaneity.

A cane and an ancient, bobbled, tartan slipper took a prominent position next to the rugby paraphernalia and choir trophies on the shelves of Mr Roberts' office. They were there to serve as a warning to us all, though only ever used on Rhys Prichard. No one dared defy Mr Roberts but him. Ever keen to have an audience, Mr Roberts would invite a few of us in each time to 'witness the action', as he liked to say, with his hands clutched tight together.

'Do you know, Mr Prichard, why I've asked you into my office? Are you aware of the charges against you, sir?' he'd say, and he'd make a show of looking angry, but he was only acting, you could tell; his mouth would twitch with the effort of containing the pleasure, the thrill it gave him really: that sweet joy of exercising his power.

It looked like agony; it sounded like it too – that clean, precise slap with the faintest echo in its wake – but Rhys never uttered a sound. Afterwards we would ask him – beg him – to tell us what it felt like. 'It doesn't bother me, honest,' he'd say with a shrug. 'I can take it, I can, no problem.' Eleanor Williams bribed him once with a fruit-salad chew: 'Now tell us, will you?' she said. 'Is it worse than a Chinese burn?'

'Give it to us then,' he said, 'and I'll say.' He held out a cracked palm – small and red and dry, as if he'd spent a lifetime washing up – waved it in Eleanor's face for his due. 'Ta,' he said, ripping into the wrapper. 'Course it is,' he said, popping the sweet into his mouth, 'but it's not a ten out of ten pain, it's not; not even the cane, that's an eight, that is,' and he held out a hand now for another. 'Ta. I've had worse. I've had ten,' he said, jumping up to his bit of wall, to the left-hand side of the school gate. 'Trust me,' he said, leaning down now so his face was level with Eleanor's. 'I've had a lot worse than that.'

Mrs Bevan, our beloved form teacher, was at the other extreme. She left having presence to Mr Roberts; he could have all the attention he liked, and he was welcome to it, because he faced no competition from her. Mrs Bevan liked to blend in. She wore beige-coloured, hand-knitted jumpers in two-toned wool, the colour of Weetabix; or grey, she loved to wear grey: the utilitarian flat kind, the colour of the filing cabinet in Mr Roberts' office, the colour of the walls in every classroom. You could go into class and not even notice that she was there until she gave a little cough to alert you. She was easy to miss: a tiny, slight woman, who stood with an apologetic stoop and was so softly spoken you had to strain to hear her. Her crinkly eyes and gold, wire-rimmed glasses made me think she was ancient, possibly in her seventies, but she can't have been: her seven-year-old daughter Gwen was in our class.

Mrs Bevan's priority, above and beyond imparting any knowledge to us, was to be kind, and she did this very well, seeking out anyone in need, even if they weren't. 'You all right there, cariad?'

'Yes, fine, thanks,' a surprised-looking child would say, double-checking from side to side just to make sure she meant them.

'Oh, I thought I saw you looking a bit sad there for a minute,' she'd say, appearing crestfallen for a moment. 'There we are then. Never mind, come by here anyway, will you, and have a good old *cwtch*,' she'd say, pulling them to her, cuddling them in tight to her Weetabix jumper. It was easy to call her 'Mam' by mistake, and we all did it – even Sara – which made Mrs Bevan turn pink with pleasure, as the child turned pink with shame. 'Thank you. I'll take that as a compliment,' she'd say, even to Rhys Prichard, which proved her kindness beyond a shadow of a doubt – really; if you'd ever met his mother you'd see.

The free milk would arrive on a cold winter's morning, the cream-topped milk bottles chilled and glistening with condensation, foil tops misted up from the refrigerated lorry, and Mrs Bevan would insist that we warm them up on the radiator, as a special treat she'd say, seeing as we'd been so good. No one wanted to, but we found her well-intentioned kindness impossible to reject, so we'd balance them, one by one, all along the vast, long radiator, and they'd warm there, gently, ineffectively, water dripping down the glass now like sweat, as the sweet, cheesy smell permeated the room.

'They'll be lovely and warm now, cariads – tuck in,' she'd say and I'd pop the lid in with my thumb, and down it through my barely opened mouth, wincing at the wrongness of the temperature – neither cold enough nor nearly hot enough. We'd mastered the art of drinking it, all of us, sieving the creamy lumps through our teeth, ridding ourselves of it in great glutinous gulps, before giving our mouths a hefty wipe with a sleeve. No one wanted to risk looking like Sianny Wyn Wyn, with her white, crusty residue around the corners of her mouth a permanent, off-putting fixture.

Mrs Bevan liked to create during lessons: there was a

shyness to her that was helped by having the distraction, I think, somewhere else to look. 'Knit one, purl one; does anyone know the answer, my cariads? Knit one, purl one – tricky bit coming up, so don't anyone speak just yet now, please.' She required absolute silence when she tackled an antimacassar: 'Tricky as buggery, this,' she'd say, through teeth clenched extra tight. We'd let her get on with it, bent double with concentration, needle darting urgently up and down, while we drew pictures, and swapped seats, and hid under our desks, but quietly so as not to disturb and interrupt the gentle rhythm of her knitting as the river rushed by outside.

Once a week everything was different with Mrs Bevan. She put on lipstick and patted her hair in preparation, and breathed a little quicker, and said, 'Right then, right then, there we go, children, there we go,' a few times over, apropos of nothing, and we knew then it must be swimming-lesson day and we'd be leaving soon, departing the school premises with her to go to the local pool. Her cheeks flushed as she coaxed us needlessly up the bus steps, as if we didn't want to go, as if we weren't all now frantic with excitement to be getting out of school and on a bus; but she didn't seem to see it. 'Come on then, on you go, steady as you go,' she'd say, clucking the words, murmuring them in a soothing whisper as she clutched her big brown tweed craft bag with both hands in front of her like a vast, oversized sporran. We were going to a leisure centre. Just the name alone was enough to get me excited. Who could not want to go to a centre dedicated to leisure?

The bus took us out of the village, cottage after cottage whizzing by until they dropped away and we were hurtling down the winding hedge-lined road to town, hazel whipping at the windows as we went. Soon there were houses again, bigger ones now, and the bus squeaked down the hill to the car park, and veered around the corner to the leisure centre. It was a magnificent building to me – flat-roofed and plain and concrete: futuristic-looking, as if it had just been dropped in from space. Inside, through the automatic sliding doors, past the welcoming hot waft of chlorine, and the pool itself didn't quite live up to the promise. It was cold and harshly lit, the water always sticking-plaster-strewn and hair-ridden and a breeding ground for veruccas, but who cared about any of that? Not us.

We all knew about *Jaws*. Lisa and Jonathan Evans had seen it, of course, twice now on Betamax – and we weren't stupid; there was no way that you would get us going anywhere near the deep end. Mrs Bevan, not liking any upset, didn't ever make us; she was happy to let us jump up and down in the shallow end while she knitted, or stitched, or crocheted away the hour, bent over, absorbed and industrious in the spectators' gallery. 'Just have some fun,' she'd say, sucking the end of a piece of cotton she was just getting ready to thread, 'go on, why don't you? Enjoy yourselves once in a while.'

We needed, of course, to be taught to swim, but even so, Mrs Bevan's lessons weren't wasted. That hour of splashing once a week, and tag, and doggy-paddling back and forth, was the one time, I think, when we were all equal. Rhys, Sianny, Sara and Lisa – the lot of us – were all on a par in the water; the hierarchies of the playground dissolved, it seemed, the minute we climbed down those steps. Even Sara, nervous of the deep end like the rest of us, forgot her fighting spirit, left it in the locker with her jumpsuit. Disparities in character, and height and weight and strength, didn't come into it; we were reduced now, all of us, to heads, bobbing up and down in the water. Stripped of anything that we were distinguished by, we were shy and awkward for the first ten minutes, as we adapted to this new, scrap-free way of being, and it was binding for us to be harmonious, to be friends, and as one for a while.

'You're coming along just gorgeous,' Mrs Bevan would say, packing up her handiwork, holding up each piece, head cocked with admiration, before she folded them into her bag. 'Tell your mams you've gone and done me proud again, will you?'

And we'd grin to each other, shivering, as we slap-slapped to the changing room, buoyed up, all of us, united by belonging, cosseted by the benign, distant love of Mrs Bevan.

6

Blimmin' gorgeous

Why did I put up with Sara Fiddick? It was never an easy friendship; there was nothing comfortable or straightforward about Sara. The truth was, I tolerated her domineering, violent ways because there was a pay-off for me, and that pay-off was our imaginary play. Sara had a talent – and a brilliant one too: she could act better than anyone I knew. She was a full-time bullshitter, so pretending came naturally to her: she didn't have to think; she just did it.

We were fans of the television series *CHiPs*, Sara and I. Though I often wondered how she actually got to watch it, without the necessary electricity, or a television as far as I could see. I asked her once and she said that her mam kept a massive battery-operated television, twice the size of ours, in the locked-up cupboard on the landing; she only got it out in the evenings, though, so as not to waste the batteries. I asked if I could see it, but she gave me one of her sideways slitty-eyed glares and said that it was a private telly only, not for me to see; and I felt embarrassed then, as if I'd asked if I could have a look at her knickers.

CHiPs followed the lives of two handsome American Highway Patrol men, Jon and Poncherello, who drove around on motorbikes, solving crime in very tight trousers. Sara and I had a deep admiration for the way that they handled their bikes, and to show our appreciation we married them, time and time again, swathed in the yellowing net curtains that Eirian kept as spares in a cardboard box under the stairs.

'Mam! Get yourself up here, will you?' Sara would yell over the banisters. 'We're playing *CHiPs* and we're getting married now, aren't we?' she'd say, adjusting her net-curtain veil in the mirror, pouting out her negligible lips. 'Bring us up some pop, will you, and something to eat for the reception?'

Soon after, Eirian would come padding up the stairs in her pale blue fluffy slippers, with a tray of orange pop and her best crystal bowl filled with ready-salted peanuts. My mother would have left the tray on the bedside table and swiftly disappeared downstairs again, no questions asked, but Eirian would stay and, to my deep discomfort, actually involve herself in the game for a while.

'I thought I should get my best bowl out, seeing as it's a wedding,' she'd say, in her trilling, made-up voice, popping the peanuts into our mouths one after the other. 'Look at this, will you? You've made it all look so lovely,' and she'd hold out the palm of her hand to the dimly lit mess of a room, with the sheets slipping from the unmade bed and clothes spilling out of open drawers, discarded in sorry-looking heaps all over the floor. Eirian picked her way through them, unhindered, shaking the hands of our imaginary guests, offering them peanuts as she went: 'No, no, take two, I insist.' Sara didn't seem to care, but I couldn't bear it. Eirian looked mad to me, but worse was how she made us look. She broke the magic when she played with us, exposed us as just two girls playing make-believe. How dare we? How dare we actually believe we were Californian women with long blonde hair who could marry Jon and Poncherello, and roller-skate backwards without looking?

Eirian loved crystal cut glass. She had a mahogany-coloured display cabinet in the sitting room dedicated to it, both functional and ornamental. It hung on the back wall behind their sofa, opposite the fire – on purpose, I think, to show the crystal at its finest, glinting prettily in the flickering firelight. The top two shelves of the cabinet were like a tiny glittery zoo: home to Eirian's collection of glass animal families; domestic and exotic all mixed in together, the cat family sitting next to the elephants, dogs and hedgehogs beside an elegant, long-legged family of deer. I loved them all, but my favourite by far was the smallest baby glass deer, with its oversized black glass eyes and tiny, sweetly bobbed tail. I would gaze at that deer with a yearning that made my heart fast-forward, imagining it sitting on my bedside table, filling my bedroom with its sparkly magic.

Sara would sometimes come back to play after school; just as long as it wasn't especially sunny, in which case there was a possibility that my mother would be mowing the lawn in her bra, or even worse, without it. I liked Sara, but she wasn't a loyal friend; anyone could tell you that. Her allegiance was transitory, readily switched to another in an instant, which was part of her strange allure. You had to work hard to keep her with you; if you were with her you were winning. I knew, without a doubt, that if Sara ever caught sight of my mother's bare breasts, then all would be lost in an instant. There would be no recovery to be had from family-related outdoor nudity, semi or otherwise – a fact which seemed to have frustratingly escaped my mother.

Sara was too proud to ask outright, so every now and then she would just get in the school taxi with us, squeezing in her cold, bare legs between my sister and me, so she could take a different route home, she said, walk to hers across the fields for a change, which was her code for coming to play.

'Hey! Shall I stop in at yours a sec then, Ab?' she'd say, just as we reached the rhododendron hedge at the bottom of our garden, as if the thought had only just occurred to her, popped into her head right then.

'You could do,' I'd say, straining to get a view of our garden through a gap in the hedge. Usually there was no sign of my mother, but occasionally there she would be, hard at work pruning a rose bush in her mismatched underwear, or halfway up a ladder in nothing but her plimsolls and a pair of bright yellow pants. I'd be forced to feign sudden illness then, and I'd be sick with panic – genuinely – so I suppose it wasn't strictly a lie.

'Huh! Guess what? I didn't want to anyway. Why would I want to do that?' Sara would say. 'Do you think I'm desperate or something?' and she'd give me a parting shove on the shoulder before stomping off down the path on her skinny twig legs, swinging her thin mousy hair ineffectively behind her as she went.

At Sara's house we played getting married, and at mine we played giving birth. I don't know why, that's just the way it was. There was a boxroom next to my bedroom, which was more or less empty, apart from some bookshelves filled with pulp fiction and Penguin Classics, and a battered old chest of drawers. We draped it in blankets and towels and made it our hospital bed, taking it in turns to lie on top with a teddy squashed underneath us, while the other delivered our baby.

Sara excelled at giving birth. 'For God's sake help me, will you? I'm having Poncherello's baby and it blimmin' hurts!' she'd shout, flailing and flapping about on top of the chest of drawers, gulping in air like a fish just pulled out from the sea. 'For the love of God, someone go and get him off that highway, will you? Quick! Before the bastard misses it!' she'd yell, glancing down at Katherine to check she was still watching, which she always was, hanging off the doorknob, staring wide-eyed from the safety of the landing.

'Come on – push it out! Do it for Poncherello!' I'd shout, snapping on my mother's Marigold gloves.

'I can't though!' she'd say, tugging at her hair, her face contorted in what looked like genuine, alarming agony, until I tugged the teddy out from under her and laid him on her stomach.

'Look at that, he's just as handsome as his dad,' she'd say, wobbly-mouthed, with real tears, or possibly sweat, running down her face. 'I'm going to call him Ponch Junior,' she'd say, as Katherine mouthed the familiar last line, and I wiped her brow with a piece of scrunched-up kitchen roll.

'See, Kath? That's how you do it. Easy. You'll get the hang of it one day. You just got to shout a bit really,' said Sara, which may as well have been her motto for life.

Katherine and I shared a bedroom at the front of the house. It was a light, sunny room: golden-tinted in the mornings when daylight shone through its pale, orange-patterned curtains. Our beds were side by side, with matching patchwork quilts, made by my mother: hexagons of patterns in yellow and orange, like a kaleidoscope. Underneath our quilts were dark pink cellular blankets, edged with a beautiful satin trim, cool to the touch, shimmery, like the fabric of a princess's ball gown. To help me get to sleep I would pull the wool from my blanket, bit by bit, scrunching it together between my finger and thumb, until it turned into pink woolly nuggets, which I kept under my pillow to re-scrunch at will. I wouldn't have thought to show them to Sara, but she saw them once when she was bouncing on my bed, as she tried in vain to hit our paper-ball lightshade with her head, sending my pillow flying and my woolly nuggets scattering on the floor.

'God, Ab, what the hell are them?' Sara picked one up and held it to the light. 'They are just . . . blimmin' *gorgeous*,' she said, forgetting for a moment to be unimpressed by anything at all that wasn't hers.

She wanted to do swapsies and I readily agreed. Of course we could, I said. If only she'd asked I would have given her some for nothing, she had no idea.

Overcome with a panicky greed, I offered her three of my largest nuggets if she could bring me my favourite thing from her house: the baby deer glass figurine from Eirian's glass menagerie. Sara crossed her heart and swore on Trixie her rabbit's life that she would smuggle it to me as soon as she could. That's what she said, and I believed her, of course I did; her voice wavered up and down as she said it, and she thumped her fist against her chest to show that she meant every word, it was heartfelt. All the same, she arrived the next day empty-handed.

'I couldn't nick it, Ab. My mam'll see, and she'll go spare, won't she?' she said, with a flick of her hair to signal that that was that, no more discussion needed. 'Don't worry,' she said, fumbling around under her jumper, 'it's okay. Look, I've got you this instead!' and she pulled out a rolled-up magazine and opened it up on my bed, unfurling it with a 'ta daah!'

There was a naked lady, with vast bosoms, the biggest I'd ever seen – bigger even than Olive's – lying in the middle of my patchwork quilt; her nakedness framed, I think now *emphasized*, by the yellow-and-orange floral field of Liberty print fabrics that surrounded her, spring-like and innocent and familiar.

'You're lucky to have that, mind,' said Sara, wagging a finger at me, as if I didn't quite deserve it. 'Keep it safe, now. My dad might want it back, you never know.' She was smiling proudly, oblivious to my breathing – shallow and quick with panic – as she delved under my pillow for her reward.

Disrespecting Sara was the source of most of the bloodshed in our playground. Skin was scratched, ripped and pinched, hunks of hair torn from heads for the wrong kind of look, a misheard word, or a wrongly perceived dig at her mother. She thrived on conflict, searching it out just for the thrill of it. Throwing away her magazine would be a slight against her judgement: a guaranteed way to get a good kicking, I knew that; so as soon as she was gone, I gave it to my sister.

Phillip Brown had come round for supper. It was Findus Crispy Pancakes with baked beans and no greens; requested by my sister because Phillip, our guest, would like it, and we must think of our guest, she said. But we weren't stupid: she was crazy about anything from Findus.

'Ooh, Phil. Well. Look at this, will you!' Olive clapped her hands together in a desperate rally of enthusiasm, as my mother put his plate in front of him. Phillip kneaded his groin, which was never a good sign, and said nothing.

'We're branching out, aren't we, Phil? Trying new things,' said Olive, nudging his hunched-over shoulder.

'Not really, I'm not,' he said, head flopping miserably towards his lap, as if his strings had been cut, both hands still shoved firmly, safely, between his legs.

'Well, *we* are – Mike and I,' said Olive. 'Mike's been a bit bunged up again lately, hasn't he, Phil?' and she started cutting up his pancake into bite-sized pieces.

'There's pink lumps in the middle of it,' said Phillip, 'look.'

'Ham,' said my mother, disappearing into the hall to call my sister down.

'You'll have to take me to Anthony's health food shop, Anna,' said Olive, nibbling her way through the rejected cubes, lined up precisely on the edge of Phillip's plate. 'Sort Mike out with a bit of roughage. Well, I tell you what, he wouldn't know what roughage was if it slapped him in the face. He had a slice of your brown bread once,' she said, 'and that did it for him. He didn't leave the toilet for a week!' and she tipped backwards as she whooped in delight, bright white trainers whirling off the floor as if she was cartoon-running.

My sister skidded into the kitchen, taking the chair in between Phillip and me as she flung a bulging scrapbook on to the table.

'I filled it up now, Mum. I need a new one,' she said, scooping in a forkful of beans, as Olive dabbed at her eyes with the bottom of her sweatshirt. We had the same scrapbooks, my sister and I, matching ones with a picture of Noah's Ark on the cover and pastel pages inside. I'd viewed my empty book as full of promise: blank pages ready to receive my works of art. I'd stuck a four-leaved clover on the first page, but hadn't bothered to press it, so it wilted and shrivelled, and I'd Sellotaped it in at an annoyingly wonky angle, ruining the book, and my artistic prodigy fantasy, just like that. My sister, though, was the sort of child who coloured in very beautifully in the same direction, and took great care not to go over the lines. She was meticulous and precise, and incredibly patient, so not a page of her scrapbook would be wasted.

'Ooh, Kath, let's have a look, shall we?' said Olive, stretching across the table with a grunt to grab it.

'It's my best ever cutting-out,' said my sister, stabbing into a Crispy Pancake, cheesy sauce erupting over the orange breadcrumbs as Olive opened the book up, its spine crackling with snapping glue.

'Oh Anna,' said Olive, and 'oh,' as she turned the next page – the pink page, where a beautifully cut-out lady, naked apart from some tights that looked as if they were made out of a fishing net, had been stuck in the middle.

'I think you'd better come and see,' she said.

'Just a sec,' said my mother, whisking up the Angel Delight, brown bubbles rising up the mixing bowl.

'Oh Kath, oh no, oh heck!' Hand to her mouth, Olive was turning to the next page – the pale green page, covered with photos of a naked blonde lady lying on some scratchy-looking hay bales, thrusting her bare bottom towards the camera.

Phillip stabbed a cube of bacon with his fork. He held it high and studied it from every angle, then perched it for a second on the tip of his tongue. He clamped his mouth shut and began tentatively to chew.

'Mam!' he said. 'Hey Mam, look, will you? I don't mind it! It's not bad at all!'

7

American Tan

I'd just come back from a two-week holiday in France, and my skin, usually the sallow yellow of a corn-fed chicken, had turned a deep nut brown. As I climbed out of my mother's 2CV, I saw Rhys Prichard waiting by the school gate. He caught a glimpse of me and swivelled round to look at me face on.

'Never! Look at you now, Ab! What's happened?' He came in for a closer look: circling me, checking me up and down, like a farmer inspecting the sheep on market day. 'You've gone all . . . *Indian*!' he said.

Rhys was always the first one to school. He waited there from first thing every morning, eating his breakfast packet of crisps. 'I like to get in early, it's good to be early,' he'd say. Early didn't come into it, said Olive; he just can't wait to be out of that house, she said, and who can blame him, when his own mother won't even get up to see him off?

More children were arriving now, streaming down the green towards the gates.

'Christ on a bike, would you look at that,' said Sara, and behind me my mother spluttered back a laugh as she helped my sister out from the back of the car.

'It's just a *tan*,' I said, trying it out on her, flipping the word out like a coin: heads meant good, tails bad.

'Where did you get it from then?' she asked, clearly unde-cided, as she scanned every inch of me with her beady little eyes.

'We got them from France,' said my sister, who had popped up next to me, a paler brown version with blonde hair that had turned almost white in the sun. 'Where did you get your jump-suit from?'

'Big Town market,' she said. 'Don't copy, mind. I got it first, I did. I got first dibs.' My sister shook her head. It went without saying she'd never dare.

Sianny Wyn Wyn was here now, and Lisa and Jonathan Evans, and all of them stopped to stare.

'That's rude, that is. Stop gawking at her, will you? Nosy parkers, the lot of you,' said Sara, pressing a hand into the small of my back, gently, firmly shepherding me through the gate. 'Don't worry, Ab, I'll look after you,' she said. 'Stay by here with me.'

'Abbie Jabby! That's what we can call you!' Rhys Prichard called after me.

'Brilliant, that is,' said Timothy Jones. 'Brilliant.'

Sara escorted me into the classroom and directed me to the front of the class.

'Stand by that white wall there for a minute now, Ab,' she said. 'Gor! Look at her now, will you? Black as anything like that!'

I was, was the general conclusion.

It was lunchtime and I was standing without my top on in the bin yard, waiting for the examination to begin. I was bent for-ward with my head down, arms resting on a bin lid, which was sticky with the remains of yesterday's rice pudding. The air vents from the kitchen pumped out hot, school-dinner-scented air and I stared down at the ground, at the sludge of rotten oranges, grey-green with mould that nestled around my feet. It started oozing into my sandals, and I scrunched my toes in.

Sara Fiddick stood next to me, a protective, pointy little hand on my shoulder.

'Stay in line and wait your blimmin' turn, everyone, *you'll all get a look at her*!' she said. 'Stand back, for Chrissakes, till I say!'

The school had formed a disorderly queue that snaked around the playground. I could see everyone, upside down, impatiently waiting to inspect me, pushing each other's heads down, craning over each other for a better look. This was an event, *I* was an event; I could tell, because even Brangwen Jenkins – who never ventured out – was in the queue. She looked rigid and uncomfortable, but she was there, blinking in the sunlight, looming large behind Timothy Jones, in her strangely grown-up-looking floral dress, identical to her mother's.

Brangwen was a large, unwieldy child with skin so pale that it looked transparent; her veins cut across it like pencil scribbles. She didn't like outside, that's what her mother told Mrs Bevan; she wasn't keen on the feel of wind, or on moving around too much. Poor little cariad, was Mrs Bevan's take on that, so Brangwen got to stay in the classroom, always, all day long. Her presence alone – just to have Brangwen there, outside! – gave a momentum to the occasion and made my head giddy with a sudden and overwhelmingly inflated sense of my own importance.

'Move forward, will you!' said Sara. 'Have a look, make it quick, then move along.'

Through my legs I could see the familiar sight of Phillip Brown's pale, shiny knees shuffling tentatively forward, and I felt him touch my back.

'Ach–a-fi!' he said. 'I don't like it.'

'Get going then,' said Sara. 'Plenty more who will.'

'What's that bit up there?' he asked. '*Her skin's falling off!*'

'That's what you're here to see! That's *peel*, Phillip, she's started *peeling*,' said Sara, rolling her eyes at the queue. 'Don't you know nothing? That's what happens when you tan.'

'Well, I'm not going *nowhere* if that's what happens, if your skin drops off like that. That's not right,' he said. There was a murmur of agreement down the queue. 'Tanning's not good, it isn't,' he said. 'Remember, Ab? When my mam went and tanned my brain?'

He was still mentally scarred from our family trip to the solarium in Wrexham. My sister and I had just felt sick and a bit hot, but Phillip had got full-blown sunstroke: he was ranting and delirious all night long, until Olive had to call out Dr Roberts. She was livid; she'd never go there again, she said, and besides, she looked white as ever and she hadn't got so much as a freckle.

'It looks disgusting,' he qualified.

'No, *YOU* look disgusting, Phillip,' said Sara. 'Have you seen what's coming out of your nose? NEXT!' and she shoved him out of the way.

Timothy Jones was after Phillip. I knew it was him, without even having to look; I could hear his Darth Vader-like breathing. He got clogged up, he said, because he was crazy about drinking his milk, and too much dairy gave you extra bogeys; that's what he said, which made me hate our free breaktime milk even more.

'Can I pull a bit off?' he asked.

'It's going to cost you, mind,' said Sara. 'We'll call it twopence a flake. Fifty-fifty split on that, Ab, if it's okay with you.' It was, I agreed, a mountain of blackjacks and fruit-salad chews looming large in my head.

Timothy wheezed and then spluttered. He must have done it in his hand, because when he touched my back his palm was damp with spit.

'Can I IOU? I'll get the money off my mam at home time, promise,' he said, his breath purring in and out of his chest, as though he had an engine running, and I felt my back prickle as he helped himself. 'Cheers, Ab. Look at that! Brilliant. I'll keep that safe, I will, in my box.'

That week gave me a glimpse, just a taste, of what it must be like to be famous. I possessed a force – I could feel it: buzzing through me like a super power. I was Magnet Girl, pulling everyone in. It felt dangerous, that strength, and I wasn't sure how to direct it. It went to my head, it went to my legs: I started to swagger instead of walk.

'There she is! Stop by there, Ab! Wait! Go on, show us that white bit again!'

I understood now what it must be like to be Evans the Butcher; I could see why he walked with his chest puffed out, and why both his kids did too. It took you over, altered you: the knowledge that you could have a hold, and easily, without needing to try.

It didn't last. That kind of glory never can. By the end of the week my skin had all shed, my tan had faded and then Rhys Prichard went and trumped me by discovering that he could turn his eyelids inside out.

I knew it was my last day at the bins when even Sara didn't turn up, and it was only Brangwen waiting: just her and a fold-up chair.

'All that queuing wears me out, it does,' she said, opening it out to sit down.

I watched her, as she went through her ritual of ladylike arranging. She began by smoothing out her skirt and blouse, and when she was happy that her clothes were all in order, she patted her hair and checked to see if her kirby grip was in place, and then, satisfied that everything was where it should be, she folded her hands beneath her already-present bosoms and looked to me, standing there scruffy and boyish in comparison, in my jeans and checked lumberjack shirt – and she raised her eyebrows expectantly and waited for me to peel off my top.

I could hear wails of delighted revulsion from the playground. 'Rhys, that is disgusting! Do it one more time, go on!'

'Sorry,' I said, 'there's no point. I don't look that brown any more.'

'I do,' she said, 'look,' and she stuck her legs out triumphantly in front of her. Brangwen's usual legs were a pale bluish-green. These legs, though, were a deep orange-brown and oddly uniform looking, not a freckle or a vein in sight, like the legs of a shop dummy.

'They're my mam's tights, they are. American Tan. I don't need to go on holiday now, do I?' she said, and she gave a little laugh. 'Do you like them?' she asked. Her voice was unexpected – soft-sounding and sing-song – I wasn't used to it.

'I do,' I said, truthfully. 'I think your legs look beautiful, like an ice-skater's.'

Colour flooded her cheeks and she lowered her head and smiled. 'Thanks,' she said. 'I can get you some if you like – my mam's got millions.'

It was as if a pipe had burst. She carried on talking then, and didn't stop. The words came pouring out fast and loud. Years of held-in conversations came rushing out, as she unclasped her hands, and then her legs, and just for a while she forgot herself. She talked until the end of breaktime, and then she stood up and folded up her chair, before giving a little nod goodbye, and that was it. I never heard her speak like that again.

8

Welsh Nash

'Hey, Ab, are you a Welsh Nash?'

Rhys Prichard and I were sitting on the wall outside our school. I had no idea what he was talking about; I was just basking in the glory of sitting next to him, just me and him, and no one else. I turned to look at him, and stared at him then, transfixed. His cheeks, always a permanent ruddy red, no matter what the weather, were coated with a thin layer of dried bogey, which had formed a glaze, like the topping of one of my nana's lemon drizzle cakes. It began to crack a little as he spoke, and I tried not to flinch as a fault line opened up from the corner of his mouth to the bottom of his ear.

'You know?' he said. 'A Welsh Nationalist! A Son of Glyndŵr!'

Still no bells were ringing; but judging from the froth of spit gathered in the corners of his mouth, I thought it was bound to be good, whatever it was – a desirable, covetable thing.

'Are you one then?' I asked.

'Course I am!' he said, swiping his mouth with a pulled-down sleeve, revealing his grin – his workable grin – wide and white and even.

If he was one, then so was I, there was no question, and the rest of the school would follow too – such was the effortless

106

power of Rhys Prichard. He had no fear, that's what marked him out; he didn't hide it – he simply had none. He was braver than anyone I'd ever met, braver even than all of the Fiddicks combined, which made him officially indomitable – superhuman – like the Bionic Man.

Once, in a red-faced, spitting rage, he'd thrown a chair at our headmaster. I can still see Mr Roberts now – our armour-plated Goliath – cowed in fright in front of the blackboard, peeping out from behind his splayed hands, whimpering softly as Rhys wielded the chair back and forth, revving up to swing it at him like a bowling ball. The whole class was silent as Rhys roared with a crazed, directionless rage, shouting jumbled-up, indecipherable insults before hurling the chair towards him. It clipped Mr Roberts' right elbow, and he yelped like an injured dog as Rhys raised a clenched fist, shouted, 'Bull's eye!' and walked out of the classroom then with a jubilant swagger, sticking up two fingers as he went.

I didn't much like Mr Roberts – none of us did, I think – but still, it was discomfiting to see him reduced like that. He just let Rhys go, then turned back to the blackboard, hand trembling as he picked up the chalk. I hadn't thought of him as a real person until then; it had been easy to see him as part of the institution, an appendage to the school, one-dimensional and fearsome and no more consideration needed. I didn't want to think of Mr Roberts as having weaknesses, anything human and imperfect like that. He'd been oddly perfect to me as he was: a perfect instiller of terror, terrifying us with ease and a peculiar kind of grace, as he stalked the corridors with his languid, territorial stride, ever ready to reduce a child to tears in a second with a booming rebuke.

Nothing was as bad for Rhys as what went on at home – poor

little lad that he was; that's what Eleanor Williams' mum said. Rhys told us his dad was a businessman, and an important, international one too. He had to travel a lot: go abroad for work, which was why he was hardly home. Prison was where he really was, said Eleanor Williams' mum, and it would be best for all of them – especially poor Eleri, would you just take a look at the state of her? she said – if that's where he stayed for good.

We knew when Rhys's dad was back; we'd see him, standing outside The Miner's, pint in hand, grinning underneath the hanging baskets, one foot propped against the wall. He looked nice, I thought – kind and funny – and you'd think he would be, being the dad of Rhys. He wasn't, though, that was the surprising thing. Drink didn't agree with him, that's what people said, and after a bender he'd batter Rhys, and his brother Wayne, until they were bashed up and bruised all over just like the windfall apples on our orchard floor.

You dirty kangaroo, what am I going to do? You pushed me down the chimney pot and beat me black and blue, we'd chant when we did French skipping, jumping over the white elastic pulled taut between pairs of knees.

When Rhys's dad really went for it, he'd whack them with his black belt; he had a studded one especially for it – Eleanor told us this when we were hanging on the climbing frame at break, and we never thought to believe her, because she talked a load of rubbish most of the time. It turned out, though, to be true. Rhys showed us the marks on his back once; they looked like chickenpox but ordered, in a line. It was fine, didn't hurt half as much as you'd think, he said, and he'd shrugged and pulled his top back down.

'Battering' was the term they used, Rhys and Wayne: 'That's my dad, that is, gave me a bloody good battering last night,' Rhys would say, to explain the wincing and the sharp intake of breath as he sat down at his desk. Intentional or not, it lightened it, made it sound cartoon-like, as if their father chased them around the kitchen with a giant oversized frying pan, silly music playing all the while. To my shame, I think it suited all of us to view it in that way. No one intervened, no one seemed to grasp the severity of what was happening, or wanted to at least. On the surface his sons shrugged it off, played it down with a deliberate, mannered cool, and, helped along by this, we accepted it, adults and children alike, I think, as one of those things, just the way things were with them.

Eleanor Williams' mum told us to look out for Rhys: be extra nice, given what he had to go through and all, but actually, there was no need. We all loved him; even, begrudgingly, Mr Roberts, you could tell. Despite his outbursts, he possessed a natural, easy kind of charm, a passionate, disarming affection for people that drew everyone to him. He would kiss, hug and clasp friends tight at will, the only seven-year-old boy I knew who could actually get away with it.

'Yeah, I'm a Welsh Nash, course I am,' I said.

'Are you? Brilliant! Welsh Nash is brilliant, innit?' he said, grinning super-wide, cheeks crackling.

I waited to see if he would elaborate, but he didn't.

'Yeah, it is,' I agreed, struggling and failing to add anything more.

'We've got to get them out, haven't we, Ab? That's what my dad says. Get those bastards off our land, send them packing to where they came from!' he said, inching towards me and giving my shoulder a tight squeeze of encouragement.

Trespassers. That's what I thought, and I was with him on that. People sometimes walked across our bottom field without asking, and there was no excuse.

'Okay, let's do it!' I said, looking around the playground to see if anyone – in particular Sara – had noticed that I was not quite, but almost, being hugged by Rhys Prichard.

'Do you want to come and burn some cottages then, Ab?' he offered as he propelled himself deftly off the wall, his black daps landing noiselessly on the tarmac like magic.

I considered it for a second. It was hard to admit, but I was starting to tire of playing Bin Hospital, a game I'd set up with my sister that had dominated playtime for weeks now.

'Yeah, brilliant, come on then!' I said, hurling myself after him, and landing with a flat-footed thump. 'Just let's go and get my sister at the hospital.'

We found Katherine all alone in the stinky back yard, whistling a mournful tune as she put her jars of medicine in a row, lined them up in order of size on the windowsill. After the business with Phillip Brown, she'd gone off nursing for a while, but he was fully healed now; *time* had healed. All the while Katherine's nurse's outfit had just hung there in her wardrobe, crisp and white and professional, luring her each time she opened the door, glinting tantalizingly bright in a sea of spice-coloured clothing. Recently she had started slipping it on again, just for ten minutes or so, to see how it felt. It felt right straight away, she said; right enough in fact to wear to school, where she could bring her healing powers to the masses.

'Come on!' Rhys shouted, his small red fists clenched tight like a boxer's. 'Let's get those English bastards! Let's burn their bloody cottages down to the ground!' he said, punching the air again and again at an invisible assailant. 'Welsh Nash rule Wales! Do you want to be one too, Kath?'

She checked her pin-on plastic watch. 'I could do, just for a bit, I suppose,' she said, taking off her cardboard hat and laying it with reverential care on the window ledge beside her, before smoothing down her hair.

Rhys leant down to her and put both hands on her shoulders. 'I think you should close the hospital down now, don't you, Kath? No one's coming any more, are they?' he said, gesturing to the playground: a seething mass of running, kicking, whooping children. 'You've made everyone better. Look at them all – right as rain.'

For two long, beautiful weeks my sister had had the whole school in her thrall. Everyone, even Sara Fiddick, had wanted to be treated by her. But the novelty had simply worn off, or, as Rhys put it, 'No one can be arsed any more, Kath.'

'But what about Timothy?' she said. 'He needs his medicine from me.'

'Timothy's better now; his eye's all good as new, thanks to you. I reckon you saved his sight – you should be proud of that,' said Rhys.

Timothy Jones had been one of her first patients; he'd come to her with a left eye so gammy – bright pink and engorged, with yellow gunk oozing from his corners – that even his best friends would make mock vomiting noises as he approached.

'Kath, sort it out for me, will you? It's blimmin' killing me!' he'd said.

My sister had studied it silently through a magnifying glass and nodded a lot, impressing everyone with her professionalism by managing to suppress her gag reflex.

For Timothy Jones to find something painful meant it was serious, that much was understood. Here was a boy who had once tried to cut off his own willy with a pair of kitchen scissors, just to see what it would be like to be a girl. He had passed out trying, and found out instead what it was like to have it stitched up by Mr Davies the doctor, which was not at all nice apparently.

'I know just what you need,' Katherine had said, and she'd soaked a tissue in her homemade medicine and laid it gently over his eye. 'Lie down now, over by those bins. Let the medicine soak in. It'll be better soon, I promise,' she said, and she was right, it was.

Word swiftly spread – *Katherine has healing hands, pass it on.* At lunchtimes a small queue gathered in the bin yard. Scraped knees, scabby chins, sore balls: all were doused in medicine and expertly bandaged up with loo roll.

'If it hurts, it's healing,' she would say, in her special soothing voice, to any patient who screamed in agony as she set about her mysterious work.

In her guise as a nurse, my sister possessed such authority and confidence that initially no one thought to question her methods, or ask her what the murky-looking medicine in the jam jars was made of. If they did, it wouldn't be easy to answer. Each jam jar had its own unique selection of ingredients, particular to the day that it was made. I knew this because I helped her to harvest it: an involved and painstakingly slow process. We collected rainwater from the upturned bin lids and thickened it up with the detritus that gathered around the top of the bins, mashing it all up until it formed a paste. One batch could be made from semolina and potato peelings, another from tinned tomatoes and the remains of spotted dick; so the recipe varied from day to day, though we always called it bin juice, because that's what it always was.

Eventually doubt began to spread. Brangwen's mother caught wind of it and banned her from going to the hospital, and that set everyone off. Sara Fiddick, ever keen to dissent, led the grumbling. Her scab should have dropped off by now, she said, and it hadn't – take a look, she said: we were rubbish. We were not healing to help. We were healing for gratitude and adoration and all of a sudden we weren't getting any. Our enthusiasm had begun to wear thin from then on.

Becoming an arsonist made sense. It seemed like a straightforward way to win back some respect in the playground. Our confidence revived as we spent a happy lunchbreak torching holiday cottages under Rhys's expert tutelage.

'Shout "Out, you English bastards, out out OUT!" real loud!' he instructed; and we did, hurling firebombs and hand grenades, and machine-gunning down the doors, as the crowds gathered round.

I was drawn to being a bigot. It didn't matter what we were against; just to be against *something,* and to be united in that, was good enough for me. *I* belonged, of course I did; it was just the others that didn't – the hippies didn't: they were English, every one of them, not like me. I was Welsh now. I could write it, I could speak it, and I had an accent too – and a strong one – at least when I was in school.

Gradually the crowd of children joined in and our voices grew more high-pitched and hysterical as we burnt all the cottages down to the ground, until the final explosion hurled us all back with a deafening bang on to the tarmac. An oblivious Mr Roberts smiled proudly on through his smoke-filled office window, and gave us a benevolent wave, delighted to see his little charges occupied, all of them, happily playing in unison.

9

White nylon socks

'God. Would you just look at your mam, Ab, she's so . . . blimmin'
. . . *tall*,' said Lisa Evans, pointing across the green with her pretend fag. I followed her gaze to my mother. She was standing
near the humpbacked bridge, chatting to Olive as she leant
against our orange 2CV, genuine cigarette in hand. She was
wearing a big, blousy blue-and-white Indian patterned dress over
a polo neck and a pair of trousers, with some of her own silver
jewellery: enamel geometric shapes hanging willy nilly round her
neck; so the less attention given to her the better as far as I was
concerned. Olive – neat and compact-looking in her navy sweatshirt and ironed jeans, and a pair of brand-new white trainers –
shrieked and bent double as if she'd just got a stitch. 'Oh Anna,
never. Stop it, will you? Honestly.'

Lisa leant back and took a long, impressively grown-up-
looking drag on her cigarette sweet. 'Really tall . . .' she said again;
any excuse, I thought, to practise her new gravelly purr of a voice,
which she used when she pretended to smoke or spoke to Rhys
Prichard. She blew out, and began tentatively nibbling away at
the end of the neon-red filter. 'I want to get tall like that one day,'
she said.

'Well tough titties, Lise, your mam's a titch, so you're bug-
gered there,' said Sara, shoving in next to her. 'Chuck us a fag,

then, will you?' she said, snatching one from the proffered packet. She made a show of pretending to light it, stuck out her chin, and blew an imaginary plume of smoke from awkwardly puckered lips, until her breath ran out and her face turned red with the effort.

'You're right though, Lisa,' she said, 'Abbie's mam's the tallest mam in Clwyd, I reckon.' The other girls nodded in earnest agreement. Confirmation from Sara made that a fact.

I looked up to see my mother waving at me. The sun was behind her and shining through her long blonde hair, which she wore straight and parted down the middle. Beautiful hair, but sadly wasted in my view. If she really wanted to, she could make it big and bouffy with flicks all over, just like Cheryl from *Charlie's Angels*. Without her shoes on my mother was five foot four. Not what you could call tall, by any stretch, but I could see what Lisa meant; she was one of those people you just couldn't miss. Indian clothing or not, she stood out; besides, anyone would look like a giant next to Olive.

It was home time, and we were sitting on the school wall, waiting to be picked up. Girls lined up on one side of the gate, boys on the other. No one was in much of a hurry to leave. It was late autumn, and the sun still shone, but weakly now: it *could have tried harder*, as Mr Davies liked to say in his one-lined, identical reports to every one of us. Even so, it was October, and here we were sitting happily outside, without our coats on. We were having an Indian summer, according to my mother. I'd had no idea what she meant, but wondered now if it had something to do with her dress.

No one seemed to want to leave. A group of parents chatted idly on the green, while we stuck to the wall, eking out the faint warmth of the concrete slabs. All the girls had bare legs, I could see now, but me. I was squeezed in tight between Lisa and Sianny Wyn Wyn, bathed in the familiar, oddly comforting warm fug of stale milk that emanated from her clothes. Sara shoved in next to her, pointy elbows sinking into stomachs either side as she clawed her way up.

'Phew, Sianny, you stink again. What do you do? Wash your blimmin' clothes in milk?' Sianny just shrugged and smiled, one eye directed at Sara, the other shooting off in the opposite direction, as she shoved her glasses back on to the bridge of her nose.

My mother was beckoning me, but I pretended not to see, returning my attentions to Lisa's white nylon knee-high socks, dazzling bright against the concrete, her scab-ridden knees poking out proudly over the top of them. I looked down the line of girls – Lisa, Gwen, Brangwen, Bethan – girl after girl in identical knee-high white socks, and then me in my tights, next to Sara, and Sianny at the end, whose socks must have been white once I think, but were grey now, and more hole than sock, like cobwebs – the thick, ropy kind that you find in the cellar.

Sitting next to Lisa was like finding yourself under one of those unforgiving strip-lights you get in service stations. I looked down at my own navy-tight-clad legs, with the gusset sagging down from under my skirt, and gave them an ineffective hitch up, bobbles ripping off from the scratchy lichen like Velcro. I hadn't minded my tights until now; they were plain, and not homemade, but there was something about that line of socks . . . there was something about Lisa.

I felt a sudden panicky, greedy, grabbing kind of feeling. *I was overwhelmed with want*, as if someone had given me the keys to a sweetshop and said, 'Here you go, help yourself, take as much as you like.' I wanted to look Welsh like Lisa, with pitch-black hair and cheeks that were flushed a permanent pink. I wanted to dress like her, wear those socks and purple padded anoraks and polyester jumpers in proper, feminine colours like lilac and pale yellow. I wanted all of that and more – much more: *I wanted to be famous like Lisa.*

There was a town about ten minutes' drive from the village: Big Town, we called it, even though it wasn't. Lisa's father had a shop right in the middle of Big Town's High Street – you couldn't miss it – with its red-and-white sign that spelled out his actual name in letters above the door: 'Evans the Butcher'. I wanted some of that: a father so important that his job was part of his name. I wanted to be one of the protected, chosen few, like Dylan in my class, whose dad was Jones the Milk. Dylan was fat, which was a novelty then; he was the only fat boy in the school, in fact. He panted with the effort of walking to school and his mother had to make him his trousers. Sara would have been on him in a shot, laughing and poking and mimicking if only she could, if only she'd been allowed; but how could she? His father was Jones the Milk.

Lisa's fame meant that she couldn't walk down the street without being stopped. 'Hiya, Lise, how are you, my love?'

'Not bad, ta,' she'd say.

'Hiya, cariad. How's your nan doing now?'

'Better now, ta.'

'Lisa, tell your dad I'll be over later to collect my sausages.'

'Will do, ta,' she'd say, answering always without obvious gratitude or pleasure. If it was me, I was sure I would be milking the attention for all it was worth, but as it was I had to make do with trailing in her wake, hoping for a sprinkling of her second-hand stardust. A part of me was envious of her self-possession, her unwavering quiet confidence; but I wanted to break her out of it too, wring some emotion out of her, make her lose control, even for a second, screech with laughter until she wet herself, perhaps, like Sianny Wyn Wyn, or yell out in terror until her voice went hoarse. But she never did.

Lisa's town wasn't much bigger than the village where we went to school, but to me it felt like the metropolis. The shops were bigger and the cars drove faster, and a permanent smell of petrol hung in the air, until you walked past the greasy spoon café with the yellowing plastic-covered tables and sticky condiment bottles on a tray in the window, where the warm stench of vinegar and stale chip fat hit the back of your throat and made your eyes sting. It was just one high street, more or less; a row of dark stone houses with lace curtains at their windows, until you got to Commerce House, the hippy commune, and then a scattering of shops and pubs. The far end of the street was dominated by a vast, dismal-looking hotel that no one ever stayed in but which resolutely remained open nevertheless, its windows getting blacker and its plastic flower arrangements more faded as the years went by.

Lisa lived in the centre of town, just below the chapel in the High Street, near their shop, in the same house that her grand-parents had lived in and their parents before them. It was a narrow, dark little house, white-fronted, with black-painted window frames and heavy lace curtains, immaculate inside and out.

It was the Christmas holidays when I first went to play at Lisa's.

'Hello there, cariad,' said Lisa's mother. 'I'm Angharad, come on in.' She looked just like her daughter: tiny and pale with blooming cheeks and black, shiny, patent-leather hair. My mother waved me off as I was ushered inside, into the muggy depths of their hallway, a narrow dark corridor that smelled of gas and tea.

'Let's get that off, Ab, shall we?' she said, wrestling my unwieldy duffel coat from me, looking as if she would rumple under the weight of it; and she led me through, small fingers poking into my back like a rudder as she steered me to the front room.

The whole family were waiting for me there; I hadn't been expecting that. Evans the Butcher himself was perched on the arm of the sofa, with the plastic shop cover still attached ('For hygiene,' said Lisa when I asked about it later, which made me none the wiser). Lisa's brother, Jonathan, lay across the other arm: two matching bookends, both of them round-faced and curly-haired like the man in the moon and his son. Lisa sat in between them, neatly, with her ankles crossed and her hands on her lap, her hair extra shiny from a recent brushing, as if she was waiting for a great-aunt to visit. Behind them, in the corner, was Lisa's nan: still, as if she was sleeping with her eyes open, filling an armchair – *part* of the armchair – in a complicated-looking crocheted cardigan, squares of colour stitched together, hands clutched tight on her lap.

I stood there on a square of the patterned carpet, and my mind emptied: wiped clean in an instant, like an Etch-a-Sketch that had just been shaken. It was the sudden, unfamiliar, weight of expectation, I think, that did it. There was nothing I could think of to say or do, so I stood there, stock-still, struck dumb like an idiot, while they waited and watched, and I thought, please, dear Lord, if you exist, show yourself, make someone say something, as the gold carriage clock on the mantelpiece ticked loud, tutted at me. Tut tut, come along, it said, surely you can do better than this?

'Sit down, girl! Sit down, make yourself at home!' (*Thank you!*) said Evans the Butcher at last, patting his hand on the limited empty space between them all. I slipped in beside Lisa, and sat there, shoulders hunched up and knees pressed together uncomfortably tight, and all I could hear was my breath moving noisily in and out of my nostrils, slow and loud like Darth Vader and Timothy Jones, so I tried to hold my breath then, until I thought I might pass out.

Still no one said anything, and I sat there, gazing down at my pale brown, toffee-coloured shoes, downcast and miserable, certain that I'd failed in some way, but at what exactly? How? I wasn't sure.

'Mam's gone to get us some pop,' said Lisa.

'Soda-stream lemonade,' added Jonathan.

'That's nice,' I said.

'It is,' said Lisa. 'Tastes real – you won't tell the difference.'

'No,' I said.

'No,' said Evans the Butcher and Jonathan together, shifting to make themselves comfy, the plastic squeaking out in protest.

'Geraint! Did you give me my pills?' asked Nan.

'After tea we can go upstairs and play if you want,' said Lisa.

'Yes,' I said, willing her mother to get a move on, so I could gulp it down and get myself up those stairs as fast as possible.

It was a bright, sunny winter's afternoon outside, but we sat there in half darkness, the heavy lace curtains at the bottom windows filtering out the sunshine as well as nosy stares. Blue and green tinsel hung in loops from the ceiling, and there was more of it wrapped around their artificial tree, which stood by the telly on a cardboard box covered in Christmas wrapping paper – small fat Father Christmases waving away merrily on sledges. It came from the hardware shop, I'd seen it in there; they were selling it in rolls in a box by the door, where the brushes used to be. The only internal light came from a small gas fire on legs with plastic logs and burning flames that were an uncosy-looking blue, tinting the room in an eerie light, as if we were sitting in a cave at the bottom of the sea.

My eyes adjusted and I could see that the room was filled with porcelain figurines, like the ones my nana liked – clusters of them in family groups, all of them deathly white and big-eyed, but oddly lifelike still, as if they might spring into action the minute you left the room.

'You liking our Ladro then, Ab?' said Evans the Butcher, and I nodded and squeaked out a yes.

'Your mam and dad collect it?' he asked. I gave a nod that could also possibly be a shake, and hoped that he would never have a reason to go inside my house – shame-makingly knick-knackless and entirely figurine-free, despite my nana and poppa's best efforts.

'A little gift to make the place a bit more homely,' Nana would say, handing my mother a china puppy sitting up to beg, or a kitten playing with a ball of wool, and once a beautiful but sad Pierrot doll weeping and lonely-looking on a log. After Nana and Poppa had left, they'd mysteriously vanish into the ether, never to be seen again. 'I don't understand. Where do they get to?' my nana would say. 'It's like the Bermuda Triangle in this sitting room – everything just disappears.'

The Evans' front room had Welsh lace on every surface. There were antimacassars on the armchairs, runners on the shelves, and the tablecloth was scattered with lace tablemats; even the top of their huge mahogany telly had a Ladro family standing elegantly to attention on a lace doily. It made me frightened to move. I was a clumsy, long-limbed child, not one meant for a small lacy room filled with delicate objects.

'Go on then. Help yourself to a biscuit, will you?' said Lisa, pointing to a glass plate that sat on top of the television, piled with an exotic selection of colourful treats: pink wafers and party rings, and important-looking mint chocolate biscuits covered in bright green foil.

'Lise!' said her nan, raising her hand. 'Lise! Pink wafer. Soft, that's what I want. For my teeth.'

It was busy on the High Street. Outside, through the upper half of the window, the tops of people's heads appeared above the lace as they walked up and down into town. Nesta, who ran the greasy café, bustled past, blonde beehive secured with a head-scarf, patting it, adjusting it here and there, stopping now for a chat with Anthony, my father's friend who ran the health food shop around the corner.

Mr Evans stood by the window, one huge finger resting on the top of the lace.

'All clear,' he said. 'No sign of the buggers today.'

'Geraint, leave it out, will you now?' said Lisa's mother. 'You're getting yourself obsessed, you are. It's not healthy.'

'Just a bit of fun, my lovely, just having myself a bit of a laugh – now tell me where's the harm in that?'

'No harm!' said Nan from the corner.

'I like to keep an eye out, I do, Ab,' he said, 'see if there are any hippies contaminating the High Street.'

'What's that you say?' asked Nan.

'Do you know what I do when I see one?' he said. 'I get my shotgun out like this,' and he aimed two fingers at the glass and fired a pretend gun, 'and I scare them bloody shitless. "Bugger off, will you?" That's what I shout. "Get back to your stinking tepees!" Honestly,' he said, with a sighing kind of laugh, 'you should see the look on their skinny little faces,' and Lisa and Jonathan laughed as I sat stiff and still with shock.

'What use are they to me, eh? Eh, Ab?' he said, when he saw my face. 'Whole house crammed full of the buggers, three doors down from my shop, and not one of them eats blimmin' meat!'

'Geraint, hush now, will you? We've got *company*, duw!' said Lisa's mother and I looked around the sitting room and back at her and blushed when I saw she meant me.

'Don't mind him, he's got a strop on today, he has. You just sit there and relax now, why don't you, Ab? I'll go and put the tea on,' she said, handing me my freshly carbonated drink, tiny bubbles fizzing around the edge of the glass. And we sat there like that, in the murky half-light, all lined up in a row, legally ruining our appetite on biscuits, until she called us through.

We ate tea in the kitchen – lamb chops and tinned potatoes – all of us squeezed in around a pale yellow Formica table, condensation misting up the windows. Lisa sat opposite me, directly under their kitchen clock: a china plate with pink and yellow roses outlined in gold decorating its edges, and I marvelled at the beauty of that clock while I chewed, pictured it hanging in our kitchen, transforming it into a room worthy of my nana and poppa.

I studied Lisa while I ate. She'd changed since she'd turned eight; something about her had altered. I watched her sitting upright, shoulders back, every movement deliberate and graceful. I straightened my back as I took in the way that she ate, which was neatly, prettily, like everything else she did; even the scabs on her knees looked attractive, like a scattering of tiny strawberries: the Alpine ones that grew in our garden in the flowerbed underneath the sitting-room window. Somehow, she'd harnessed some inner power, discovered without telling how to take possession of her entire body. She'd lost something too; her childishness had gone: that's what it was. And me? I wasn't nearly ready; I was several stages down the evolutionary scale, still inhabiting my head more or less; what my limbs did, what my mouth did, was of no concern to me. I left all that to instinct – at least I had done, until now.

Evans the Butcher demolished his tea, pausing to suck the end of a cracked, greasy finger every now and again, pointing a chop in my direction to ask me yet another good-natured, sweat-inducing question, Lisa kicking me under the table all the while.

'So, I hear your mam and dad are learning Welsh then, Ab? That's good then. Angharad, pass us the brown sauce, will you? Ta. How are they getting on then? They got the knack of it yet?'

'Does your dad watch the rugby then? Did he see the game on Sunday?'

'Never seen your dad down The Miner's. Where's his pub then? Is he a Nag's Head man?'

The answer was a shameful no to all, but I nodded nonethe-less to every one of them, grateful for a mouthful of gristle.

'Dad, shut your mouth, will you? Ignore him, Ab, why don't you?' said Lisa at last, pushing her bone-laden plate to the middle of the table. 'Mam, we're done here now, aren't we then? Can we have our dessert in front of the telly?'

'Of course,' said her mother, and in a chorus of 'tas' we rushed through the wood-chipped hall and on to the sofa. Jonathan prodded the power button with his special magic stick, his home-made remote control: a long piece of bamboo with Blu Tack stuck on the end. The television burst into life: the sound of strum-ming music fading out, and there was a man, behind a desk, in a brightly coloured V-neck geometric-knit jumper and tie.

'Hello again!' said the man, and he gave a grin and a wink to camera, as Jonathan squeaked his legs underneath him, sending the antimacassars sliding to the floor.

'Oh, *Newsround,* is it then?' said Lisa's mother, ladling out fruit salad from an industrial-sized tin into cut-glass bowls on the sideboard. 'I do love a bit of John Craven,' she said, topping each one with a Teddy boy quiff of squirty cream.

'What? You got the hots for him, have you then, Angharad?' Evans the Butcher was standing in the doorway. 'Look at him, why don't you? He's wasting away, if you ask me. He needs some meat on his bones!' he said, cupping his gargantuan stomach.

'Get over, will you?' she said, pretending to be offended, as she passed us our bowls on individual trays with what looked like a beanbag attached underneath – for comfort, said Lisa when I asked her later, as well as added extra purchase to the knee.

'He's wearing a jumper with a blimmin' tie! Bent as anything, if you ask me,' he said, settling into an armchair with a painful-sounding grunt.

The gas fire had warmed up, and the flames had turned a more believable orange; everything looked peachy to me now, even the Ladro had taken on a healthy-looking glow. I sat there, happy, wedged in tight between Lisa and Jonathan, slotting in comfortably between them as John Craven delivered the news personally to me, staring straight into my eyes, and I felt the dry heat make my cheeks flush pink, like Lisa's.

10

John Craven

The day after I first visited Lisa's house, I decided that I wanted to be John Craven. How can it be explained? I can only think that at eight years old, and too young to love him exactly, it made some twisted kind of sense to me to embody him instead. All logic blinkered by his handsome, clean-shaven face, I knew only that I wanted to pay tribute to him; to acknowledge my appreciation for what I thought he stood for, which was what I wanted my family to stand for: respectability, properness and *all things right and dutiful*.

I asked my mother if I could have my hair cut short, and she delightedly complied, scrabbling around immediately for the stiff kitchen scissors in the sideboard drawers: any excuse to cut hair. Noisily, squeakily, she followed my instructions, lopping off my wonky, long pudding basin into a shorter, wonkier version of John Craven's, side-parting it and combing it forward so both ears were covered, like his. A tie was found, an old one of my father's, and I wore it then, every day, with a shirt and a jumper and my smartest-looking trousers. If eyelids were batted I didn't notice, and I was called John from there on in, no questions asked, none to my face at least.

Our telephone was in the hall. It had its own area dedicated specially to it under the stairs, my mother's domain, where it sat below a cork noticeboard on a small table made from bamboo. Next to it was my mother's diary, and a ringbound notepad with a pen tied on to it with baling twine, just in case anyone thought to steal it. The phone itself was a dark greeny kind of brown, the colour of a wet cowpat, with a dial that clicked around and spun back into place as you dialled the three-digit number. My mother was to be found 'on the phone' most evenings, settled in the rattan chair, calling friends and family one after the other. Sometimes I would sit with my sister at the top of the stairs, where we'd fish for titbits, catching tantalizing snippets here and there; down a few steps and we'd get the whole story, hear her perfecting it as she went along, making it better, funnier still with every phone call. We'd sneak a peek at her through the banisters, cigarette tapping away on the scallop shell, a glass of white wine waving around for extra emphasis, as she talked about her other, more exciting-sounding life.

I saw being 'on the phone' as a glamorous, adult pursuit, something to aspire to, like smoking purple Silk Cut or going to get a perm at the hairdresser's. So it was an honour when my nana rang on Sundays for her weekly chat and actually asked to speak to me in person, on the phone.

'Fill me in then, my darling, come on. What have you been up to?' she'd say, and I was grateful that she wanted to know, delighted that she cared. She did care, of course she did, though there was another element to these chats, I think, that bypassed me entirely: wily Nana, the super-sleuth, was checking up on us. She was making sure that her family were all still safely on the rails, convinced as always that my father was going to push us off them any minute now. My sister and I – biddable and unwitting, the both of us – were her perfect moles. It was almost too easy: all information required flowed from us in a torrent, and all of it, thanks to flattery, entirely uncensored and unchecked. If Nana thought that I was grown up enough to be on the phone, then I would sit up straight like Lisa and tell her who my parents had been spending time with, cross my legs like Lisa, and describe the parties they'd been off to. Whatever she asked, however prying, she was guaranteed to get the honest truth.

'How are you, my darling Abbie?' she said this Sunday, as I settled on my knees in the chair. When I corrected her to John, she said nothing; there was silence, just the hiss and rustle of our phone line.

'What do you mean, darling? What's going on?' she asked eventually, her voice breaking into a cough like it did when she made it squeaky-high. 'Les, my love, pass me a light, will you?' she said, and there was a click and a deep breath in, and a muffled exchange with my poppa, and then she asked me to go and get my father.

My precious five minutes had been horribly curtailed. This wasn't how it was supposed to be. Our calls usually ended with my sister begging for me to get off the phone, desperate for her turn, while Nana fired question after question at me, cooing and ahhing at pretty much all that I said. Everything I did was somehow turned into an achievement by Nana. 'You've gone up a shoe size? Oh darling, well done you! You're growing so well.' I was used to being praised to the hilt, lauded till my chest swelled; and I'd pass the phone to my sister, certain, for a short, sweet time, that I was an exceptional and astonishing child, nothing short of superhuman. Affronted, I disentangled myself from the springy phone cord to call my father, raising my voice above Joni Mitchell, until the kitchen door opened and he came with a roll of his eyes to the phone.

He grabbed the receiver and huffed at the ceiling, one hand scrunching his beard as she spoke.

'Ma, what? Don't be ridiculous. Relax, will you?' he said, perching one bare foot on the chair, a royal-blue trouser leg unfurling like the sails of a yacht.

We had a glass wall by our sitting-room door. My parents had put it in when we moved in. It was just a small one, the width of a person, but big enough to let in some light. I liked it. I thought it looked futuristic and glamorous, like something Buck Rogers might have in his house. I hid myself behind it and sat down, cross-legged, on the dark brown carpet.

'Of course not. Jesus!' he said. 'Wiggy, do you mean? That boy he was with was called Sasha – that's a *unisex* name; it's not a girl's name,' he said, shifting his weight from foot to foot, and glancing longingly towards the kitchen door. 'We're just letting her *express herself*, that's all, Ma. No, don't say that – that's outrageous. It's not. Not at all.'

I swiped greasy smears down the window with my forefinger; fat, streaky lines marking the glass, one after the other like warpaint, as I mulled that one over.

What, exactly, was it not? I didn't want to 'express myself'; it sounded like something a hippy would do, and for some reason faintly rude. I'd grown used to Nana being my personal cheerleader, waving her pom-poms for me regardless: two, four, six, eighting me all the way. I'd come to expect her full, blinkered, unwavering support – something she rarely granted to my parents but had always, until now, given to me.

My father called my sister to the phone. Nana didn't want to finish off our conversation; that was that, we were done and dusted, so I took my dented pride outside. I ran out of the back porch, along the gravel at the front of our house, and then left, to where the swing and wooden climbing frame looked out over the lawn and the mountains, their tops blurred with mist and streaked white with snow like messily iced cakes. I climbed on to the swing and tipped myself back, skywards, as I swung higher and higher, wind whipping my cheeks. I could see the red-tiled roof of Olive's house, crusted with a crunchy layer of ice. I swung higher, and below it there was Olive, outside in her back garden, in black fingerless gloves. She was breaking up a Battenberg cake into tiny, bite-sized pieces, laying them on her window ledge to feed to the birds. I had to turn the other way. Some people have it all, some *birds* have it all, I thought. Me? I wasn't even allowed sugar on my Weetabix. My mother had told Olive off when she saw her doing just that with a Wagon Wheel and an orange-flavoured Club biscuit. 'Anna, you crack me up, you really do!' said Olive. 'Honestly! What are you on about? I thought you knew your nature. Birds haven't got any teeth!'

I swung on, breathing in the cool, frosted air – and out again, my breath magically visible now, streaming out in front of me like puffs of cloud against the bleached-out, heavy-looking sky. The stillness that surrounded me was interrupted when the rhododendrons at the bottom of the lawn began to shiver, the leaves shaking, dripping freshly melting ice, revealing themselves again: dark green and shiny new like plastic. I slowed the swing down to a gentle sway, as grunts and strains of effort came from somewhere deep within the bushes, and the branches in the middle parted to reveal Sara Fiddick.

'Oi! Bitch!' she called, finger pointing towards me, in case there were any other bitches to be confused with. 'What the flimmin' 'eck do you think you look like, eh?' she said, her voice squawkingly high with disbelief.

I kept my head down and said nothing. No reply was

expected; like all of Sara's questions, it was rhetorical, requiring nothing other than a shamefaced nod of acknowledgement, which she wasn't going to get from me. In Sara's world there were no questions, just answers – hers of course – and all of them, always, unquestionably, right.

'I tell you what,' she said, as I carried on silently swinging, fixing my stare on the shoe-scuffed, bald patch of soil beneath me, 'you look like a bloody, flippin' nut job, you do.'

I contemplated that, stomach sinking, as I watched a trail of armoured woodlice winding their way across the packed, shiny earth under the swing. Like it or not – which mostly I didn't – Sara could be relied on, always, to make things crystal clear. For her, as for my nana and poppa, there were simple rights and wrongs. I skidded the swing to a halt, shamed, but sure at least. I faced her briefly and, blood rushing in my ears, I swiped her my middle finger. Her face froze briefly with disbelief, and then she gave a little shiver of delight. Sara was made for this: there was nothing she loved more than a good face-off.

'Bloody lezzer,' she said, meeting my gaze with defiant, narrowed eyes. 'Do you want a scrap, do you then?' she asked, raising her bruised, bony fists in front of her.

I turned and ran then, skidding up the steepest part of the lawn, pulling off my tie as I went. 'Chicken! Lezzer chicken!' shouted Sara, squawking and clucking at my fast-retreating back as I hurled the tie into the box bush. I clomped my feet through the gravel, towards the sunroom door as fast as I could, head down to hide my tears. I didn't want to be John Craven; I could see that I was done with that now. I didn't want to be a chicken or a lezzer either. I wanted to be *the same*, that was all – and if not, just similar, even, would do.

Part Two

11

Pac-a-mac

It was early summer, and we were sitting in our back garden, Matthew Martin and I; side by side, with our legs dangling into the pond, waiting for the leeches to latch on. It was a muggy, buzzing Sunday afternoon, and the only place to be was outside, immersed in water. Matthew's parents, Anthony and Bethan, my parents' closest friends, had come over for lunch. It was almost teatime now, but still they were all sitting at the table in the sun-room behind us, around the empty plates and crumpled-up napkins and the last remaining crumbs of pudding. Every now and again their laughter would echo down the lawn, and there would be the clink of glasses as they helped themselves to more wine.

'What are they *doing* in there?' I said. 'There's nothing left to eat – why don't they just get down?' It was for something to say, really, to test out my voice, which I'd been trying hard to make deeper and less babyish since my sister had tape-recorded me while I chatted to my nana on the phone. She'd played it back to me doubled up with laughter: I sounded like Pinky or Perky, she said, and, in a fury, I'd shoved her to shut her up, because she was right, absolutely, I did.

Matthew turned and looked behind us. 'Your dad is par-taking in the wacky baccy by the looks of it,' he said, giving me a slow, weary roll of his eyes, as if to say 'What's he like?' I wanted to roll my eyes back at him, silently reply 'I know!' But I daren't, because what he'd said had just whizzed right on over my head; and I knew better, thanks to Sara, than to admit it. If you didn't know, you didn't ask: that was the golden, unspoken rule. Asking made you look weak, and could earn you a thump in the mouth. So I nodded and said, 'Hmm,' and then added an experimental 'uh huh' in the lowest voice I could summon up, because it was the sort of thing an American might say; the way a Charlie's Angel would reply.

Matthew was almost a teenager and a boy, so he was pretty much an alien to me: a different species entirely. I considered him with covert, sideways glances; studied his checked cowboy shirt and sticky-up blond hair, and tried not to stare at the sprinkling of fine hair that grew above his top lip, glittering gold as it caught the sun. It made him look older, possibly fifteen, and he was tall for his age too, like me. I was lanky-limbed now, gangly and big-footed, which made me clumsy and uncoordinated: tallness didn't sit well with me yet, and wouldn't for years to come.

Matthew went to school in Bala, so none of my friends knew him: *he was exclusive to me*, or that's what it felt like at least. It was an honour, but a burden too, to be with him; and the weight of it, the almost impossible task of trying to be grown up like him, gave me an uncomfortable awareness of myself, a horrible consciousness of my every move, as if I were on stage in front of an audience, all of them watching, waiting for me to muck up. I needn't have worried: no one was looking, not even Matthew – transfixed as he was by the cool dark water. The only spectators were our cats, that was all, once in a while peeping out from behind the laburnum, regarding me with a steady gaze and a dismissive twitch of a whisker.

I stretched my legs out and swept my feet through the water, duckweed collecting between my toes like underwater cobwebs, and wished that Sara Fiddick would walk down the lane now, cheekily sneak a peek through the bushes at the bottom of the lawn; she was nosy by nature, and could never resist a quick sticky beak whenever she passed our garden. I pictured that sweet sight: Sara gasping in wonder, agog with disbelief from the rhododendrons as she took it all in: a blond, teenage-looking boy, American-looking, like a film star, sitting here, in our garden, and chatting, just to me.

The mountains around us were quiet and still and empty, but it was busy in the pond, jam-packed and heaving with life. Water boatmen twitched across the surface, and beneath them brown clusters of mosquito larvae jerked back and forth like animated commas. Occasionally a dragonfly swooped on to a lily pad in front of us, a surprising flash of bright metallic blue against the pond's prevalent green.

'Have you got a leech yet?' said Matthew, scrutinizing his pondweed-covered legs, water dripping shiny black splats on to the hot slate flagstones.

I raised my legs out of the pond too, sending the boatmen darting for safety. Suckering on, under my right knee, was a large leech, chocolate brown and glistening. I resisted my instinct to tear it off, and instead moved my leg towards him for inspection.

'Disgusting!' he said, breaking into a grin. 'Hey, I know what we can do! Let's leave our legs in for ages, until they are *covered* with leeches, and then they'll drink all our blood, and we'll pass out!'

We were still full from our lunch, but even so we had stockpiled a mound of sorrel leaves, gathered from the verge outside the gate, to munch our way through as we waited. Sara Fiddick called sorrel Sour Duck, and for some reason it had stuck; everyone – even my mother – called it that. We endured, more than enjoyed, Sour Duck; it was a challenge, always, to eat as many as we could in the most casual way possible, without balking at the sourness of it or retching it back up into our hands like Phillip Brown couldn't help but do.

'Do you know how ladies get pregnant?' Matthew said as he bit into a leaf, scrunching one eye shut despite himself.

This was a murky area for me. I knew the odd, alarming detail about sex, thanks to Sara Fiddick and her dad Dave's magazines, but none of those details seemed to fit together, nor made any sense in a way that didn't appal me.

I spotted a snail egg sac, stuck to the underside of a lily pad, irresistibly odd-looking, like a translucent slug peppered with hundreds and thousands. 'Sort of,' I said, feeling my cheeks colour, and I leant forward to hide my face, carefully peeled the sac from the leaf, placing it on the slate beside me, where it glowed luminous against its black background, and I busied myself by checking the underside of the lily pads for more.

'Men are like farmers,' said Matthew, plopping his legs back into the water.

I looked across at Colwyn now, in the cab of his tractor, juddering down the lane towards us.

'They have ready-made fertilizer,' Matthew said, bending down to roll his sodden trousers further up his legs. 'They spray it on to the ladies to get them pregnant.'

There was a sudden burst of inappropriate laughter from behind us – *there was nothing funny about this* – and my mother's raised voice, distorted from behind the glass.

Olive was 'trying for a baby' now, so I'd heard her say to my mother. I pictured Mike coming home from the sawmill with a backpack filled with fertilizer from Colwyn's farm, aiming his spray gun at her as she opened the door to welcome him home.

'Look, I've got some more eggs for you,' said Matthew, lining up two more next to mine. 'Men's willies work a bit like crop spreaders,' he said.

'But when does the spraying happen?' I asked, a rising sense of alarm making me forget to pretend to know anything at all.

'Any time,' he said. 'That's why men have to wear johnnies full time.'

There was a grinding roar as Colwyn's tractor turned up our lane, and he drove past us now, tipping us a nod as he went, eyes on the road all the time.

'Do you know what johnnies are?' Matthew asked.

I shook my head, too miserable to talk, and stared down at my bare legs, ghostly white in the water. There were three leeches on me now; the first one had turned a darker brown and looked twice the size of the others.

If he was Sara he'd have revelled in my ignorance, but he just nodded and carried on: 'They're like little anoraks that men have to wear down there to stop the spray getting everywhere,' he explained, chomping into another leaf.

'Have you got an anorak on now?' I asked, shifting as subtly as I could a little further from him.

From behind there was the scrape of chairs against floor tiles as the adults finally got up from the table.

'No, not yet, but I'll probably wear one full time when I'm thirteen, just to be sure,' he said.

I stared fixedly ahead of me. Water snails swivelled around the pond's edge, creating slow but constant movement just beneath the surface, their shells shiny black and pointed like tiny witches' hats.

There was the creak of the summerhouse door.

'Matthew!' His mother, Bethan. 'Come on, it's time for us to be getting back!'

'Better go,' he said. 'Shame I didn't get a leech. See you soon,' and he leapt up, straightened up his shirt and brushed it down, though there was nothing to brush off that I could see.

'Bye then,' I said, sounding back to squeaky normal, as he ran his hands through his hair and bounded barefoot up the lawn in his soaked-through rolled-up trousers, our cats springing out from the bushes to follow him, weaving in and out of each other behind him as he went.

I thought of the teenage boys that I knew, and Simon Parker sprang to mind – my mother's friend Sheila's mainly silent thirteen-year-old son. Simon had close-cropped hair and a pierced ear, and a hearty dislike for everyone who wasn't Leonard Cohen. I pictured him sitting in his dark attic bedroom – wallpapered all over with newspaper – hunched over his desk, writing another poem about death, with a tiny Pac-a-mac in his underpants. That image of him made him seem a lot less frightening to me, and yet, in another way, infinitely more.

12

Hippy dinners

'Hang on a sec, girls, I just need to pop into The Happy Pear,' said my mother as she swerved the 2CV off the High Street and into a parallel parking space, where it juddered and then stalled to a halt, nowhere near the kerb. Rubbish parking, even by my mother's standards, confirmed by the lorry behind with a long, low blast of its horn.

'No, Mum, please! Let's just go home. You'll be ages!' I said, tugging at the roots of what could still be described, disappointingly, as my pudding basin (despite my many frantic, futile attempts at adding flicks). My sister just banged her head against the window again and again and wailed. She was right to: the word 'pop' was my mother's coded warning; it really meant *Grit your teeth, girls; prepare yourselves; I'll probably take for ever, knowing me.*

The Happy Pear was a health food shop, so we hated it, my sister and I, with its dried-up bits of fruit, its jars of smelly herbal tea and its sorry-looking pretend cakes that were sweetened with apple juice instead of sugar and had no buttercream or jam in, or anything else that might have tasted nice. All the food in there was brown. We wanted food from the Co-op – bright, colourful, happy food loaded with fat and sugar, food to make the heart sing. Worst of all, my family had an *association* with it: Anthony was the owner – as in Anthony and Bethan, who were Matthew's parents and my parents' closest friends.

Lisa Evans' mum tutted and huffed when she walked past The Happy Pear; I knew because I'd seen her do it once, while I waited for my mum outside the Co-op, which, like yin to yang, heaven versus hell, was only on the other side of the road. I'd been sitting on the window ledge as my mother queued for the till, my feet propped up on the polio boy collection box. Opposite, Anthony was fiddling about with the display in his shop window, squatting down as he rearranged bags of rice in a pile, aiming for a pyramid, I think. He was in his waistcoat of many colours, which was hand-knitted by Bethan from a pattern by Kaffe Fassett. My mother and Bethan were crazy about Kaffe Fassett. Anyone else, a man especially – my father, say – would have looked like a joke in that waistcoat. Not Anthony. Somehow he wore it with authority. It was something to do with the way he held himself: upright and proud as if he was in the army. That and his pleasingly smart hair, which was formal hair like my maternal grandfather's, short back and sides and super straight, the last visible trace of his past life as a stockbroker in London.

Lisa's mum had been heading off down the High Street. She looked smart for the shops, in pearly lipstick and court shoes and the tights that I loved called American Tan. Anthony had given her a cheery wave, but she'd turned her head the other way – in my direction, though she didn't see me – and said 'Honestly!' and she'd made a spitting noise, and she looked like she spat, though I saw that no spit actually came out. Still, that was cross for her; livid even. Lisa's mum didn't get any crosser than that. Anthony waved again, though, smiling, craning his head, thinking she'd just not noticed him. It belittled him in my eyes: made him look suddenly a bit weak. I thought grown-ups were supposed to get things, *understand*. He didn't – while I did. The rush of power I felt from the topsy-turviness of that made me feel uneasy, because it wasn't welcome; I wasn't ready for that yet.

Anthony had owned his shop for a few months now; he took it over from Llewellyn the Tobacconist when he finally retired. Llewellyn – who looked one hundred and ten, with his caved-in face and yellow, tobacco-stained skin – would have carried on till he dropped down dead if he could, I heard Lisa's mum say once, but it was the cataracts that did for him. I'd pictured Llewellyn falling down when she said that, keeling over, flat as a plank, in the middle of serving a customer – me, say. I thought of him lying dead on the flagstone floor: face up, eyes wide open, still clutching my bag of flying saucers. They scared me, his eyes: all milky and blue like moonstones. Would I take my bag of sweets from his hand before I called the ambulance, or would that be wrong, I wondered?

Anthony had found the perfect position for a health food shop – ideal, being right next to Commerce House. It could be like the commune's corner shop, somewhere for hippies to buy their soya milk and pumpernickel bread and herb toothpaste and other essentials like that. He'd start local, that's what he said, though long term he had bigger plans than that. He wanted people to travel far and wide. North Wales needed to be woken up to health food, and it was down to him, he said: the doors were wide open, because when it came to competition he didn't have any, not yet.

His shop stood out in the High Street, with its dark brown shiny paintwork, just two doors down from the Evans' red-and-white-painted butcher's, and next to the General Stores, which was painted a navy blue. It was its chiller section that got the Evans so het up: crammed full of its 'phoney bollocks', as Evans the Butcher called it; *making a mockery of meat*, he said, which amounted to pâté made out of mushrooms, and sausages made from beans, and strange-looking make-believe bacon that looked plastic, the meat bits a cerise pink as if they'd been painted on with coloured ink.

'Is it any wonder these hippies look so friggin' pale and ruddy goddamn ill, when they live off a pile of shite like that?' he'd said when I was round at Lisa's the week before for tea; and there was silence and I looked up from my pork chops and he was pointing a greasy knife at me. 'Eh?' he asked, and I just nodded, and felt my cheeks crackle hot, not sure if he was trying to catch me out. Did he know about my connection, my link to the shop of shame?

'I know. I couldn't eat that stuff, no way,' I said, shoving in a big forkful of meat. 'This pork tastes delicious,' I said, my words mangled through the mouthful, but needs must as my nana would have said.

'Do you think?' he said, raising one woolly eyebrow in what looked like suspicion to me.

Evans the Butcher was a member of the Round Table, and the Round Table knew everything about everyone, so said Eleanor Williams' mum; they even knew what colour knickers you were wearing. The injustice of it all made me boil hot with anger: I was being tarred and I wanted no part in it, that's what I thought as I took a long, deep swig of my Kola, draining my glass in one.

'Want a top-up, Ab?' offered Lisa. 'Mam'll fizz up some fresh for us now, she will, if you do,' she said, and I nodded and grinned in reply. This was me, right here, couldn't they tell? I loved Kola; I loved meat; I loved packet food; health food meant nothing to me.

*

We'd been living in North Wales for seven years now, and still I'd found no one exactly like my family; no one with our peculiar, off-kilter mix of a little bit of this and that, and neither one thing nor the other. The most similar, though, the only family remotely like us, were Anthony and Bethan and their sons Matthew and John. They had a touch of hippy too, and listened to Simon and Garfunkel, and Anthony came from London like us. I liked them, very much; they were friendly and funny, and knew everyone, and most essential of all, despite the health foods they fitted in, mainly thanks to Bethan, who was born and bred in the village. Her brother owned the chemist shop in town: Morgan the Chemist, no less. Bethan spoke Welsh, and loved Wales with a passion; she sang about her love for it in Eisteddfods. She was a big part of the local community, and because of her, Anthony was too.

I knew, deep down, in my core – *in my waters*, as my nana would say, whatever they were – that my parents weren't hippies, but to me they were still worryingly on the cusp. My mother made her own hummus and brown bread, and loved a good forage. 'Like a gypsy,' I overheard Nana say to Poppa once, curling her lip and giving a little shiver, which I took to mean wasn't good.

I worked hard, I tried tirelessly to retrain my parents, specifically my mother; to steer them in the conventional direction, which, foodwise at least, meant the Co-op. My sister and I would accompany my mother there – to lend a hand, we said, but really it was to guide her, direct her, push her, even, towards the Angel Delight, or the Findus Crispy Pancakes, something breaded and orange-coloured like that. Just looking at The Happy Pear – from the back of the car as my mother drove, painfully slowly always (*dangerously* slowly, my father said, which unnerved me, and puzzled me too: what was dangerous about going slow?) – a fleeting glimpse of that shiny brown façade was enough to make me tense with irritation.

'I won't be long, girls, I promise. I just want to stock up on a few things,' my mother said, and she actually sounded excited, as she grabbed her patchwork bag and her shopping basket from the passenger seat. 'You can stay here and wait if you like,' she said, in a light kind of voice, as if she was doing us some kind of favour. She squeaked open the car door and I watched her bounding barefoot up the steps to the pavement, taking them two at a time, nimbly avoiding a small mound of dog poo – trotting now, *because she couldn't wait to get there* – and I felt the pang: the dull twinge of worry that came now when I thought about adults and their peculiar, alien ways. I didn't want to be a grown-up; it wouldn't suit me, I felt pretty sure about that.

'There's no point waiting here, is there?' said my sister, giving a final thud of her head on the window, and she was right. Without one or other of us trailing after her, imploring her to leave, my mother could be gone for evermore.

'Let's go then,' Katherine said, her voice drenched in misery, opening the car door in slow motion, tipping herself out on to the road.

'You never know,' I said, 'he might have got something new in, some doughnuts filled with custard or something like that. Maybe . . . ?' My voice trailed off as I scuffed up the steps behind her, bowing my head as I went, in case Sara or, God forbid, Lisa – *please God not Lisa* – were to see me.

At the top of the steps Matthew appeared from around the corner, cycling past the General Stores on his BMX, which he'd just got new for his birthday.

'Oi!' shouted out a teenage boy, leaning against the phone

box outside Commerce House. He was smiling at Matthew, thankfully, not me. '*Hippy Dinners!*' he called, taking the hands out of the pockets of his Harrington jacket. 'You okay there?'

'Gwyn!' Matthew shouted back – *answering to that.* 'How's tricks?' he said, grinning and doing a wheelie, then speeding up towards him.

Hearing Matthew's nickname always gave me a sick-making thump in the stomach. We weren't so different, Matthew and I, so it offended me by proxy, that name. It didn't bother Matthew, though, not a bit. 'It's just a name,' he said, 'so what?' He'd been Hippy Dinners for a couple of years, since his last year at our school, when he'd taken in a packed lunch for the first time ever. Hawk-eyed Neville Fiddick had spotted the contents of his lunchbox – brown homemade-bread hummus sandwiches and a nice healthy slice of Bara brith.

'Matthew! What the frig have you got in there?' he'd said, grimacing and baring his pointy teeth, but Matthew had just shrugged and smiled.

'I don't care what you think, Nev,' he said. 'Tastes good to me!' and he'd taken an extra-large bite of his sandwich and given a thumbs-up and a wink as the dinner hall erupted in shouts of '*DISGUSTING!*' He just smiled and carried on eating, bigger and bigger mouthfuls. 'Delicious,' he said in between bites. 'I love it!'

'Tell you what, I'd rather eat a sheep-shit sandwich, I would, than have one bite of your hippy dinners,' said Neville, and Sara's screech of delight sealed it. That was it: his official re-christening. I didn't, I never would, but all his friends called Matthew Hippy Dinners from then on.

Anthony was kneeling on the floor, opening cardboard boxes, deep in conversation with my mother by the time we finally ventured in: me first, and then my sister; the bell rattling out its distinctive sound – its *vegan ring* as Eleanor Williams' mum called it once: hesitant and a bit weedy, like the mewl of a new-born lamb.

'Ah, girls, lovely to see you!' he said, clapping his hands together. Anthony was someone who clapped a lot – not applause, just a one-off, solitary clap; and he'd leave his hands there, clutched together, and shake them back and forth when he needed to say something important.

'How long would these need to soak for, do you think?' asked my mother, frowning at a bag of black lentils.

Why would you bother? I thought. As Nana said once, 'Why soak food? Life's too short, Anna. Soaking is for pans and stains.'

'Maybe overnight,' he said, running a Stanley knife along the middle of a box, 'just to be safe.'

I sneaked a monkey nut out of a box on the shelf and won-dered what could be unsafe about lentils? My mother was drawn to dangerous foods; that's why she liked picking fungi. 'It's like Russian roulette!' she said once, putting a fungi salad on the table. 'Don't worry, just joking. I'm almost definite it's chanterelle,' and she laughed as my sister and I just sat there, staring at our lunch. 'Tell you what, I'll eat it first, and if I drop dead, don't touch it, okay?' she said, scooping up a mound on to her plate.

'Carob bars!' Anthony said, pulling out a bag from the box. 'There you are!'

'What I actually came in for,' said my mother, finger trailing along the jars in the chiller cabinet, 'is tahini. Do you have any?'

'Yes!' he said, clapping, and clutching. 'Well, I *will have*. You'll have to hang on a sec – it's in this lot somewhere.' He stood up to survey the boxes, swiping a hand through his Second World War hair.

'Shall I pop back in twenty minutes?' said my mother.

I thought that I groaned inside my head, but it must have been out loud, because Anthony turned to look at me. 'Tell you what, Abs,' he said, 'I'll have a treat waiting for you when you get back, okay? I promise.' He tapped the top of a box. 'Would you like that?'

'Yes!' I said.

'Yes!' echoed my sister, and she star-jumped into the air, plaits flying. We got overexcited, always, when it came to treats, which was all down to my nana and poppa. They'd set the bar high. They'd elevated the meaning of treat, promoted it with their endless generosity, so it meant something extravagant and indulgent to us now – a big box of chocolates with a gold satin bow; or better, something unsuitable for children, like, say, some shoes with a bit of a heel.

Outside the shop and in the sunshine, the air was heavy with incense. The windows of Commerce House were open, blankets pulled back, and Maya and her daughter Nell were sitting in one of the top windows, pale-skinned and red-haired, and both of them in purple dresses.

'Anna! Come on up,' shouted Maya in her husky voice that always surprised me: it didn't fit her; she was too small for a voice like that.

'Shall I?' said my mother.

'Yes!' said Maya, raising a chipped, white enamel tin cup. 'Come and have a cup of tea.'

I hated those cups. She'd given me a drink in one last time we went, and the chips were rusty and made the water taste funny. I drank it all the same, to be polite, but sweated quietly away in the corner after that, worrying that I'd been poisoned by rust. That was the only time I'd seen Sara Fiddick cry: when she scraped her leg on a barbed-wire fence. 'Mam!' she'd shouted, even though we were in Colwyn's top field and Eirian was miles away. 'Help me, Mam! It's rusty, I've got *tetanus* now, I have!' I didn't know what tetanus was, but Sara was crying, which made it something she could die of, that was definite. Sara was tough as boots: she could stick a needle in her finger and draw blood and she'd even *laugh* when she was doing it. I rushed her home then, as quick as I could, guiding her by a bony elbow, down the winding track to her house.

'Ta,' she'd said, when we got there, her eyes still wet with tears. 'Don't tell no one about this, all right?' and she pushed her back gate open and swiped her nose with her sleeve. 'You're dead if you do. I mean it. *Dead*,' she said, drawing a finger across her neck. 'Okay?'

'You need to come in, Anna.' Maya wasn't giving up. 'Wiggy's finished his mural now – you have to see.'

'Yes, I heard!' said my mother. 'Just a quick pop in . . .'

And in my head I shouted the rudest word I could think of at my mother: 'Whore!' I shouted, 'You stupid whore!' (Which meant idiot, according to Rhys Prichard, but not just idiot – a *massive* one, he'd said, and he knew that, because that's what his dad called his mum.)

My mother carried on, though, oblivious, pattered towards the open door of Commerce House in her turquoise and blue Paisley-patterned skirt. She swished through the doorway, skirt fanning out behind her in a wave, and was gone.

'Remember the treat, just think about that,' said my sister, as I double-checked left and right, up the street and down; and there were no witnesses, so we followed her in, because we had no choice, and I wondered how old I would have to be before I didn't have to do this: trail around after my mother doing idiotic things.

We went in then to the musty, narrow, bright-green-painted hallway, past the bikes piled up on each other, past the dog-eared posters of Joni Mitchell and Jimi Hendrix and the Rolling Stones. I knew who they all were now, all of them, even the ones Eirian wouldn't have heard of, like Captain Beefheart and Joan Baez, who looked beautiful even though she had short hair. I'd been educated in the who's who of music now, thanks to Matthew, who'd tried to teach me, using my parents' album covers like flash cards, when he came over to babysit.

'Up here,' shouted Nell, 'main sitting room!' and we followed my mother up the open wooden stairs, and I wobbled and had to stop when I looked down through the gaps, so I focused on the abandoned objects left on every stair: a sandal, a packet of tobacco, a comic called *Fat Freddy's Cat*. Nell was waiting for us on the landing, grinning.

'You really don't like those stairs, do you?' she said, and I shook my head and stared at her, because it was hard not to stare at Nell. My mother had a postcard of the *Girl with a Pearl Earring* pinned to the cork board above our phone. Nell reminded me of her; beautiful, in a quiet, pale kind of way, with her huge dark eyes set wide apart. If she covered up her red hair, wrapped it up in a blue tea towel, then she'd look identical.

She took my hand as I got to the top, and then grabbed on to my sister's, and I wanted to say, 'You're twelve. *That's not what you do* – you don't hold hands!' But she was home-schooled, and that's what happened: home-schooling made kids a bit weird. Eirian had said that, tutting away as she tapped the ash from her cigarette when she was round at Olive's last week, 'taking the weight off', as she called it, with her cup of tea, which was nice – always nice – and her fag, which was always, without fail, the last one. She was on one of her rants about the communes. *Ooh, don't get Eirian started,* Olive would say. *Please don't get her started on that!* But she'd be grinning when she said this, because she liked it really, loved it when things hotted up.

So Nell wouldn't know, that was all; it wasn't her fault. She wouldn't know about things like holding hands, and when not to: which was never when you were my age and above.

The main sitting room was probably the best room in Commerce House, and I didn't like it much even so. It was a big, light room, with its two windows looking out over the street, but still it felt cluttered and cramped. Every available space was covered with books and guitars and homemade-looking wooden instruments, and abandoned half-drunk cups of something with mushed-up leaves at the bottom like compost. There were spider plants everywhere – more and more of them each time we visited – hanging all over the place in teeny, tiny baskets made by Maya out of rope. 'It's like the Hanging Gardens of Babylon in there,' said Olive after she'd dropped in to visit once, which I think she meant was good. I hated those plants: I didn't see the point of bringing the outside in; it felt all wrong to me, especially when their leaves were matt with dust and you could hear the chunterings of the busy High Street outside. Nature felt unnatural in a place like that.

'What do you think, then?' asked Maya, nodding towards a sofa with one arm missing, and draped with a yin and yang throw. Wiggy's mural was above it, covering the entire wall: a giant rainbow, spanning either side of a hill in a moonlit, star-filled sky. The hill was covered all over with wild flowers: dandelions, daisies and celandines, growing through blades of grass, and clumps of sorrel and stones half covered in moss. The detail was extraordinary: every petal of the flowers perfectly painted, perfectly real and life-sized.

'Rainbows only come in the day, I thought; when it rains,' said my sister, head cocked to one side as she stared at it.

'Ah, but it's not a *rainbow*, Kath,' said Maya, tucking her hennaed hair back behind her ears, which were a tiny bit pointed and Spock-like, I noticed; they were hidden away usually – perhaps that was why – behind her big red blanket of hair. 'It's a *moonbow*. They're very magical, very spiritual and life-giving,' she said in her growling voice. 'We saw one once when we were star-gazing in Yosemite. *Oh my God!*' She made the word God go on for ages as she threw her head back to the ceiling. 'You wouldn't believe what a sight that was,' and she shook out her hair. 'Just incredible.'

'It's wonderful,' said my mother, and she was being truthful; she was only ever truthful – well, if she lied, which wasn't often, you could tell. 'He should paint more!' she said. 'He can't waste a talent like this.'

'I know,' agreed Maya, and she sat down, cross-legged, on a cushion on the floor. 'Talk to him, Anna, tell him! He needs a good old kick up the arse,' and I was wincing as I thought of that – of my mother publicly kicking Wiggy's skinny little bottom with her new cork wedges, him buckling head-first down on to the High Street – when Nell beckoned me towards the door.

'Do you two want to come see my bed?' she asked.

'All right . . .' I said, waiting to hear if there was any more to it than that, but there wasn't, and I was nosy, so I didn't really mind seeing her bed.

Nell took my sister and me down the corridor, holding our hands again, past a bedroom with a big double mattress on the floor, and in the middle of it, there was Wiggy, lying face up and fast asleep.

'He's zonked out,' said Nell as we both stopped to stare in, and she whispered 'Idiot', that's what it sounded like, under her breath.

'But it's *daytime*,' said my sister.

'Don't worry about it,' said Nell, swatting the air with her hand, 'that's just Wiggy; that's what he does.' He was her father, but she obeyed the unspoken hippy rule of calling her parents by their first name – or nickname in the case of Wiggy. His real name was Christopher Wigmore, my mother had told me, which made him sound quite grand – and he was, or used to be, though you'd never think it to look at him, said Olive. His parents had a big house in Surrey, and stables and lots of land. Wiggy didn't visit them any more – he couldn't because he'd been disowned, which I thought only happened on TV. I'd found that last bit out from Maya; I heard her telling my mother in the orchard when she came over once to collect windfalls.

Wiggy's father had tried to make him join the family business, just like his older brother had, she'd said, checking the apples for bruises and putting the good ones in her skirt, which she'd gathered up in front of her like a makeshift basket. I could see her stripy knee-high socks when she did that, and her pale little knees as well. I was hanging upside down on the climbing frame, swinging back and forth, which made it difficult to catch it all, but Wiggy wanted to go to art college, from what I could gather. His parents didn't want him to, but he went and did it anyway: moved to London and stayed with his old schoolfriend Freddy – the same Freddy who now lived in The Mill. They shared a squat – which I took to mean was a tent, and I pictured them camping on a patch of grass next to Big Ben. That was years ago, said Maya, and none of his family ever spoke to him now, not even his brother, who had two houses now, one of them in Greece, with a boat, I think she said, or was it a goat?

'In here,' Nell said, taking us into a room without a door, the last one at the end of the corridor. It was a narrow room, with a tiny, low-down window and a chest of drawers in one corner, two mattresses on the floor and one bed. That was it. Its walls were bare plaster – the colour of an actual plaster – and were covered from ceiling to floor with writing and drawings, in biro and pencil, and fingerprints in multicoloured paint.

'Ta daah!' she said, spanning out her hands in the direction of her bed, which was wrought iron with a sleeping bag on it, and a velvet beanbag instead of a pillow. 'Welcome to the only proper bed in the whole of Commerce House. Do you love it?'

We did, we said. 'Come on, then, sit on it, why don't you?' she said, stepping over the mattresses on the floor. 'It's really comfy,' she said. 'I just nagged and nagged until they had to give in. I was so sick of sleeping on the floor.'

'Who sleeps there?' asked my sister, looking at the two mattresses side by side on the floor.

'Kit and Sasha,' she said, 'my half-brothers: Wiggy's sons from before Maya. They're not happy down there, though; they want a proper bed now, like me.'

'You don't know how lucky you are. I'd *love* to sleep on the floor,' said my sister.

'The novelty wears off, believe me,' said Nell, opening up the top drawer of her chest of drawers. She sounded like a grown-up when she spoke sometimes. I liked that about her. I would practise saying 'believe me' in the bathroom mirror later, and then try it out on Lisa and see what she thought of that.

'Do you want to see my books?' Nell asked. 'I have to hide them all in here, or they'd go walkies,' she said, handing me a hardback book without its cover, with the words *Pride and Prejudice* embossed in gold. 'Wiggy and Maya got me this for my birthday.'

If I was Sara I'd have said I'd read it ages ago and added that it was a bit shite too. 'We've got this one at home, I think,' was all I could say, opening it up. The print looked tiny and crammed together and there were no pictures to break it up.

'Read it!' she said. 'It's all to do with love and class and stuff: things like that.'

'Have you read any Just William?' I asked.

She hadn't, she said, taking out more grown-up-looking orange-and-cream books from the drawer, stacking them up in a tower so the Penguins on the spines lined up, before lifting out an important-looking hardback. '*Middlemarch*,' she said. 'I've just started it,' and she hugged the book to her chest.

Underneath the books was a crumpled-up brown T-shirt and a shoe box without its lid on, packed tight, filled with what looked like treacle toffee: cling-film-wrapped blocks of rectangular dark brown chunks.

'Do you get to have that?' I said. 'Your own box of toffee in your bedroom?'

'I wish!' she said, laughing. 'That's *black*.'

'What's that?' asked my sister, taking a piece out and holding it up to the window.

'You know, the squidgy stuff,' Nell said, and we stared at her, waiting for more.

'Liquorice, do you mean?' said my sister.

'No! It's *dope*, isn't it?' she said. 'Drugs! You ninnies.'

I'd heard about drugs and I'd thought that they were against the law, but Nell didn't look ashamed or embarrassed or even worried that we'd seen them, which made me wonder if I'd got that bit wrong.

'Wiggy sells it, you know, to Freddy and Angelica, and that lot who live up at The Mill,' she said. 'He smokes half of it, though

– he's really pissing us all off actually. Especially Maya.'

'You can't say that!' gasped my sister, clapping a hand to her mouth and giggling through her fingers. 'That's such a bad word! That's swearing!' she said, and Nell told us all the other swear words that she knew then, which was way more than we did, as it turned out. She could use them, too – that was the thing that shocked us – even to Wiggy and Maya, because that was fine: *her parents had said it was fine for her to swear at them!* It was freedom of expression, they'd said.

'Look, I've made you a present,' said my sister to Nell, handing her the lump of black, now shaped into something a bit like a duck.

'Sweet!' said Nell. 'Thanks!' And my mother called us from the sitting room then, shouting that we needed to go.

Anthony was beaming: radiating happiness when we went back into The Happy Pear.

'Task done! Tahini found,' he said, sounding triumphant, 'in the bottom box, naturally. Of course it had to be,' and my mother thanked him, in a really over-the-top way, I thought, like he hadn't located a jar of tahini at all; like he was a deep-sea diver and it was pearls that he'd found: actual treasure that he'd given her instead.

'And girls, I haven't forgotten about your treat,' he said, and my sister was looking at me, grinning, tongue sticking out of the corner of her mouth. 'Hold your hands out now for your surprise,' he said, and he gave us each a piece of wood: a twig with its bark still on.

'It's edible!' he said, clapping his hands. 'You wouldn't think to look at it, but try it! Just chew!'

I was supposed to be grateful, and I would have been once, like my sister. She'd cheered up now, just like that. She was tucking in, munching away, giggling, happy as Larry, because she was only seven, which was a baby practically, and seven-year-olds were easy, more easy to please than I was.

'This is what it's like to be a dog,' I whispered to her.

'I'd *like* to be a dog!' she said.

'Save me!' I muttered – to myself, not her – and I began to chew, and imagined myself in another life, a life without stupid sticks pretending to be sweets, a perfect life where I was the daughter of a Charlie's Angel and we lived in a brand-new bungalow in Florida, possibly, and we had a kitchen with matching units, and a fridge with an ice-machine, and it was bubble gum I was chewing, because Farrah Fawcett would let me have bubble gum – she would *encourage* me to have it, she wouldn't think I was too young for it at all.

'Keep going!' said Anthony, totting up my mother's bill with a tiny, worn-down pencil. 'It's hard work all right, but stick with it – it's worth it.'

I carried on, gnawing at the stick, only a faint taste of sweetness my reward, and as I swiped the drool gathering at the corners of my mouth I spotted Lisa Evans coming out of the Co-op on the far side of the road. She looked happy, half walking, half skipping on the sunny side of the street, swinging a bag from her elbow as she tucked into a bright pink packet of Monster Munch, pickled onion and the best flavour, so tangy it made your eyes squint shut with the vinegariness.

I shoved my stick in my shirt pocket, shut my eyes and prayed then for her to keep on walking past, but when I opened them again she was crossing the road and heading straight towards the shop as I stood there, next to the till, still like a musical statue. As she approached, her step slowed and she stalled and then came to a stop in front of me.

'Look, Abs,' said my mother, 'Lisa's outside!' and I gave a low, quiet groan of acknowledgement, as my mother waved. 'Can she see in?' she said. The sun was eye-squintingly bright outside and, opposite, the Co-op's shop windows were like mirrors reflecting the light.

I watched her, unaware of her audience as she lifted the crisp packet to her mouth and tipped it up to get the last little bits at the bottom. She caught sight of her reflection then; she must have done, because she blinked and then widened her eyes and checked her newly pierced ear lobes – still pink – with a stud in the middle, gold balls like the ones Olive used to decorate her trifle. The Co-op plastic bag swung on her elbow. There were sweets in it. I could see the white paper bags through the thin plastic. Evans the Butcher asked her to buy him his fags, and his payment was always sweets with the change.

She rubbed the crisp crumbs from her lips, and finally she turned her back, and I breathed out then as she headed off up the hill, past the chapel to her house. From behind she didn't look like Lisa; she looked like someone else, like a fully grown woman, in her anorak – a new one – that went in and out at the waist, and her shoes, which had a bit of a heel. Gwyn and Matthew were still chatting by the phone box, and Rhys Prichard had joined them now, and they stopped, all of them, and turned to watch her, even Rhys – *especially* Rhys – as she pushed open her front door, and tipped her head towards them, smiling at them over her shoulder.

13

Yackety Sax

It was lunchtime, and Lisa and I were standing in the school hall, in the dinner queue, sandwiched tightly in between Jonathan Evans and Rhys Prichard. One of them, I couldn't tell which, was wearing aftershave. I guessed it might be Jonathan because he was wearing gel in his hair today; and aftershave and gel seemed to go together, to *happen* to the boys just like that. His curls looked curlier than ever, but shiny, as if he'd worked up a sweat. He grinned at me when he saw me looking and patted his hair. 'Proper gel, that is now, Ab,' he said. 'It's not lard – that's what Aled Fiddick said it was, but it's not, I swear. I only tried that the once, honest to God,' he said. 'Are you liking it?'

It was unexpected. I was taken aback to be acknowledged by him and my cheeks burnt red to reveal it. As with all his sister's friends, Jonathan ignored me most of the time: benignly, rather than rudely, as if I hadn't even occurred to him, and it had been natural to ignore him back.

'I'll take that as a yes,' he said, which it wasn't, so I didn't reply. The silence between us didn't feel comfortable any more. He cleared his throat.

'I like your shoes,' he said at last, which embarrassed me because I couldn't bear for him to look at them. They were hateful shoes, shoes a boy might wear: chunky lace-ups with ridged rubber soles and the colour of cooked pastry. I'd done my best to try to lose them, but my mother kept tracking them down, delighting in finding them every time. 'Here they are! Abs! I've found your shoes – what a relief!' My nana had winced when she'd first seen me wearing them, and taken a sharp breath in, as if she was looking at a nasty wound. 'Ooh,' she said, and finally, after a long pause, 'they look *comfortable*,' which meant *terrible* coming from Nana.

I looked up at Jonathan, expecting him to be laughing, but he wasn't.

'Thanks,' I said.

'Pleasure,' and he stretched out the word as he raised an eyebrow at me. He was the only boy I knew with curly eyebrows.

'Stop pushing, will you all now?' shouted a dinner lady from the kitchen. 'There's no rush, there's plenty enough to go round,' she said.

'Yeah . . . like we're gagging to eat that cach, now aren't we?' said Jonathan, but quietly, into my ear, so no one else could hear, because he never wanted trouble, not like Rhys Prichard, who liked to create a ruckus; he'd have shouted it out loud, knowing him.

An industrial metal vat was shoved through the hatch from the back, and I caught a waft of our lunch: the sweet and savoury blast of mushy peas, neon green, bubbling and glooping away in front of us like some stinking primordial mass.

Brangwen's mother was on dinner-lady duty. She only came in on a Monday, because she didn't need the job, she said; she just liked to get out of the house. Brangwen's mother, like Brangwen, always looked smart, 'put together' as Olive would say, and she stood out in her fitted dress with covered buttons, next to the other dinner ladies: all hot and wilted-looking with their scraped-back hair, in their baggy polyester blouses with sweat marks under the arms. Her white paper hat was perched on top of her new hair-do, her 'power set', as she liked to call it, and she kept cupping it, checking it was in place. She had it done every Saturday in Hairway to Heaven, the salon in town, two doors up from the greasy café. Lisa would see her in there, she said, sitting under a dryer, eating biscuit after biscuit for an age.

Rhys Prichard was next to be served, but he turned to Lisa behind him. 'Go on then, Lise, ladies first,' he said, showing her the way forward with the flourish of an eczema-covered hand.

'Ta, Rhys,' she said, slinking past him.

'Yeah, shit before the shovel,' said her brother, and she flicked him the Vs over her shoulder. Everyone flicked the Vs all the time, but Rhys Prichard looked at Lisa like she'd just done the funniest, cleverest thing he'd ever seen.

'Nice one, Lise, good call,' he said, clapping until Jonathan knocked the wind out of him with a thump in his lower back.

'Boys! Cut that out, will you now?' Brangwen's mother was wielding a mash-covered serving spoon in their direction.

'His fault, wasn't it?' said Rhys Prichard. 'Oi! Lise! Save us a place, will you?' he shouted after Lisa as she crossed the dining hall with her loaded plate and said nothing.

'Hey, Mrs Jenkins, guess what?' said Rhys, holding out his plate to Brangwen's mum. 'You've got hair the spit of Maggie Thatcher's, you have,' he said, and she blushed as she walloped on a mound of mashed potato, and said, 'Thank you, Rhys, I'll take that as a compliment.'

'I wouldn't, mind,' he said, grinning and pointing at the potato for more. 'My dad reckons she's a lying bitch, he does.'

'Not nice! Bad word, Rhys,' she said with a frown. 'We don't like that word now, do we?' She peeled two discs of pink speckled

Spam from a tray with big metal tongs, and on to his plate, slap, slap.

'What, *bitch*? Bitch is *nothing*,' he said in his raspy, broken-down voice as he headed off to the knives and forks. 'He's called her tons worse than that.'

'No hope, no hope,' she muttered, shaking her head as she rearranged the Spam and then turned her attention to me. 'Hiya, cariad,' she said, sing-song high, 'we've got a *gorgeous* lunch for you today, we have!'

'No peas for me, please,' I said, staring up at her transfixed. She looked much wider than our prime minister and strangely see-through too: the strip-light above her worked like an X-ray, making the skin on her chest transparent like a jellyfish. I could see a road map of red veins branching out all over under the surface, creeping out above the neckline of her dress.

'Sorry, pet, you got to eat your greens, you have. They keep you healthy and strong, don't they?' she said, and she squelched the white plastic ladle into the vat, upper arm juddering with the impact.

On the far side of the hall, next to the double doors, I squeezed in around one of the chipped white Formica trestle tables, where everyone sat in industrious silence, carving smiley faces in their Spam. Rhys Prichard was on the far end of the table from Lisa, on a seat clearly not saved by her.

'Look at that then, Lise, will you? Spitting image of you, I reckon,' he said, holding up his plate with his carved Spam likeness of her. Somehow he'd managed to get the hair spot on.

Lisa stared back at him for an uncomfortably long time. 'What do you want me to say?' she asked at last, and the smile dropped from his face.

'I don't know. I thought you might like it, that's all. You can keep it if you want,' he said, proffering the plate.

'No,' she said.

'No,' he echoed, shoulders sinking. 'I'll eat it then, shall I?'

'Don't care,' she said with a shrug.

'Get a move on now! Clear those plates or none of you bug-gers will get a dessert!' Mr Roberts, our headmaster, had appeared behind the hatch for second helpings. 'You know the rules,' he said, loading up a pyramid of mashed potato. 'If your plate isn't empty, *no playtime!*' he shouted, which made spit spray out of his mouth in a fine mist, like Lisa's Impulse Body Spray when she sprayed it out in front of her to walk through – the only way to get a *smell all over,* she said. Impulse was a deodorant, but a perfume too; either way, she didn't need it yet, said my mother.

None of us spoke as we sat, heads down, concentrating, elbows stuck into faces, as we shoved the food in, gulping it down in painfully large lumps as fast as we could: anything to avoid the indignity, the humiliation of a playtime spent alone in the dining hall, left out.

Lisa Evans, with her neat, efficient eating, was first to clear her plate; and she sat back with a satisfied sigh, folding her hands behind her head, as if she was relaxing on a sun-lounger.

'Jonathan and me watched an amazing programme last night,' she said, barely above a whisper, which made everyone at the table stop eating, knives and forks suspended mid-air. The quieter Lisa spoke, the more important the information: everyone knew that but Sianny Wyn Wyn.

'What's that you say, Lise?' she asked, blinking quick-time, face twitching, as she shoved her glasses back on to the ridge of her nose. 'Speak up, will you? Can't hear what you're on about.' She licked a line of mushy peas from her knife.

Jonathan and Lisa Evans's lives were superior in most ways to pretty much everyone I knew. Life wasn't fair, I was beginning to get that now, but there was a limit, surely; there had to be, in terms of having it all? My sister – who had moved on now from worshipping the Queen and Princess Anne to God – had a theory, and she put it all down to the Lord. Lisa and Jonathan had been *chosen*, she said, with a shrug, as if that were explanation enough. (Why? For doing what? I wanted to know, but she just shook her head as if I was an idiot for even asking.) God shone his light on the Evanses, she said; he blessed them with things, like soda streams and an 8.30 bedtime, and their two massive televisions that they could watch whenever they liked.

Unlimited access to television was nirvana to me, and to every other child that I knew. Eleanor Williams' mum would tut – any excuse to tut: it wasn't right, she said, for children to watch what they liked, that's what she said. But I didn't agree. Television had made the Evanses all-powerful in my eyes, filled them to the brim with knowledge of the adult world, knowledge that I didn't have. The rest of us were weak and lacking in comparison, and Lisa and Jonathan knew this and loved it too, and didn't try quite hard enough to hide it.

'It was brilliant,' murmured Lisa, splaying out the fingers of one hand to examine her nails, which she'd painted a pearly white, as we stared at her, mouths open, and waited; desperate, all of us, for her precious little nuggets of gold.

'*The Benny Hill Show*, it's called,' she said, addressing the Duralex water jug, slipping her bottom to the edge of the seat now so she was practically lying down, ankles still primly crossed. She sighed and let her gaze wander around the room, to the ceiling and the strip-lights hanging in between the wooden beams. She hadn't noticed – that's what she wanted us to think – that we were rapt; hanging like needy little monkeys on every one of her softly uttered words.

'What's that? What's the show called, Lise?' gargled Sara Fiddick through a mouthful of gluey mashed potato. Lisa ignored her, stretching out her legs along with her moment, but Sara pressed on, unbowed, noisily gulping down her mouthful and said, 'I think I know it, yeah. I think I've watched that one. Tell me the name again – I think it's my favourite.'

'Benny Hill,' said Lisa, and the way she said it, the way she elongated the words, in a deep, gravelly kind of voice as if she was announcing the winner of an Oscar, gave it instant status. It was incredible, the way she did that: hooked us into something, *anything*, like a show we'd never seen, never even heard of until now. She had such power: the influence to sway, the authority to rule supreme.

The next week, and all anyone could talk about at school was Benny Hill. Rhys Prichard scurried around the playground, black daps in a whirr as he hummed the frenetic theme tune, slapping the girls' bottoms as he went, his eyes trained on Lisa all the while. He was Benny through and through; he'd got him down to a tee, that's what everyone said. Katherine and I tried as hard as we could, we laughed along with the rest of them, but I worried that we sounded weak and unconvincing compared with them. *We didn't know what was typical of Benny*, that was the thing, because our mother – and our mother alone – had refused to let us watch him.

'It's just not suitable,' she'd said through a mouthful of pins as she sat at the kitchen table hemming a homemade sundress for my sister.

'Why though? *Explain*,' I said, my hands balled tight into fists; and it was hard to hear her properly through the pins, but she mentioned something about half-naked women and sexism and an absolute lack of respect.

'Why is it suitable for everyone else,' I said, 'but at the same time not for us?' I wasn't trying to catch her out; I genuinely didn't understand. I saw right and wrong as wholly indiscriminate – what was right for everyone else should therefore be right for us.

'I don't *care* what anyone else does,' my mother replied, and she even dared to give a little laugh, as if she wasn't nuts for thinking that at all, as she started tacking along the hem. There it was: the crux of it.

'But you *should*,' I said.

The Benny Hill game would be a phase, I had to hope, like Bin Hospital, or cottage-burning; it would pass in a couple of days. I carried on hoping, on and on, as day after humiliating day Katherine and I were forced to join in every lunchtime, pretending that we had the first clue. We suffered like that for two weeks; two weeks of indulgent eye-rolling at the mention of his name – 'Benny! He's just so crazy, isn't he?' – of humming along to the second-hand theme tune and debating our favourite bits, 'definitely the same as Lisa's'.

It was Nana who finally saved us. 'What's the harm, Barry?' she said. 'Just let them watch it! It's just a bit of fun – where's the harm in fun?' I heard my father gruffly relaying this Sunday-afternoon phone conversation to my mother that night.

'Honestly,' she said, 'why should I take advice from someone whose idea of fun is Bob Monkhouse?' I despaired when I heard her say that, because the Evanses loved Bob Monkhouse, the Browns did too, and Eleanor Williams' mum had even been to see him live at the Palladium; and she had taste, she knew about taste, because she wore knee-high boots and had blonde hair styled to look like Sapphire from *Sapphire & Steel*. Somehow, though, in the way that she often could, Nana managed to work her witchy kind of magic, and the unheard-of happened: my mother actually changed her mind.

So here we were, my sister and I, in the study, on our dark brown velvet sofa. We sat in a nest of Kelim cushions, clutching each other's clammy hands, heads pressed together, craning close – too close – to our tiny portable TV as it blasted out the familiar theme tune which we knew now was called 'Yakety Sax'.

'Aagh, I might just pass out!' said my sister, and I knew what she meant: the build-up had almost been too much.

'You never know,' I said, giving her hand a reassuring squeeze, 'it might not be that good.' I spooned the lumpy bits from the homemade banana milkshake into my mouth. But it was.

My sister and I laughed, long and loud, as Benny – cheeky, funny-looking Benny – chased ladies who were practically naked – *nearly nude!* – around a park, until we were choking and gurgling, tears streaming down our cheeks; with relief, I think, as much as amusement. I looked back at my mother, behind us, leaning arms crossed against the doorway. Her head was pulled back, mouth open; and she was frozen still, as if she'd looked at Medusa and had been turned, just like that, into stone. If ever I saw Medusa, I'd try to remember to keep my mouth shut, I was thinking, as she came to life – *jolted* back to life – and gave an indignant yelp, as if someone had pinched her, as if Benny himself had slapped her on the bottom.

'Good God, what am I *doing*?' she said. 'I can't let you watch this!' and she rushed forward, as if it were some kind of life-saving emergency, leapt towards the television as if it were a bomb about to explode, and patted it all over, saying, 'Where is it, for goodness' sake? Where is it?' Her wooden bangles clacked together, her string of amber beads went swinging, banging into the screen, as we wailed and refused to show her. But she found it anyway – it wasn't really that hard to locate: the red button on the bottom right-hand side – and she pressed it and said, 'There!' and turned it off; and went marching into the kitchen.

We shrieked out our protests, rolling around on the Moroccan rug on the sitting-room floor, really going for it, letting it all out in the way you could only ever do at home, with no one else watching. I was outraged still, but also enjoying the sound of my own voice, when I heard my mother's perky-sounding singing from the kitchen.

'She doesn't give a damn about us, does she?' I said, and my sister gave a sad-looking, despairing kind of nod.

'She doesn't even *like* Dr Hook really, does she?' she said, swiping tears from under her chin with the pulled-down back of her sleeve. 'She only knows it because Olive's put it in her head – that's Olive's song, not hers.'

It wasn't just the singing but the choice of song that seemed so insensitive to me. The tune was so upbeat you could only really sing it, I reasoned, if you were feeling completely happy, with nothing weighing you down, like two daughters sobbing in your sitting room because you'd ruined their lives for ever.

Sometimes it hits you, some things just make you feel it: the sheer powerlessness of being a child; and this was one of those times.

'*I decide.*' I hated those words. Being beaten up, having my eyes scratched out in the playground for not knowing about Benny Hill, was not the best for me. *My mother didn't know what was best for me*, which frustrated me beyond belief but alarmed me even more.

I would make my mother care, I thought as I picked my way up the stairs to my bedroom: make her despair like me. If she wouldn't feel sorry out of the goodness of her heart, then I'd force her to. I'd run away. She'd be sorry if she lost me, she'd have to be: there'd be no dancing about in the kitchen, no singing Dr Hook then.

While my sister went to run the bath, I found my sleeping bag and filled it with all the essentials I'd need. In my moneybox was a pound note and a few pennies of change. I took my green-and-red S-belt from my top drawer, and a handful of my most impressive pink blanket nuggets. At the back of the cupboard, stuffed behind my trainers, were a pair of cork wedge sandals, another unsuitable-therefore-beloved present from my nana, hidden away from my mother, and I took them with me too. I was going to live with Nana and Poppa, I decided – *I* decide! – and everyone wore heels in the city.

My sister was calling me from the steaming bathroom as I padded back downstairs. The larder door, next door to the kitchen, was open, and I crept in to search out provisions – though pickings, I knew, would be slim. Jars of dried pulses and fungi lined the top shelf; and the shelf below was crammed with all things pickled: beetroot, walnuts and gherkins, and jar upon jar of unidentifiable vinegar-soaked vegetables. Somehow Sara Fiddick had never found this room when she came over to play; she'd never nosily sniffed it out, and I was grateful for that. On the cool slate floor were bottles of my mother's elderflower cham-pagne, and two cobweb-covered kegs of Mike Brown's homemade lager – last year's Christmas present from him, as yet untouched. I scanned the stone sideboard and, in amongst the tinned chestnuts, I spotted a packet of digestive biscuits: normal, not chocolate, but biscuits at least. I shoved them in with the rest, and took the torch that hung on a meat hook by the door.

The sun was just setting when I pushed open the back door.

I cast a glance behind me, but there was no sign of anyone pleading with me to change my mind – no mother calling me: not yet. I slammed the back door as hard as I could, to make them hear, just to make it definite and let them be in no doubt I was gone.

A warm breeze hit me as I stepped outside the porch. From the sitting-room window, with the lights on, the garden had looked darker: gloomy and shadow-filled, but the lawn was bathed in a soft pink evening light. I headed across the grass towards the back gate and our tree house, where Olive and Mike's house nestled in the dip below our garden. I peered over the hedge to their back garden – I had to, I couldn't help it. It was blue-lit by their television, I could see. A burst of deep laughter and Olive's distinctive high-pitched squeal of delight confirmed to me what they were watching. Phillip would be with them too, sitting in between them on their slippy-slidey beige leather sofa, taking all of it in.

Buses wouldn't leave until the morning, I knew that much, so I settled in for the night, hidden away under our tree house, and watched as the sun disappeared behind the Berwyn Mountains. I pictured Nana and Poppa's faces as I turned up unannounced at their door.

'Darling, we hoped you'd come, one day, we always hoped,' Nana would say, cupping my face, eyes all teary with love. Nana and Poppa would be on my side, they were always on my side, and they'd tut and cluck around me, saying, 'I know, oh you poor thing, I agree,' and they'd let me watch Benny as I ate lemon drizzle cake with cream, and some extra cream if I fancied it, just for extra goodness.

I should enjoy the silence; take it all in, I thought, because it would be broken soon enough, by frantic shouting, searchlights and police with sniffer dogs. In the distance the lights of the village glimmered, and silver clouds scudded across the darkening sky. Colwyn Parry had been burning brambles in the field next door, and a sweet, scorched smell hung in the air. I leant back against the tree trunk and watched as the mountains slowly turned from dark purple to charcoal. Car lights flashed up the road, swooping the length of the rhododendrons, once, and then again. Minutes and then maybe an hour or so passed; and as the sky darkened, I saw glow-worms: their tiny lights gleaming in the tall grass at the bottom of the plum tree. I watched, transfixed, as they flared up, soft bluey-green like sea glass, and faded away again.

In front of me a frog, shiny in the moonlight, gamely attempted to jump through the uncut grass, struggling determinedly towards our pond. I lifted it up and placed it by the edge, and it quietly plipped into the silver water, making the bulrushes quiver. I made my way back to the hideaway under the tree house, squeezed myself into my almost full sleeping bag and snuggled down, feeling around me for the packet of biscuits, imagining my new life in Liverpool, which would involve cinemas and hair salons and boutiques full of clothing that Olive called *à la mode*. Still no one was shouting for me.

I bit into my biscuit and looked up at the sky as a cloud shifted to reveal the moon. The garden was spotlit now, shadows springing across the lawn. The moon was bright and perfectly round, and I stopped mid-crunch, looking around me then at the very different garden, less familiar now with its dark shadows, which had turned from a watercolour grey to an inky, impenetrable black. I looked back to the moon and I thought of Mr Davies, our supply teacher, and the horror story he'd read out in class about a werewolf hungry for blood. It was a good example, he'd said, of how to write with suspense. 'Was that really appropriate?' my mother had said when I told her; rhetorically, though, addressing the kitchen window and the field outside full of sheep. 'Yes!' I'd said. I was nine now, old enough. I was *glad* he'd read it. It was good to know – forewarned is forearmed, my father would say – as panic rose in my chest.

There was a rustle, and a crunch of twigs in the rhododendrons, and then I saw what might well have been the glint of an eye. I lay there prone, rigid with fright, like a giant slug in my sleeping bag: the easiest of prey; a snail had a shell on at least. This would serve my mother right, I thought, as I shuddered uselessly in my sleeping bag: I would be torn limb from limb, and it was down to her. She would be left to pick up my pieces, if there was any of me left, and she'd regret not letting us watch Benny Hill; there'd be no way then she'd not regret it.

Now I wanted to go home. I wanted my mother, and at the thought of that the blood rushed to my limbs and I leapt up, pushing myself out of my sleeping bag, and I legged it then, stumbling up the lawn as fast as I could, to the haven, the safety of the back porch.

I pattered through the pitch-dark sitting room, towards the strip of orange light leaking out from under the door into the hall. From the kitchen I could hear Stevie Nicks singing about thunder and my mother joining her for the chorus.

In the hall the smell of warm spices and nicotine and candle wax reached me from the open kitchen door. Wiggy and Maya and Anthony and Bethan were all there, eating supper with my parents in the candlelight. The table was full with the remains of their meal: a Moroccan tagine, and an almost empty bowl of rice and a few leaves left of the salad.

'The wanderer returns,' said Wiggy, tipping his glass towards me, and everyone clapped.

'Welcome back!' said Bethan, who had new short blonde hair: quite styled and proper, though her blouse was Indian and had elephants on it.

'We saw you – well, we saw your torch, flashing about in the garden when we were driving up,' Wiggy said, filling up Anthony's wine glass.

'Yes, we thought you were a burglar, until your mum said it must be you,' said Maya, scooping another spoonful of rice on to her plate. 'Isn't it lovely, Abs,' she said, 'to be out on a night like this? Perfect for star-gazing!'

'We were just saying that,' my mother said, turning to the window. 'It's the most beautiful evening out there, so clear!'

'Bedtime now though, I think, my honey bun, don't you?' said my father, kissing me on the top of my head. 'You smell of wood smoke.'

'I'll come and tuck you in,' said my mother. 'Pudding in a sec, when I'm back,' she added, over her shoulder. She wrapped a bare warm arm around me and gave me a squeeze as we walked up the stairs, and she felt warm and smelled of her, which meant lovely.

It was Monday and I was desperate to get to school; desperate to impart my knowledge gleaned from three full minutes of Benny Hill. The tantalizing glimpse had expanded into an entire episode in my mind – my sister's too; we knew him now, not much, but enough at least to blag with conviction.

I arrived at the gates to see Lisa and Jonathan Evans clambering out of their dad's meat truck, the fatty smell of lamb drifting after them from the open passenger-side door.

'Did you see the show last night?' I asked, skipping towards her, too happy to remember about skipping and how it was only for babies.

Lisa looked at me, studied my face with her peculiar, detached, blank stare.

'Didn't watch it,' she said, head to one side.

'What do you mean?'

'We never saw it,' and she hitched her Dunlop sports bag on to her shoulder.

'Why?'

'Gone off it,' she said, pushing into the stream of children, past Sara and Eleanor Williams. 'We like *Not the Nine O'Clock News* now – it's way better,' and she murmured it so I had to lean forward to catch it. 'You seen it?' she asked, lining up for class.

'The nine o clock news?' I pushed past Sianny Wyn Wyn to be next to her.

'No! *NOT the Nine O'Clock*,' she said, and shook her head. 'Don't tell me you haven't seen it?'

'I don't think so, no.'

'It's *brilliant*, isn't it, Jonathan?'

'Oh yeah, it's amazing, Ab,' he said from behind me, shaking his curly hair. An image of Leo Sayer popped into my head, the disco glitter on his curls catching the light as he danced.

'You're going to love it, you are.' He pushed in next to me, putting his hand on my shoulder. He was wearing a different aftershave today, something spicy and unbearably sweet. 'I tell you now,' he went on, 'I can't wait to see Rhys Prichard playing *that*,' and I made my way to registration with a sweeping feeling, as if a river was carrying me off, away downstream from everyone else, towards a wide-open, empty sea.

14

Baby doll

Katherine and I were walking along the back lane towards the Fiddicks' house, both of us transfixed by the goddess ahead of us. She didn't belong here. She looked like a lady from a film: too beautiful to be real, I thought, too beautiful certainly to be walking down a muddy lane; there was something obscene about it. She needed be carried on some kind of stretcher at least, or in a golden carriage pulled by two white horses as a servant peeled her grapes. She stopped, and bent down to pick a pebble from the heel of her white stiletto, framed by rosehips and bryony in the hedgerow behind her, the sun highlighting her glossy, long, dark hair. As she stood up straight again, she smoothed down her tight red pencil skirt, which elegantly restricted her, forcing her to sway rather than walk – majestically, though – like a bright red poppy in the breeze.

'She's so *lovely*!' said my sister, in a gravelly whisper.

'I know,' I said. 'She looks like Wonder Woman in her relaxing clothes,' and my sister nodded in double-quick time.

'Imagine if she *marries* him,' she murmured, 'just imagine that.'

I did. I pictured her marrying my uncle, in a frothy white ball gown, saying, 'I do, Malcolm, oh I do!'

'We'd be related then,' I said, and I flew down the road, that's what it felt like, as I pictured being officially linked: bound together for ever to Jackie. Lisa Evans had a brand-new sandwich-maker: it melted the cheese and toasted the bread and made the sandwich come out shaped like a clam, *but she didn't have what I had; she didn't have a goddess in her family, did she?*

We watched as our Uncle Malcolm reached up to her and took her hand in his, squeezing her lozenge-shaped red finger-nails tight in his plump little fist – double-checking that she was real, I think – and when she didn't vanish into thin air he gave her a gaping grin, and blinked a few times as though he had some-thing in his eye, and she was *still* there, so he led her with small, shuffling dance steps around a giant cowpat, crusted over in the middle, its soft edges sprinkled with rust-coloured flies.

She turned now and looked back towards us, and we craned our necks up and tried to catch her eye, but she didn't see; she was gazing over us, towards our house, with a look that reminded me of Eleanor Williams' dog when he wanted to climb up on your knee: pleading and big-eyed and a little bit desperate.

'PSSST!' It came from the stile next to the hazel hedge on Colwyn's field side of the road. 'PSSST! Ab! Bitch!'

I crouched down to see Sara – who else? – peering up at me from behind the hedge. 'Know your name!' she said with a tri-umphant cackle. 'Brilliant, that is!' She sighed and shook her head. 'You always fall for that, you do.' She was wearing one of Eirian's shirts again, and it was huge on her, and blue and flowery, with collar points that stuck out like paper aeroplanes.

'Who are them then? Up by there?' She gestured towards my parents, with Nana and Poppa and Uncle Malcolm and the vision, making their slow but steady progress towards the oak tree.

'That's my uncle and his girlfriend from Liverpool,' I said, my pride uncontainable, revealed in a face-splitting grin.

'Is it?' she said. 'Is that right, is it?' And she stood up and cupped a hand to her mouth.

'Oi!' she yelled, and they turned, and looked taken aback as this small, wiry girl with straggly hair and oversized clothes confidently alerted their attention.

'*CITY SLICKERS!*' she shouted, and she turned her back and wiggled her bum at them. 'PONCES!' she called over her shoulder, and she scrambled off, squealing down Colwyn's field towards her house, leaping over molehills, shirt sleeves flapping over her hands.

Uncle Malcolm and Jackie had arrived earlier that morning, before Nana and Poppa even, and earlier than my parents had expected, by a couple of hours or so at least. We were lying on the bedroom floor when they came, my sister, me and Phillip Brown, mouths poised over our father's portable cassette player, about to record our best ever version of Pink Floyd's 'Another Brick in the Wall'. Phillip had needed coaxing – he always needed coaxing. 'I don't like it, that's all,' he'd said, picking at a scab on his knee. 'It's too sad-sounding for me. Why don't we do "Bright Eyes?" he suggested. 'Something with a nice tune like that?'

Outside there was a faraway roar, a powerful engine sound, like an aeroplane's – Uncle Malcolm's sports car, in fact – and we heard its tyres crackling over the gravel, and then the bip, bip, bip of a horn.

'No!' Phillip said, stumbling up on to his feet. 'That's your *family*, that is.' He swiped his palms up and down the side of his racer shorts. 'And look,' he said, 'I'm still here!' and he pushed at our bedroom door, juddering it open over the ridges of the sisal carpet. I didn't like our bedroom carpet; its brown-ness and the ridges made me think of a freshly ploughed field; and soil wasn't cosy for a bedroom.

'I'm gone, I gotta go, I'm off now, out the back,' he said. 'I need a wee, I do.' He was nearly eight, and still this was his knee-jerk response to panic.

We didn't know Uncle Malcolm like we knew our nana and poppa, so we felt too shy to run down to greet him straight away. We loitered there, in our room, leaning on our windowsill, and looked down at his car, with its big black fin sticking out of the back, and silver bits in the middle of the wheels, and no roof.

'I bet it's got an ejector seat,' my sister said, as my mother shouted for us both to come down.

Downstairs, the front door was open and filled with the bulk of Uncle Malcolm.

'Girls! How are ya?' he said, in what sounded like an American accent. He *looked* American too, with his orange-brown skin and Tippex-white teeth, but he wasn't. He lived in Liverpool, and always had done as far as I knew.

'Come here, you two,' he said, but he came to us, short arms outstretched as he slip-slapped across the cork tiles of the play-room floor, grinning, open-mouthed, a flash of white chewing gum rolling on and then off the tip of his tongue.

'Look at ya!' he said, tousling my hair, which made it impossible to know what to say next. I wanted to say 'Look at ya' back, but I worried it would sound rude, because since I'd last seen him he looked like he'd doubled in size. His burgundy trousers seemed tight; uncomfortably tight, not intentionally: the fabric all shiny from stretching across his thick-set legs, so they were glossy and purple like aubergines. I'd seen Nana ironing a pile of his pants once in her sitting room. They were satin-looking and very brief at the sides, the sort that touched where they fitted as my nana would say – or was it fitted where they touched? I was never sure. I pictured Uncle Malcolm standing, hands on hips, legs proudly apart, as good as naked in a pair of those snug-fitting pants, glistening and dark brown all over, like a saveloy sausage fresh from the deep-fat fryer.

Behind him there were muffled squeaks of protest, and the dented brass handle on the door of the downstairs loo rattled up and down.

'Just give it a really good shove, Jackie, will you?' called out my father, as he came in with the cases.

'It just jams a bit,' said my mother, kicking the door with her heel, and it banged open; and there she was. A shimmering red butterfly burst out from the dark brown cocoon of our hideously painted downstairs loo. She was seven foot tall at least, with one foot of it hair: a vast, flicked, backcombed mass of it.

'All right, girls?' she said, fluttering eyelids that were metallic blue like beetles' wings.

'Hello,' we said, our voices high and gaspy-sounding with immediate and reverential love. My sister gave her a low curtsy, pulling out the side of her dungarees as if they were a skirt, touchingly oblivious to her lack-lustre-in-comparison outfit. She was dressed, like me – like a boy – in cereal brown: a muesli-coloured two-tone jumper, and dungarees the shade of Weetabix.

Jackie smiled at us with lips that shone gloopy cherry, and we watched as she crossed the playroom floor on her spiky high shoes, sinking with each step into the cork tiles, indenting them with dots like a path on a treasure map – the trail of her progress towards the door to the kitchen, where Uncle Malcolm marked the spot.

'Girls, meet my baby. This is Jackie, *my baby doll*,' said Uncle Malcolm.

I looked at the toy box, where my sister's own baby doll lay.

It was almost bald, with just plugs of hair dotting the scalp, and scribbled all over with biro, one eye wide open and the other jammed shut. I'd mind quite a bit, I thought, if I had a boyfriend and he compared me to something like that.

Jackie scanned the room through her heavy lashes. I followed her gaze and took it all in with her: its terrible plainness, the white walls, the oversized paper-ball light shade, and the sploshy painting of nothing identifiable that hung in a wooden frame by the front door. There was nothing for her here: no crystal chandeliers, no shag-pile carpets, no nightclub serving cocktails down the road.

'Are you from the television?' asked my sister, still staring up at Jackie, head back, mouth open, like a fledgling waiting to be fed.

Uncle Malcolm let out a machine-gun laugh. 'Ha! Ha! Ha! Jackie, what do you think of that? Don't ya just love that?' he said. 'She's not on television *yet,* Kath, but one day maybe. Ha!' He reached across to Jackie, buffing her bottom as if he was trying to get a shine on it. 'But she *is* in magazines, aren't you, Jack? Jackie is a *glamour* model,' he explained, saying the last bit extra slow as if we were hard of hearing, as he pulled her towards him, looking at her as if she was a great big chocolate cake covered in chocolate buttons.

My sister and I nodded at each other. That made sense. She looked just like someone who should model glamour, I thought, as we followed them through to the kitchen.

'Hey, Baz, did I tell you I played McEnroe and Borg last week at the tennis club?' said Uncle Malcolm as he settled, with an urgent-sounding grunt, on to a chair next to Jackie.

'No! Really?' replied my father in a voice that didn't sound like his: higher than it should be, like a boy's.

'McEnroe said to me, he said, "Malcolm, you're a great player," and I said, "John, you know you're not so bad yourself." Ha! Ha! Such a personality!' And my father made a vague-sounding 'hmph' of acknowledgement as he pressed the foil milk-bottle lid in with his thumb and the milk drummed into the jug.

'And I didn't tell you, did I?' continued Uncle Malcolm, stabbing the air with his cigar. 'Kevin Keegan dropped over to my place last week, just rang the bell, just like that: the very man. He stayed for ages, didn't he, Jack?'

She nodded, while she examined her fingertips. 'He had lovely hair, Anna, honest to God, just as curly in real life,' she said. 'And so much of it, too,' she added, as Uncle Malcolm swiped his hand through thinning locks, briefly hiding his tanned bald patch with a slick of sticky-looking hair.

'He just sat there with us at the table, didn't he, Jack? Just chatted away, drinking tea with us, just like that. So down to earth, you wouldn't believe it,' he said, shaking his head and casting a regretful glance down our kitchen table, so sadly devoid of any sporting legends.

'Hey, love,' he said, turning to look at me, 'guess what? I've got a little something for you,' and I stepped forward, suddenly self-conscious, as he smiled at me with his super-bright teeth and placed a burnt match in my hand. 'There you go – I thought you might like to put that in the bin; and can you get us an ashtray, sweetheart?'

I liked the *idea* of Uncle Malcolm; but now that he was here, now that I was standing like an absolute lemon with his discarded match between finger and thumb, I felt the unexpected, slightly nauseous dip of disappointment. He was family, and family should be loved without condition, but there it was: I wasn't sure I liked him even so.

Outside, there was the indignant peeping of a car horn, and through the window a tide of sheep rolled away, a frothy white wave retreating to the hills, revealing an expanse of muddy field. Nana and Poppa had arrived and there was no one there, no welcoming committee to greet them.

My father leapt to his feet. 'Ah, great, they're here!' he said, sounding genuinely pleased, as he rushed out of the door with my sister, and me following after them, delighted to be out of the room.

'The sun's out – why don't we all go on a walk before lunch?' my mother suggested, when the suitcases had been unpacked.

'On a walk?' said Nana, as if she was just checking that she'd heard her correctly. 'Where would you want to *go*, Anna?'

'Oh, not far – down the road. It's such a lovely day, I just thought it would be nice to get out,' she said, heading for the porch.

'That's a lovely *idea*, Anna, but I think Les is quite keen to watch the golf,' said Nana, looking to my poppa for back-up.

'It's not on till four, Ed,' said Poppa, raising his eyebrows in an apology, 'but there might be some racing on first, you know. I should check, I'm not sure.'

'Well, just a quick walk then – twenty minutes,' said my mother, one foot in a welly already.

Nana and Poppa didn't understand walking; I could see that now. For one thing it didn't suit their clothing, which was always uncompromisingly dressy. All of my dad's side of the family viewed practical clothing, and the wearers of it, with contempt. They liked to see people making the best of themselves, and in their minds someone in outdoor clothing – anorak, say, or walking boots – had either let themselves go or was undergoing a mental breakdown. They didn't mind walking if it was to a destination, like the casino; or if it was incorporated into a sporting activity, like golf. But you could tell that a walk just for the sake of it confused them, lacking purpose or reward.

'Does anyone need wellies?' asked my mother.

Jackie recoiled, shrinking back against the wall. 'Why?' she said. 'Will there be mud?'

'Probably not. I just thought you might want something a bit easier to walk in, that's all,' my mother said, gesturing to Jackie's stilettos.

'Oh no, ta, these are *dead* comfy – they're like slippers,' said Jackie, clutching on to the gold chain strap of her handbag with both hands, as if my mother might snatch it from her and force her into an anorak too while she was at it.

My father and Uncle Malcolm were standing waiting for us outside. They both looked Jewish, you could tell, but that was it, the only clue that they might be related. My father looked like the typical Bob Dylan fan that he was: lanky and bearded, with his sticking-up hair, in clothes that had been made in Tibet. Next to him, in his Pringle golfing jumper and burgundy slacks – both stretched to their full capacity – Uncle Malcolm looked small and squat, and had a glossy, European kind of glamour. He was shiny all over, with his Brylcreemed hair, gleaming, clean-shaven face, pointy patent-leather shoes and gold jewellery: neck chain, bracelets and signet rings, all of them glinting in the sunlight. I wanted my father to have some of that shine, just a bit of that gloss to highlight him as the clever, funny man that he was. Next to Malcolm he looked a little misrepresented somehow: too low-key for who he was; a background kind of matt.

My poppa walked up to his sons and put his arms around their shoulders, squeezing his pink Pringle jumper in next to Malcolm's lemon one. Two French fancies next to a flapjack.

'So, son,' he said to Malcolm, 'how's business?' Straight in there, just like that, with his favourite topic.

'Business is good, Dad, yeah, it's going real well,' Malcolm said, nodding towards his car.

'That's great, son. You're doing well – you deserve that, you really do,' said Poppa, beaming and patting his back.

We were never sure what it was, exactly, that my Uncle Malcolm did for a living; he was always vague when pressed. There were businesses connected to sport, and that particular combination made his parents, my poppa in particular, pink-faced and beaming with pride.

'He's just like his papa: an *entrepreneur*,' my nana would say, lowering her voice when she said the hallowed word. 'It takes a special person, a very special person indeed,' she said, 'to be an *entrepreneur*.'

Later, at supper, my mother brought a roast chicken to the table.

'Oh, would you take a look at that,' said Nana. 'Les, get your camera; take a photo, please! It looks like something from a recipe book, doesn't it?' The highest accolade you could give to home-cooked food, according to my nana. 'Well done you, Anna – your cooking is really coming on,' she said, clapping her hands together. 'Don't you think, Les, Anna has really come on?' and she pointed a frosted, peach-tipped finger towards my mother, as if my poppa might have forgotten who she was.

'Oh definitely, yes, Anna, just super, oh yes,' said Poppa, shoving an overloaded forkful into his mouth. 'Delicious,' he added, less clearly this time.

'So what do you like to cook, Jackie?' asked Nana, fixing her with a hard-eyed stare.

Jackie paused to consider. 'Don't know, really. I just eat out.

I don't like cooking much really, Edna,' she said, pushing a piece of chicken around her plate with her fork.

Nana looked at her, incredulous. 'Don't joke with me! You're pulling my leg! You must cook! Every woman cooks,' she said, 'don't they, Les?'

'Of course they do,' he said, laughing. 'She's just having you on, Edna.'

'Ma, give it a rest, will you?' said Uncle Malcolm. 'Jackie has to watch her figure.' He swiped his sleeve across a dribble of gravy streaking down his bottom-shaped chin. 'Just let her be,' he said, and he grunted to his feet to push past my chair towards the loo.

Nana presented her trifle with a flourish, holding the glass bowl high as she wiggly-walked into the dining room. 'Here we are, my darlings, here it is!' she said, lowering it slowly to the table. 'Nana's speciality!' She stood back to scrutinize it with her head cocked to one side. 'Awww,' she cooed, clasping her hands together, as if she was admiring a sweet little baby.

'Oh Ed, you've gone and done it again. Unbelievable, your mother, don't you think, Baz? Well done you,' said Poppa, clapping and nodding at my father to join in. 'Easy on Malcolm, though, when you're dishing out – half the amount for him,' he said, as the spoon squelched in.

'What's *happened* to him? He's just got so *fat*!' said Nana, heaping a quivering mound of trifle into a bowl as Malcolm came back into the room, squeezing his way past my chair to his place. 'Darling, we were just saying you need to keep an eye on that waistline, so just a little taste for you, okay?' she said.

'You got me,' he said. 'Just a spoonful then, Ma, just the one.'

'Well done, that's the way, and I'll just splash a bit of cream on it, darling,' she said, plopping on a couple of extra spoonfuls before she did. 'A pudding does feel naked without it,' and she flooded the bowl with cream.

Malcolm shrugged and started tucking in, cramming one mouthful on top of the other as my nana looked proudly on.

'It's portion size you've got to watch, darling,' she said. 'Lose the weight, and they'll be queuing up.' She was smiling at Jackie now, who was staring out into the garden at one of our cats squatting down in the herbaceous border.

'Don't worry,' said my sister. 'He'll bury it in a sec, you'll see.'

That night I was woken by the sound of hissing; low and urgent, like a burst pipe spraying out water. There was silence, and there it was, back again, but louder: Jackie's voice – a raised whisper – raspy with anger. 'Bugger that, Malcolm, and bugger you!'

My sister lifted her head from her pillow. 'Someone just swore – I heard that,' she whispered, her voice slurry with sleep.

The door to the green spare room slammed, and I heard Uncle Malcolm's voice, soft and coaxing, like my mother's when she was rounding up the hens.

'Come on, baby, come on,' he said, 'don't be mad at Malcolm.'

The next morning I was woken again, by the thunk of a car door being shut. My sister stirred in the next-door bed, and I yanked a curtain back to see Jackie already sitting in the passenger seat of the sports car, her shiny red mouth set straight, elbow resting on the side of the door, hand tapping on the walnut dash as she looked towards the house.

'Kath! They're sneaking off!' I said, as the front door opened and Uncle Malcolm appeared, pattering over the stones in his slip-ons as if he were navigating hot coals. He opened his door carefully, glancing back at the kitchen window as he squeezed himself in behind the wheel and unzipped his padded body-warmer, allowing for breathing space. I watched their silent, animated conversation, and tried to read their lips. 'She said bugger again just then, definitely,' I said.

'I thought they were supposed to be staying all day,' said my sister, squishing in beside me at the window.

'Well, they *were*,' I said, and we looked at each other then and gasped with the thrill of it; the amazing, heady rush of adults being rude.

Malcolm had his head on the steering wheel now. Jackie gave him a shove, and he lifted his head and his face looked saggy and sad, like a bloodhound. He gave a final glance at the house, then drove off, super-fast, at ninety miles an hour it looked like, wheels spinning, sending up a cloud of pale brown dust as he revved off down the lane. The sheep ambled lazily back towards the fence, and as I watched the dust settling I was hit by a worry that perhaps my family were in some way to blame. We weren't up to scratch, we weren't shiny enough for them, it was true.

We didn't see Uncle Malcolm for a long time after that. There was a lull: an Uncle Malcolm-shaped void, so quite a big one. Time flattered him. Katherine and I even missed him after a while, softened as he now was in our memories, re-imagined as a funny, jet-setting uncle who told non-stop fascinating stories. It was a year at least before he came back to stay, arriving this time with Nana and Poppa, crammed into the back of their bright red, smoke-filled Nissan Sunny.

He was different a year down the line; a little bigger over all, but in every other way reduced. His shine had gone, all glossiness lost, along with the tan and the jewellery: no chunky chains around his flesh-swollen wrists; the signet ring somehow prised from his finger, an indented ring of pale skin in its place. Business wasn't good right now, a bit slow, he said, but it would be picking up soon, he had no doubt about that, no doubt at all, as Nana and Poppa nodded in frantic agreement, and Nana placed a supportive hand on his knee.

'The rough with the smooth – that's business, son,' said my poppa. 'You know how it is, how it goes.'

He'd moved back in with Nana and Poppa, back into his old bedroom, the tiny room at the top of their stairs, where *Beano* annuals lined the shelves and an Airfix model of a biplane hung from invisible thread above the single bed. Nana said it kept her busy, bringing him his breakfast to his room on a tray every morning, with grapefruit ready-cut to save his energy. He needed to relax, she said; and he did, very well, watching golf with Poppa while Nana ironed his underpants and passed his cigarettes to him, ready lit.

'You're too good to me, Ma, that's the problem. What woman could ever match you, eh?' he said as he patted her leg.

'Aww,' said Nana, 'stop it,' eyes welling.

'He's got a point, Ed,' said Poppa, 'he really has.'

'You better watch it, Ma, or I'll never move out,' said Uncle Malcolm, rasping out laughs through a cloud of cigarette smoke; and true to his word, he never did.

15

New girl

Mr Roberts was taking class registration but no one was concentrating this morning.

'Jonathan Evans?'

Silence.

'*Jonathan Evans*, I said!'

'Here.'

'Lisa Evans?'

Silence.

'LISA! ARE YOU PRESENT?'

'Yes! Sorry. Here.'

'CONCENTRATE, will you?' said Mr Roberts. 'Eyes to me!'

There was a distraction. A stranger – a new girl – standing to attention, that's what it looked like, at the front of the class on the raised bit of floor by the blackboard. She had her hands held behind her back and was staring out in front of her, like a soldier waiting to be inspected.

'Wendy Finch?'

'Here,' she said.

'Children, this is Wendy. She has just moved here all the way from *Manchester* . . . Let's . . . welcome her!' said Mr Roberts, holding both his hands out in front of her, as if he were a game-show host presenting her as the prize-winner's trophy.

'*Bore da,* Wendy!' we said, as loud as we could, all of us craning to get a better look at her. She *looked* like she was new, fresh out of a box: all polished and pressed in her bright white knee socks, and a navy satin bow tied in the middle of her blonde curly hair, like a show dog.

'Look at her,' hissed Sianny Wyn Wyn from the back. 'How do you get to be like that? All smart and done up like that?' She looked down at her own ancient, hand-me-down, patterned red-and-white pinafore dress, bobbly with wear, with the hem falling down at the front.

'Her ribbon looks *cach*, though,' said Sara, patting her own Big Town-market hair accessory: an oversized white stretchy hair-band, like a giant, slightly grubby bandage, which she thought made her look like the girl from the BBC test card.

'*Croeso, crrrrroeso!*' Mr Roberts was singing now, warbling out some welcoming Welsh song that he'd forced us all to sing at the last Eisteddfod.

'He's gone into show-off mode, hasn't he?' said Sianny Wyn Wyn, resting her chin in her hands, her knees poking out either side of her desk.

'Sianny, *you're* in show-off mode and all,' said Sara, turning back to look at her. 'Do you think we all need an eyeful of your filthy kecks? Do us all a favour, will you? Shut your legs, for chrissakes.' But Sianny kept them just like that, because she didn't hear her. Something had gone a bit skew-whiff with Sianny's hearing; she might have glue ear, she said, or it could be grommets. She'd prefer it to be grommets because they were just tiny little ear pebbles and they fall out in the end, in the middle of the night, she said; not like the glue which might just stick around in there for ever.

'Duw! He's embarrassing himself now – he should take a

look at himself,' Lisa said, shielding her eyes with her hand, as Mr Roberts added movement to his singing, his hands rotating back and forth like pistons now, as if he was some crazy, singing, red-haired train.

'Round of applause now, boys and girls. Let's hear it, let's put your hands together for Wendy!' he proclaimed, his hands squelching wetly against each other. His hair had gone all sweaty round his forehead, and had slicked into dark little curls. I didn't like it when it went like that: it didn't feel teacherly, somehow, to have a headmaster covered in sweat.

At playtime Wendy was the first one out of the doors, and she was down the steps, stalking, sturdy-legged, across the playground to the right, towards the goalposts.

'Oh Duw, what's she doing going by there then?' said Sianny Wyn Wyn. 'Never! Look at that, will you? She's going to the *boys'* playground, she is!'

The dividing had been gradual. Over the last year or so there'd been a sifting of the sexes: boys right, girls left, and whoever baggsied the middle playground got it first. It was natural to begin with, a practical thing: we just wanted to play different games. The girls liked to play Charlie's Angels in the climbing-frame headquarters, and the boys had just gravitated to where the goalposts were. Now, though, the separation felt more deliberate, like an intentional pushing away from each other, and was riven with tension: a negative force, like magnets facing the wrong way.

We followed Wendy, boys and girls together, and watched as she hitched herself up on to the wall.

'Why d'you move here?'

'Dad's new job.'

'What's that then?'

'Gamekeeper.'

'What's your favourite colour?'

'Burgundy.'

'Why's that?'

'Because it's ace,' she said, giving an exasperated roll of her eyes, 'why do you think?' And she took a packet of chalks out of her pocket and began drawing on the concrete slabs: cartoon characters of bald little men with big noses looking over walls.

'You can draw just like Rolf Harris, you can,' said Rhys Prichard. 'You'll have to teach me how to do that, you will.'

Lisa wrinkled her nose in disgust and mouthed 'brown noser' at him, and he looked stunned, and his eyes shone with tears. He was a tough nut, so it was surprising how often Rhys had to fight back tears: clenching his fists and blinking them away, so we didn't ever see him properly cry. Wendy carried on drawing, singing 'Mamma Mia', segueing neatly then into 'Dancing Queen' as she covered the wall in faces.

There was a distant rumble and the ground juddered, and Wendy's musical medley was drowned out by the low growl of an engine as an ancient-looking red double-decker bus arrived on the green opposite, smoke belching out of its exhaust.

'What the friggin' hell is *that*?' asked Rhys Prichard, as it swung backwards and reversed noisily towards the swings.

'It's a *house bus*,' said Timothy Jones. There were curtains in the windows and a wonky-looking chimney bent out from the middle of the roof.

'That's hippies from The Mill, up by us, that is,' said Sara. 'My dad saw them doing up that bus, he did. He reckoned they made a right balls-up of it.'

I felt a sickening lurch in my stomach as I recognized the

driver. My parents knew him: he was Freddy, Wiggy's best friend from The Mill.

'Look at that man driving, will you?' said Sianny. 'He's the spit of Jesus Christ Superstar, he is,' and everyone laughed, even Wendy.

'Don't reckon they can park there, do you?' said Rhys Prichard.

'That's illegal, that is, they'll get arrested,' confirmed Sara, as she scaled to the top of the climbing frame and tipped herself upside down, her thin, greasy fronds of hair hanging down like tentacles.

'Look at me! Real high up here. Wendy, look how fast I can swing!' she called out, flashing her greying nylon knickers as she grappled with her upturned skirt, while Wendy steadfastly ignored her.

Sara righted herself, pink-cheeked and indignant, as though she'd just been slapped in the face.

'So, what's your favourite telly programme then, Wendy?' asked Rhys Prichard, and Lisa rolled her eyes. Wendy carried on drawing for what felt like an age, tongue sticking out in concentration.

'*Top of the Pops*,' she said at last, 'no contest.'

'Good one,' said Sara. 'We all like a bit of *Top of the Pops* round here, don't we?' *Yes*, we all said, *we do*.

'Funny that, when some of us have got no TV,' whispered Lisa, jutting out her chin towards Sara.

Sara hitched herself up next to Wendy, squeezing right on in so their legs were pressed against each other.

'I reckon you'll fit in round here,' she said, just a little bit too close to Wendy's face. 'Stick with me. I'll look out for you,' she said.

'And me! I will too and all, you know,' said Rhys Prichard.

'Rhys, come by here, will you, a sec?' said Lisa. He looked at her for a second, before bounding towards her with a dopey-looking grin.

'What can I do for you, fair lady?' he asked, and he gave a deep bow.

'Can you give us a hitch up on the wall?' she said. 'I got my best shoes on. Mam'll kill me if I scuff them.'

'Delighted to be of service, ma'am,' he said, bending down to give her a fireman's lift.

On the other side of the green the bus door had opened, and Freddy came down the steps, and then Angelica, his tall, blonde wife, who reminded me of Carly Simon. She was holding a tiny newborn baby to her chest.

'Don't you know them by there, Ab?' said Sara. 'Your mam and dad are mates with them, aren't they now?'

'What?' I said. 'No way!' Squeaking out the words in outrage.

All eyes were on Angelica as she sat down, cross-legged, on the grass by the swings, and undid the top of her kaftan.

'My God, how gross is that?' said Lisa, as we watched Angelica lifting her baby to her breast and latching it on.

'Lads!' shouted Rhys Prichard. 'Over here! We've got boobies at three o'clock!'

'Yep. Rude as hell, that is.' Sianny Wyn Wyn was leaning forward, face scrunched up with the effort of taking it all in with one eye. 'Rude as blimmin' hell.'

'It's not like this in Manchester,' said Wendy, jumping down from Sara's side and heading for the slide, as Sara stared after her, open-mouthed.

'There's Northerners for you,' said Lisa. 'Mardy buggers, the lot of them.'

I was desperate not to lose her. 'Wendy!' I called out to her before I'd even thought of what I'd say. 'Guess what?' and she actually turned around and looked me straight in the eye, so I had her full and undivided attention.

'What?' she asked, perching one hand on her hip as I tried to conjure up something – anything – to catch her, and it came to me then:

'*My Uncle Malcolm makes* Top of the Pops.'

All heads swivelled in my direction.

'You never told us that,' said Sara, her eyes narrowed into little slits.

'Yeah, I did – I have, I'm sure.'

'That fatty I saw with all the jewellery?' she asked.

'That's the one.'

Wendy was looking at me from the top of the slide.

'So . . . if you want to be a dancer in the audience you can if you like!' I called up to her. '*I saw him last weekend and he said he can get me and my friends on it whenever I want!*'

Wendy tipped back, pushed up her legs and slid down to the bottom.

'Go on then,' she said, straightening up her skirt. 'Tell him we'll do it.'

'Okay, I will!' I said, grinning wide, thinking 'Shit! Shit! Shit!'

We all lied at my school; it was part of the culture: just something that everyone did. The landscape must have played some part: the isolation over-fostered our imaginations, I think, and made them work overtime. Outrageous claims were made all over the place: vampires and werewolves were spotted, UFOs landed in back gardens, and famous singers – Rod Stewart and Elton John mainly – dropped in for tea willy nilly. Fact and fiction merged pleasingly together in a blur, and these tales were accepted more or less, not as the truth exactly, but as entertainment, necessary to pass the time. All of us were complicit, all of us happy to choose a middle ground, a benign state in between not quite believing and not wanting to ruin a good story, because really, why would you want to do that?

Wendy was a trendsetter. She'd brought her roller skates in on her second day, and we'd watched her – while pretending not to – swooping confidently this way and that across the playground, skating perfect arcs forwards and backwards, blonde hair billowing bright against the mustard backdrop of the school wall. By the end of the week nearly all the girls were wearing them: begged, borrowed or dug out, long lost and forgotten, from the bottom of the toy box.

I was sitting on the wall in mine – bright yellow strap-on ones; they'd given me blisters that were starting to rub. I loved sitting on the school wall. From a distance it looked like nothing: a featureless expanse of grey concrete; but close to, it teemed with colour and life. Its surface was dotted with lichen: paint-bright splats of yellow and green, scratchy like a loofah on the underside of my legs. In amongst it ladybirds wheeled in and out of cracks, and tiny luminous red spiders magically skimmed the surface on legs too small to see.

I found a scrumpled, crunchy old tissue in my waistcoat pocket and I spat on it like my sister taught me – spit heals, spit on everything, she said (not including her, she added) – and shoved one half down the back of each boot, and kicked the roller skates' wheels against the wall again and again, listening to the ball bearings make their satisfying, rhythmic whir.

Across the playground, over by the bins, my friends were a blur of arms and legs as they skated around in circles. They looked good from a distance: professional almost, until Sianny Wyn Wyn came bashing in and out between them all and crashed to the ground with a gristling crunch of jaw. She lay there, face down and still on the tarmac, as everyone skated around her. Eventually she picked herself up. In silhouette, with her skinny legs and oversized skates handed down from her brother, she looked like the letter L. Her chin was scraped pink, and a dark streak of blood trickled down one of her legs. She gave both a perfunctory wipe with the back of her sleeve, straightened her glasses, squinted up into the sun for a second, and then skated off again without a word. Sianny was the runt of the litter; that's what she always called herself, just in case you got there first. Both her brothers were big and strong – proper farming boys – and they battered her sometimes till her legs were a ruin of bruises and bumps. She was tough, thanks to them. She prided herself on that.

I'd been spotted. Wendy's hot pink face came zooming towards me.

'Hey, Ab, have you heard back from your uncle yet?'

'My dad left him a message to call,' I said. 'He's busy, but he'll call, I promise.'

'It'd just be nice to have a date,' she said, 'so my dad can book the minibus.'

It wasn't her fault; she just didn't know the rules. In her own particular underwhelmed way, Wendy believed me, absolutely, and there was something about her character – a sureness to her – which made everyone else then go along with it too.

'Dance practice starts in five minutes at the front,' she said, spit spraying out from her mouth. It was something medical, an excess of saliva, she said, which meant she had too much spit to know what to do with. She sweated a lot too, but I wasn't sure if that was connected.

'Come on, girls, time to get to it!' she shouted.

'One week in, and listen to her,' muttered Sara. 'She needs to know her blimmin' place.'

It was a disco in the playground. Wendy's tape recorder was propped on a bin and Cliff Richard's voice rang out, through the fuzzing crackle of white noise, wondering, mournfully, why it was that they didn't talk any more. The boys were playing football round the back, so we could relax and dance like no one was watching, and we did. We swayed and swivelled and shuffled, and I imagined myself dancing like this in front of the camera, and Dave Lee Travis saying, 'Wow – everyone take a look at that girl. Now *she* can really dance!' I *could*, I could really move. I was amazing.

'Try clicking your fingers, Abs, that might help you get the rhythm,' Wendy said, moving her hips round and round, holding her hands high as if she was hula-hooping. 'Look at this,' she said. 'This is what they were doing last week.'

Eleanor Williams did it the best; when she moved she looked like syrup being poured from a tin.

'Imagine if we get on camera,' said Wendy. 'Practise your face.' So we smiled in a confident, pouty kind of way, like Lisa would have done. She wouldn't join in though; that was thanks to Wendy being a bossy cow, she said.

'Don't take this the wrong way, but I think you should take that plaster off your glasses when we go, Sianny,' Wendy said. 'You know, just to make sure they let you in.'

Mr Roberts was yelling at us: '*Girls! Off! Turn that racket off!*'

We gasped, and clapped our hands to our mouths, and Wendy jumped to it and clicked the recorder off, but it was too late: he was out through the doors and powering down the steps.

'This is a schoolyard, children!' he shouted. 'What did I just say it was?'

'A schoolyard,' we all chimed together.

'And what is it *not*?' he asked, stumping us into silence with the limitless options to consider. 'A *nightclub* is what it's not!' he said.

'Sorry, Mr Roberts,' we chorused, sing-song exaggerated sad.

'We were practising for *Top of the Pops*,' explained Wendy.

'Were you now?' he said.

And when she told him about my uncle, Mr Roberts gave one of his alarming, not at all amused laughs – short and urgent-sounding, as if someone had winded him in the stomach.

'Is he now?' he said, nodding thoughtfully to himself as he looked at me, as if he was re-filing me in his mind under 'trouble'.

'Okay, inside now. All of you. Playtime's over. Just give me a shout, will you,' he said, turning to go, 'if you want me to get you all on *Tiswas*. Don't think I told you, did I? My uncle's Lenny Henry!' and he allowed himself a little smirk then as he silently took the steps in his shock-absorbing rubber-soled shoes.

Wendy watched Mr Roberts' retreating back, and looked back to me then and stared. She wasn't angry. I wanted her to be angry: anger would have been easier to deal with; she looked *disappointed*. I mouthed an apology, and she was about to reply, but Jonathan Evans came shooting out from the boys' playground then, straight-backed, elbows powering up and down in his self-conscious professional-runner kind of run.

'You're never going to *believe*,' he panted, breath heaving out of him so hard he put a hand on the wall to steady himself. 'You got to come,' he said, 'this is such a shocker,' and there was no time to waste, so he started running back again, beckoning to us as he went, and a small crowd of us followed him as he shouted over his shoulder, 'Sara's *snogging* Rhys Prichard!'

'No!' we shrieked.

'Yeah!' he yelled, nodding his head frantically as he ran. 'Proper full on, on the mouth, behind the shed.'

'That's *filthy*, that is!' shouted Wendy and we eughed in agreement, all of us, gleefully revolted, and ran as fast as we could to where the boys were.

16

Down the lane

Every school day Katherine and I walked the quarter of a mile or so down our lane to the main road, where we would wait for Idris, owner of the Gwalia shop in the village, to pick us up in his taxi and drive us to school.

I never tired of walking down our lane. It changed character on every corner, beginning as a makeshift track dissecting the scrubby, sheep-filled fields beyond our house, and when it reached our gate a slightly more substantial thoroughfare emerged. Earth and stone gave way to crumbling, pock-marked tarmac, framed by rhododendrons on the mountain side, and the long, lichen-clad wall of our garden on the other. From here, we would follow the lane to the right, where overgrown hedgerows buzzing with life edged the fields that spread out wide and flat in front of Olive and Mike's house.

When we reached their house we would dawdle for a while, hoping to catch Phillip and Olive heading out of the door, but more often than not we just heard Phillip's wails of protest from his bedroom and Olive bellowing at him to get his blimmin' bum down the stairs and fast. We would carry on without them, scuffing our shoes down the hill, where the lane cut through a tangle of cow parsley and meadowsweet, and then went down-wards, steeper still, as it altered again and became a cool, dark incline, overshadowed by the dense trees that interlocked above it like a tunnel as it reached the main road.

We called it the main road even though it was narrow and winding and, most of the time, empty apart from the odd mouse scuttling fearlessly across it. We took our time to get there, always stretching out a five-minute walk into ten, rummaging in the hedges as we went, delving in for bits of treasure, and slaloming down the last steep bit like skiers.

When we eventually reached the bottom we would sit on the large flat rock that poked out of the verge and wait there, as we surveyed the riches we had gathered along the way. Snail shells, iridescent green beetles, the occasional snakeskin or slow-worm carcass, half-eaten and stinking. All were lined up on the rock and scrutinized as we listened out for the sound of Idris' pale blue Ford Escort chugging towards us. Occasionally another car would drive past and we would leap up to have a look, certain that we'd know who was in it and where they were going, and most of the time we did.

To the left of where we sat, set back from the not-especially-main road, was Colwyn Parry's farm. If we clambered up the rock and pushed back the tall grass, we had the perfect vantage point of the farmhouse and its garden, and from there, crouched down in the safety of the grass, we would speculate. The Parry family and their farm held an endless fascination for us.

From the road the farmhouse looked oddly grand, out of keeping with its modest rural environment. It was a large, formal building, with extravagantly proportioned windows, totally at odds with the unassuming stone cottages that dotted the same road to the village. In front of it a vast, skewed monkey-puzzle tree grew right in the middle of the lawn, dominating the garden. It had grown taller than the house, and it leant awkwardly over it, casting strange, angular shadows across the roof. Even on the sunniest day the house and its garden were always in shade, the forest of fir trees surrounding it helping to bathe it in a permanent gloom.

Under closer scrutiny, the house looked far less impressive. Render crumbled from the walls, the once white paint had turned grey, and sorry-looking curtains hung faded and torn behind grimy windows. If you craned your neck enough you could catch a glimpse of incongruous, industrial-looking farming sheds at the back of the house, scrappily made out of corrugated iron and seemingly held together with baling twine. It was a place of contradictions. The house looked as if it had been designed for pleasure, for leisurely tea on the extensive lawns, or drinks parties in the drawing room, and yet it appeared to be used, unremittingly, for work; the enduring smell of farming chemicals permeated the air, serving as a constant reminder of this. Even the wooden swing in the garden was unused, its seat covered in a carpet of moss, the frayed rope that held it up green and untouched.

Colwyn Parry was older than my parents, although how much so was hard to tell. His greasy tweed cap was always pulled down over his eyes, so an adult couldn't really get a look at his face. From the viewpoint of a nine-year-old, his eyes were unavoidable, a startling bolt of blue against his khaki-coloured clothing, and above them, curling, untamed eyebrows that grew thick and surprisingly white.

He was lean, and so tall that he stooped, as if even his bones were so skinny that they couldn't keep him upright. Katherine and I called him Jack Spratt, who would eat no fat, and it pleased us that his wife, whose name we never knew, looked very much as if she would eat no lean. She was a small, tight ball of a woman with closely cut curly hair and brown-speckled skin like a hen's egg. We only ever saw her in a sleeveless housecoat with her large upper arms bursting uncomfortably out of the top, and she was always carrying something, laden down with washing, buckets, or bottles for the lambs. 'All right there,' she'd say, if she happened to walk past us, giving us a cursory nod as if to signal that was the end of the exchange, and nothing more was required. We understood, and said nothing, nodding to her retreating back as she scurried onwards into the gloom.

They were both the same, Mr and Mrs Parry. Neither had time to stop and say hello, nor to ask how our parents were, or what we had been up to. As I got older I recognized that their busyness, although real enough, also served them well. It suited them just fine to be forever in a rush, because in fact, more than they were busy, they were both overwhelmingly shy. Even immersed in the shadows, I could see their cheeks flush red on the rare occasion that we spoke. It was catching, that shyness; they passed it on to whoever they came into contact with, making them mutter and blush and look to the ground as they did.

'I saw her, Abbie! She's there at the window, look!' said my sister, standing up on her tiptoes, and she nudged her way through the cuckoo-spit-covered grass towards their garden gate to get a closer look. I clambered up next to her and peered in, but as far as I could see the top-left bedroom window was empty.

'Look *now*! She's back there again!' she said.

There she was. Olwenna, the Parrys' daughter; standing in her nightdress, her white-blonde hair hanging loose around her shoulders as she stared blankly out across the fields.

'What do you think she's looking at?' wondered Katherine.

I followed her gaze. The field on the opposite side of the road was often home to a neighbouring farmer's Shetland ponies, but it was empty now and the forest of fir trees at the end of the field obliterated any potential view.

'Nothing,' I said.

'Do you think she's happy or sad?'

'Neither,' I said. 'She looks nothing at all,' and she did: she looked barely there. She didn't fidget, or pull faces, or twirl around pretending to be a ballet dancer. There was no lightness to her at all; she didn't behave like a nine-year-old child.

'She's not coming to school today, is she?' my sister said.

'I doubt it.'

'But it's not fair though, is it? We have to go, even if we don't want to. Why does she get to play all day?'

'I think she must have to help out on the farm.'

'She doesn't look like she'd be much help,' she said, which was true. Olwenna's limbs were pale and spindly like bamboo, and the hollows under her eyes made her look too delicate to lift a bucket.

'That's what you look like if you don't see sun, all pale and shadowy like her,' I said.

'She probably needs some fresh air,' said Katherine, aping our mother's favourite refrain.

In the distance we could hear Idris' taxi spluttering its way towards us. When Olwenna heard it too, she turned and glided back into the gloom of her room as smoothly as if she were skating on ice.

'Wait there, Idris! Wait for us!' It was Olive at the top of the hill, pulling a now silent Phillip behind her, his tear-streaked cheeks bulging with cola cubes, red sweet juice dribbling down his chin.

Just once in a while Olwenna would come to school with us, noiselessly appearing from nowhere by the overgrown side gate, always just as we had got in the car, and Idris was about to pull away. 'Olwenna's coming! Stop a sec!' one of us would cry.

She would hesitate at the door and then squeeze in beside Katherine and me, sending us both shuffling up to the other side, as fast as the plastic-covered seating would allow, scared that we might squash her, or snap one of her limbs by mistake by pressing on her when the car went round a bend.

'Hiya,' she'd say through a curtain of hair.

'Hiya,' we'd say, suddenly as shy as she was, and then an awkward silence would descend: nothing but the sound of Phillip happily crunching his placatory sweets from the front. Idris would always drive more cautiously when Olwenna was on board, taking the bends at a noticeably slower pace, anxious, I think, that he too might somehow damage his fragile cargo.

She was the same age as me, and she only lived at the bottom of our lane, so by rights she should have been our friend. But the Parrys liked to keep themselves to themselves, as Eleanor Williams' mum would say, and as she said this she would roll her eyes heavenwards, making it clear that there was a lot more to it than that, believe you me.

It was autumn, Katherine's birthday, and she was having a fancy-dress party. She and I dressed up as gypsy girls – kitting ourselves out entirely from our mother's wardrobe. We tied Indian pat-terned scarves around our heads, and clanked with wooden beads and bangles; I thought I looked good, like a proper gypsy, until Sara Fiddick came swaggering up the road dressed as a Charlie's Angel. She was in her Big Town-market jumpsuit, nipped in at the waist with an S-belt, and she'd put flicks in her hair like

Farrah Fawcett's. She looked like a grown-up woman and she knew it, I could tell: her chest was all puffed up with pride – and what looked like socks in a trainer bra. My outfit felt ridiculous in comparison: babyish and embarrassing and wrong. Her brothers, Aled and Neville, shuffled self-consciously behind her; Aled, as a builder, was in a hard hat and an orange council jacket; Neville, in one of his dad Dave's flat caps, was clutching one of his ferrets to his chest.

'I'm a poacher, aren't I?' he said crossly, in answer to our collective quizzical look.

'Maaaam, I told you, didn't I? I *said* I don't want to go! I hate parties, I do; you know that. Take me home, Mam!' Olive emerged from behind our house, her mouth set determinedly as she dragged her reluctant-looking cowboy towards us. The wailing continued, but she ignored him and propelled him forwards. Propelling Phillip was a regular occurrence for which her sturdy forearms were perfectly designed.

In the distance I could make out two figures walking through Colwyn's field towards our house: Colwyn with his daughter Olwenna. We'd always invited Olwenna to our parties, but she'd never come, never even responded to an invite, and now here she was. I watched her holding her father's hand as she stepped up and over the stile. She hadn't dressed up, or perhaps she had; it was hard to tell. Under her coat I could see she was wearing a long dress with ruffled sleeves. It made her look like someone from *Little House on the Prairie*, though that was the sort of thing she wore all the time.

No one knew quite what to say to them. Colwyn blinked at us from under his hat, attempted a smile and then muttered something in my mother's ear.

'I'll look after her, don't worry,' she said.

A war-cry echoed from the bottom of our lane, and a grinning Nell appeared with Maya, both of them in matching cardboard headbands with wonkily stuck-on hen feathers. Nell patted her hand over her mouth and whooped again and waved.

Colwyn leant close in to my mother. 'You want to be careful,' he murmured, 'with people like that.'

'What?' said my mother and she gave an embarrassed, hemmed-in kind of laugh.

'I'd keep my distance if I were you, that's all I'm saying,' he said, and he turned to Olwenna. '*Tara*, cariad, I'll be back to get you later,' and he stroked the top of her head; then he was gone, loping off down the lane before my mum even had a chance to invite him in for a cup of tea.

Fifteen or so of the kids from the village were there, and we all crammed into our sunroom, with the views of the wraparound mountains: terracotta now with the last of the bracken and dotted yellow with late-flowering gorse. We loaded our plates with Hula Hoops and stripy jelly and Rice Krispie cakes, and chatted as we stuffed it all in, pausing only to refill our plates.

Olwenna sat in between Lisa and Wendy, silent and watchful: participating, but only just. She ate slowly, and carefully, as if it was a chore that just had to be got through. Later, she passed the parcel, along with the rest of us, but we had to nudge her – 'Olwenna, your turn!' – and she jolted, as if she'd been sleeping with her eyes open. 'Sorry,' she said every time, as she took it and passed it on. My mother timed it so it was Olwenna who won the prize in the middle – a packet of felt-tip pens – and when she unwrapped them she whispered a thank you. They were wasted on her; I could see from the look on her face, she wouldn't use them, wouldn't cherish them like I would have done.

*

On Monday morning Katherine and I were eager to be off and down the road. We wanted to be there, waiting by the gate next to Colwyn's back garden. Olwenna had been to our house now, which in our book made her officially our friend.

'She doesn't have to be shy with us now, does she?' said my sister, racing along our verge, jumping down when she got to the corner.

We slowed down, as we always did, when we reached Olive's house, and this time – the first time ever that I could remember – Olive was there and Phillip too, dressed and ready and waiting, leaning against their gate.

'Shhh!' said Olive, holding a finger up to her mouth. 'Have a listen,' and a shot rang out, and then another.

Phillip clapped his hands over his ears and wailed, like he did on fireworks night. 'Stop!' he shouted. 'Mam! Tell him to stop!'

The double-decker house bus had moved, and here it was, parked up at the bottom of Colwyn's field.

'Is it allowed to be on Colwyn's land?' my sister asked.

'The shooting would suggest not,' said Olive, in a pretend serious voice, and she looked amused – she always looked amused – but then a little shocked, as Colwyn strode into view, approaching the bus, with his shotgun aimed at the front window.

'Oi!' he shouted. 'Ten minutes you've got to pack up and be off!'

A curtain was pulled back from a window at the back and Freddy appeared at the door. He looked more like Jesus than ever today, standing there with his shaggy beard and long sandy hair, in big baggy white pants like a loincloth.

'Can you believe it?' said Olive. 'Poor them. There's no

dignity in that, is there? Having to move from pillar to post like gypsies.'

'What's wrong with a council house, that's what I want to know?' said Mike from the doorway, bending down to put on his work boots. 'No one's forcing them to live in a bus – they *want* to, Olive; *they like it,*' he said, shaking out each leg of his overalls. 'You've gone soft in the head, I reckon, if you feel sorry for people like them.'

'I'd love that,' my sister said, 'to live in a bus. Either that, or a boat would be good.'

We were late for Idris now, and we ran down the lane, as fast as we could, as the bus choked back into life and trundled slowly off along the line of alders, towards the bottom gate to the road.

Olwenna wasn't there when we reached the bottom. Idris was waiting for us, engine running as he smoked his fag out of the window.

'In you get now, kids, get a shift on,' he said.

We looked back at the gate, and still there was no Olwenna, but Colwyn appeared from the front of the house, half in, half out of his oily wax jacket.

'Excuse me!' my sister called, scrabbling up the verge to the gate. 'Is Olwenna coming to school today?' and he shook his head.

'Not today,' he said, addressing the house, not her. 'She's had a bit of a turn, she has,' and he buttoned up and strode off towards the sheds.

'Chop chop!' shouted Idris from the taxi, flicking his fag to the ground. 'Come on now, chop chop.'

We were watching John Craven's *Newsround* when my mother told us. You remember, don't you? What you were doing when you hear unforgettable news. She said Olwenna had died in her sleep.

She'd been ill for a long time; it wasn't unexpected, my mother said, and hot tears sprang down our cheeks. That was obvious now – *why hadn't I guessed?* But I'd never been told, and illness – *an illness like that* – wasn't something that would have occurred to me, ever. I'd known it could happen, but never believed it: that children – a child that I knew – could die.

My parents went to Olwenna's funeral. Olive went too, and so did most of the village. Later, at our kitchen table, Olive did a roll call of the names: Idris and his wife Gwen – *didn't she look good in black?* Eirian and Dave – *did you clock Dave was miming to the hymns?* Nerys Williams – *what about that dress? Just a touch too much chest for the church, didn't you think?* And on and on she went, with snippets of what everyone said and how they looked and what kind of sandwiches they ate, which made it sound like more of a wedding. And then from nowhere she was crying, and I'd never seen Olive cry. The coffin, she said, did you see how small it was? *Poor little lamb,* she said.

I sat behind them on the sideboard, looking out of the window at Colwyn's tractor, parked up in his field; and soon it was just the rhythm of Olive's voice I heard, as it went up and down and up again: fluid and comforting and familiar. I peeled an apple, then chopped it messily into slices and ate it piece by piece, and the rhythm stopped, and I heard the scrape of Olive's chair as she pulled it in closer to my mother's.

'Okay then,' my mother said, 'but volume control: keep it down – you know walls and their ears.' And I listened in properly now, which was easy because Olive couldn't keep it down if she tried.

There was one person at the funeral that everyone had been

talking about. Do you know the one? Olive said. She was young, in her twenties, with long, straight blonde hair, and had been standing with Colwyn and his wife. After the ceremony she was the first to leave, and she wasn't there for the wake. Nobody knew her, that's what Olive said, and my mother agreed: she said she'd wondered who she was too. The dining room of the farmhouse was just a touch too cold, didn't you think? said Olive – off on a tangent – but it was a lovely spread and the sausage rolls looked homemade.

Nerys Williams – mother of Eleanor – was the one who'd filled Olive in.

'You'll never guess, Olive,' was what she'd said. 'You won't guess in a million years who she is.'

The young woman was the Parrys' daughter: *their only daughter too*, said Olive, and she took a great big gulp of tea as she watched the news sink in.

She'd fallen pregnant at fourteen years old, and that didn't go down well with Colwyn. He'd sent her away, banished her, to relatives in Oswestry, Olive thought it was, and the baby, her baby, Olwenna, was sent back to live on the farm.

Nerys had made her swear not to tell a soul, Olive said, topping up her cup from the pot, 'but it's just you, Anna, so that's okay, isn't it? I'm telling you and then no one else.'

17

Marlboro man

Trigger was a horse in a hurry. He galloped through the forest with his head down, nostrils steaming as if his belly was on fire, trashing the undergrowth. Our route was a mess of obstacles: crumbling tree trunks soft with rot, chocolate-brown puddles as big as ponds, and boulders spattered with lichen, but nothing slowed him down. He leapt and swerved his way forward, undeterred, frantic to be reunited with his master, who had ridden off into the distance without him.

I clung to his mane, shrieking, as the forest whizzed past in an indistinguishable blur of green. When I dared to lift my head, I caught a glimpse of a far-off flash of red on white: Matthew on Missy, waiting for us at the neck of the woods.

The gallop slowed to a canter and the darkness switched to brilliant, midge-filled sunshine, and we were ambling out into a meadow: a tangled mass of long, damp grass steaming in the sun, where Trigger delivered me to his master like a shipwrecked passenger clinging to a raft.

I heard Matthew clearing his throat, and then there was silence. Trigger filled it with a triumphant snort and swished his tail, victorious, as he nuzzled up to Missy, lowering his head down next to her to munch on the neon-green grass that poked out through the brambles.

'Are you okay there, Abbie?'

I lay on Trigger's back, and stared down at my dangling, mud-splattered legs.

'Not bad for a first gallop; you managed to stay on at least,' said Matthew, as he rootled around in his shirt pocket, eyes scrunched into the sun.

I nodded, and mouthed a silent yes.

He smiled as he fished out a packet of cigarettes – not the sweet kind, but the real kind, purple Silk Cut like my mother's, and from another pocket, a box of matches.

I pulled myself upright. 'What are you going to do with those?'

'Well, what do you think?' he said.

All the parents smoked, without exception. Every day, in every house, a well-deserved fag or two was puffed with relish and apparent guilt-free pleasure. For us, the children, it was both a duty and a joy to tell them off about it. We basked in the moral high ground, revelled in the glory of our parents being in the wrong.

Matthew shook his head and looked pretend regretful.

'Look, if I could stop myself I would, but I can't. I'm addicted. If I don't have a cigarette at least every week it makes me feel really sick. Okay?' He scratched a match to life and offered it to the end of his cigarette, as it wobbled up and down to avoid it. 'I'm not being rude, I'd offer you one too, but you're too young.'

Too young. That stung like a Chinese burn.

When it lit, he inhaled, long and deep, and blew a steady stream of smoke out from one side of his mouth.

'Anyway, you should be pleased. It keeps the midges away,' he said, waving it above us, clearing a brief patch of blue in the mass of grey that had surrounded us.

His sprinkling of upper-lip hair looked less sprinkly now: thicker, almost verging on a moustache. That wasn't the only alteration. He used to dress just like my sister and me – the only other child who did – in dungarees and corduroy, but recently, since he'd discovered riding, I think, he'd started to dress like the Marlboro Man. He wore tight, checked shirts with metal-tipped collars and a brown leather Stetson, and chaps. It was the cowboy boots that I admired him for most. It took strength of character and a lot of self-belief to wear boots with a heel when you were a thirteen-year-old boy in North Wales. All of it, he said, was genuine, authentic cowboy clothing, sent over to him from his cousin in America.

He took a final deep drag of his cigarette, brushed the long tube of ash that fell on to his chaps, and flicked the butt into the grass, beckoning me on.

'Head rush. Wow. I needed that. Oh, and not that I care what my mum and dad think about anything, but this is our secret, okay?'

The gorse- and heather-covered moors stretched out ahead of us like a vast purple-and-yellow eiderdown. I scanned the horizon for something that would contain Trigger, but there was nothing, no roads or fences, just an entire planet, it looked like to me, of unrestrained, open moorland waiting for me to be hurled into.

'Come on. We've got to get a move on,' said Matthew. 'I've got another lesson after this.'

'With who? I thought you only taught me.'

'I did,' he said, 'but I'm going to start teaching Nell now. You know her, don't you? Nell from Commerce House?' and he squeezed Missy on with his heels, and trotted off down a sheep trail. I followed on, and pictured Nell, the Girl with a Pearl Earring, riding on Trigger, like me; and as we lumbered into a wobbling, teetering kind of trot a rage rose up in me and just hovered, with nothing – no one – for me to attach it to. I liked Nell. I liked Matthew too. Anger didn't make sense.

I squeezed Trigger's stomach with my heels, and shouted at him to move on.

For the next riding lesson with Matthew I wore a checked shirt knotted around my ribcage and tied a handkerchief around my neck. I kept my riding boots on until my mum dropped me off, and then hid them behind the long grass by the gate to Matthew's house, and took out from my backpack the pair of high-heeled cork wedge sandals given to me by Nana.

Matthew was saddling up Missy as I walked into the courtyard. He gave the leather strap a final heave against her belly and turned to look at me, once, and then again.

'Have you got your boots?'

'Just these,' I said, looking down at the ground, which seemed now so much further away.

'No,' he said, shaking his head. 'You can't ride in those, that's ridiculous – they won't fit in the stirrups. I'll have to get you some boots,' and as he walked off I heard him tutting over the clacking of his spurs.

In the tack room he chucked an ancient-looking riding boot towards me, which missed my upturned hands and thudded to the ground.

'How did it go with Nell last week?' I asked, shoving one foot into the too tight boot.

'Fine.' He hurled the other towards me. I missed again. 'Think it's gone a bit crap at Commerce House,' he told me. 'Wiggy's been up to his usual business so Maya's turfed him out again.'

'Oh.' I wondered what usual business it was.

'Nell's a nice girl,' he said.

'She is,' I agreed, forcing my other foot inside.

'I don't know,' he said.

'What?'

'I think that was a one-off.'

'Oh?'

'I just don't think riding's her thing,' he said, and I straightened up, sat tall on the bench and the Hallelujah Chorus came into my head: many voices singing 'Hallelujah! Hallelujah! Halle-ee-lu-uu-jah!' High-pitched, and joyful, and jubilant.

18

Yogic flying

The moorland stretched out before us, mounds of bilberry bush, heather and gorse, and the sun shone down, warming the yellow flowers just enough to release their scent, which was tropical coconut, like sun lotion. I could feel a monumental sulk brewing in the pit of my stomach – sulks were becoming a daily occurrence – and I wanted to go with it, abandon myself to the torpor and misery, but I couldn't. It would be hard to get the most out of a good sulk, impossible really to enjoy one in front of Deirdre and Joe.

'Join in, Abbie, come on, please,' said Joe, beckoning me over, but I shook my head and jumped down on to the path. He gave a shrug, and looked at my father as if to say 'I tried', and shouted out, loud and hoarse: 'One, two, three, go!' Then he was off, grunting with the effort of it, with my parents and Deirdre in painfully slow pursuit, all of them bum-shuffling over the heather, as they attempted to yogic fly.

If Joe was my father I would have told him, shouted right back at him, that it was a stupid waste of time, that walking was quicker and that they looked like idiots, all of them. That's what I would have said, but I wasn't Sara Fiddick so I didn't. I didn't dare say a thing. I just walked behind them in a fury along the sheep trail, kicking sticks and stones and sheep poo out of my way. I was too old for this, too old for my parents to be acting like idiots and expecting me to join in.

'*Keep going*, Anna!' shouted Deirdre, as my mother stopped and shrieked with laughter. 'You can do it!' she said, fist clenched. 'Tap into your life source!'

I watched them shuffling forward, making clumsy, faltering, unproductive jumps over clumps of heather, like rabbits with myxomatosis.

'Look at this!' cried Joe, still ahead, blond hair bouncing as though it was attached by springs, his Thai fisherman's trousers flapping out behind him. 'I'm doing it! I'm yogic flying!' he yelled, his words buffeted and faded out by the wind.

Deirdre joined in: 'Feel it! Breathe it! Release yourself!' She was panting, raising both hands in the air. 'Here's to freedom!'

'Fuck Newton!' Joe shouted, clearing a bilberry bush, bouncing over it like a space hopper. 'Fuck gravity!'

Deirdre and Joe used to work in advertising with my father. They'd met, years ago, when they'd all worked at Saatchi's together. My father eventually moved agencies, but Deirdre and Joe had stayed on, until now, when they'd decided they needed a break. They had to because they were '*burnt out*', they said, which made me think of the blackened Ford Fiesta that had been dumped over the ravine on the main road to Llangollen. They needed some space; they needed time off – a good stretch of time, at least, to get their heads together, to *reassess*, to think about different pathways in life. I picked this all up from a conversation I'd heard my mother having with Olive, as they drank tea and ate digestives in the sunroom. 'Bless!' said Olive, when my mother told her. 'I wouldn't work in advertising if you paid me, would you?' she said, dunking her biscuit once, and then again, into her milky-but-strong cup of tea.

Deirdre and Joe were staying, self-contained, in our annexe for a while. My mother had tried to convince them against it, but they insisted even so. It was 'work in progress', that part of the house, my mother said, and not much had yet progressed. The back kitchen, as we generously referred to it, was our utility room in fact, which also doubled up as a junk room. Tools hung from hooks on the walls, remnants of the working farm the house had once been. There was an old mangle in one corner, and ancient, rusting implements in difficult-to-open drawers. It was draughty and dark, and a little creepy too.

'I don't know why you're apologizing, Anna – we love it. It's *amazing*,' said Deirdre, when I thought she should have said cach. 'Anyway,' she said, addressing her reflection in the window, 'we're not here for long,' and she gave herself a doe-eyed look and a quick little pout, like a kiss.

But how long? That's what I wanted to know. A week? A month? A year? They'd been here for weeks already and there had been no mention – well, none to me – of when exactly it was they might go.

Each morning, when we opened our bedroom curtains, there would be Deirdre and Joe. They were up and perky and dressed already: not looking burnt out at all. My sister and I would watch them as they stood there looking out across the fields, breathing in deep as if they were preparing to dive; 'centring', they called it, which just looked like standing and breathing to me. They'd wave up at us if they saw us, and smile, spreading their hands before them to alert us to the view. I never knew what to do back. Yes, there were the mountains, so what? A thumbs-up? Was that the right response? And just the one? Or maybe both?

Sometimes Colwyn would be there, in the front field, shifting sheep or mending a fence, and Deirdre would shout out 'Hello there, Colwyn! Lovely morning,' even if it wasn't especially, and Colwyn would keep his head down, always, and pretend he hadn't heard. She was beautiful, Deirdre, and not used to being ignored by anyone, especially a man, so Colwyn's doggedness, his sheer determination to avoid communication, made her straighten with surprise every time.

My father had been working in London now for three days in a row. That was the way it was panning out these days: part-time advertising, part-time writing at home. He was due back home at any minute, and my sister and I waited for him outside the house, fizzing with excitement, jumping on and off the wall, taking turns to dash down the road to the corner and back again, so we could be there, right beside his car, running next to him, as he drove the last part of the hill. We shouted out, delighted, when we saw him, emerging from his car rumpled and smiling; familiar, but foreign too, after three days away in the city.

'There you are!' he said. 'At last!' as if he hadn't been at work at all, but had spent days out hunting for us, and he'd found us now, finally, here. We flung ourselves on to him, and he grabbed us tight as we each balanced on one of his feet: our ritual, well worn and reassuring, to re-establish him as our own.

'Hold on!' my sister said as he walked towards the front door, slow and steady like a deep-sea diver, the weight of a daughter on each foot. Progress was halted when he was halfway there by the squeak of the back-kitchen window opening, and Joe's grinning face peering out.

'Barry! Thought you were back! Fancy a sun-downer?' he said, waving a bottle of wine.

'Love to, in a sec,' my father said, lifting me and then my sister off his feet, as my mother appeared at the door.

'Supper's ready actually, B,' she said, as he bent down to kiss her and wrap his arms around her, lifting her up in a hug until just her bare toes were touching the ground.

'Come and see us round the back when you're done then,' shouted Joe.

'Who knows?' said my mother, over supper, when I asked her when they'd be leaving. 'A few more weeks perhaps?' She said it as if I might be the one who knew the answer, not her, the adult, who'd most likely invited them.

'Something like that, yes,' said my father, helping himself to seconds of cauliflower cheese.

It was their vagueness that alarmed me; it felt deliberate for some reason, intentionally underplayed. My parents were more definite than that. I went to bed fretful and uneasy, while from outside, around the back, my parents laughed with Deirdre and Joe, stopping me from concentrating on sleep, from thinking about anything else but them.

The next day a terrible, sick-making thing happened: my father took up yoga. It was Joe's suggestion: it came from him, but my father hadn't resisted. Wiggy came to teach them, trudging through Colwyn's fields with three rolled-up mats in a backpack. I sneaked a peak at them from my bedroom window while my father, Joe and Wiggy practised on the bottom lawn. The sun wasn't out, but they were all bare-chested, my father and Joe just in their pyjama bottoms, but still overdressed compared with Wiggy, who was nearly naked in his pant-sized, cut-off denim shorts. I'd never seen his legs before; they were milky white and skinny and bent oddly one over the other, as if his bones were made of rubber. I looked on, breath misting up the glass, as he helped my father contort himself into unpleasant-looking positions, coaxing him on all the way: 'Come on, Barry, down a bit further, that's it, you've got it, hold it there!' I watched my father, head down, purple-faced with the pressure of it, bum sticking up in the air, as Olive clapped and whooped from the other side of the gate, and I drew the curtains on them then.

After that my father practised in his bedroom every morning. When he was home I'd go in early to wake my parents up – which I viewed as my God-given right – but he'd be out of bed already, sitting cross-legged on the carpet in his underpants. I found this very disturbing. It wasn't *fatherly*, that's what I thought, though I wasn't quite sure why. My sister and mother seemed unconcerned, relaxed enough even to laugh about it, and that bothered me even more. I tried to picture John Craven doing yoga: tie-less, *topless*, in his sweatpants in the praying lotus position on his immaculate, gnome-filled lawn. He wouldn't do it. He had more self-respect, more dignity than that, I was sure.

'Describe it again, darling,' said Nana, on the phone in one of our weekly Sunday chats. 'Is he *meditating*, do you think?' This wasn't good: meditating could make you blind, I thought – so said Rhys Prichard.

'I don't know,' I said, stretching out the phone cord as straight as it would go. 'He hums a bit, and sort of whispers under his breath, if that's what you mean.' I kept my voice purposefully low, aware of my sister lurking on the stairs above, left ear poking out between the banisters.

'Who got him on to it? Was it that couple who live in the barn?'

'Annexe,' I said, 'and they're not *living* there, they're *staying*, just staying for a while.'

'Either way, it doesn't sound right to me,' said my nana, 'none of it does.'

'No,' I agreed, relieved and then shamed by the prognosis.

It wasn't right. *They* weren't right, so *we* weren't right. The wrongness of it all spilling out, *spreading out*, to cover all of us like spilt ink invading blotting paper.

'When are they going to leave, do you think?' asked my nana.

'Soon,' I said. 'Not long.'

'Good,' she said, and she gave a tight, nervous-sounding laugh. 'Glad to hear it! Do you know, I might even get some sleep now,' she said, pausing to take a drag on her cigarette. 'Your paps bought me some lovely goose-down pillows, so soft; it's like resting your head on a cloud. Send them back, I said. They're wasted, Les, I said. What's the point? When I can't sleep? When I'm sick with worry like this!'

'What do you mean?'

'Enough now, Ed, come on,' I heard my poppa say behind her.

'Tell me,' I begged, squeezing the phone cord so tight that I couldn't feel my fingers.

'Nothing, darling,' she said, which meant *something,* said like that, which meant *commune*; of course it did.

'He's thirty-four now, Ed: old enough to make his own mistakes,' said Poppa, or something like it; it was hard to hear exactly, with the sports commentary blaring away in the background and the hiss and crackle of the phone line. I thought at first he'd said steaks.

My father had a past that was 'colourful'. I'd heard his friend Anthony referring to it at Wiggy's art exhibition at Commerce House once, catching the snatched end of a story '. . . yes, that's Barry for you, Barry and his colourful past,' he'd said to Maya, and they'd laughed as she passed him the end of her skinny, bent cigarette. He would have said more, he was just about to, when he saw me hovering by the plate of flatbreads and dhal, bored enough to think about tasting it. He clamped his mouth shut at the sight of me and I had to stand there like an idiot as he gave Maya a comedy warning cough. They turned their backs to me then, and pretended to be entranced by one of Wiggy's paintings: a hippy woman, who looked suspiciously like Maya, lying topless in a pile of autumn leaves.

'It's so evocative, isn't it?' murmured Maya, which I thought meant provocative or erotic or something sexy and forbidden like that, and I walked off with a mouthful of mushed-up spicy lentils, sickened by the taste and the fact that she could be so overtly rude, so horribly uninhibited in front of another man.

So what if he'd had a colourful past? That's what I thought as I navigated my way down the crowded, open wooden stairs towards my parents. My father *loved* colour, I knew that. My mother knew it too; she was always trying to rein his love of it in. 'Not the purple socks with the red trousers, B, come on, can't you see? One or the other,' she'd say. It was hard to imagine, embarrassing to imagine, a more colourful version of him, in primary colours head to toe: a professional clown perhaps? So I was grateful to my mother, glad she'd come along and helped him tone things down.

Much later I discovered what it meant in fact, picking up pieces here and there from overheard conversations and the odd letter not intended for me. My father, the great brain, the apple of his parents' eye, had run away from home, given up his pristine, suburban life, the promise of a professional future, for a beatnik-filled squat in London. He went to university, but it bored him, that's what he said – once I'd safely finished my own degree – so he dropped out and went to live in Ibiza for a year, to experiment with hallucinogens instead. My poppa was the captain of the golf club and all his friends' sons were training to be doctors.

Poppa went to London to rescue him from a commune once, desperate to save the family name, touchingly dressed up in a suit to give the right impression. It didn't work. My father didn't need rescuing thanks, he said; he was happy as a clam right there. It was July, apparently, but there was still a Christmas tree up in the commune's sitting-room window, and Nana would recount this detail to my mother time and time again, appalled, as if it was the very worst crime she could imagine.

Those years, the loose ones, before my father had pulled himself tightly together, got himself a good job and met my mother, they were long gone, but they'd conditioned my nana and poppa to worry about my father no matter what. There was a sense of expectation always in those phone calls. They were waiting, I can see that now: just waiting for it all to go wrong.

We had a large garden, about an acre in all, but still, it didn't feel big enough that summer. Deirdre and Joe took it over, the two of them, and claimed it as their own, invading it by stealth, like ragwort. The garden was our domain, my sister's and mine, somewhere where we could play unobserved, which really meant unimpeded. Deirdre and Joe were an intrusion, that's what it felt like, and they intruded more and more: their presence magnified, more noticeable with every day that they stayed on.

Why were they still with us? I'd hear them talking about their future plans: they did it all the time, and with great intensity, as they sat by our pond with a glass of wine, and shared a cigarette, sucking away on it urgently, as if it were the last cigarette on earth. Deirdre would marvel about India, and talk about staying on an ashram next: somewhere where they could really find themselves. *Well, go on! Why didn't they put their money where their mouth was then? Bugger off!* That's what Sara Fiddick would say.

Joe agreed – he always agreed – and then they'd kiss each other in much the same way that they smoked: intensely and urgently, and with a fair bit of sucking too. They didn't care that we were watching, or that it was our garden, because they were settled in. It felt like their garden now, and late at night, when I couldn't sleep, I wondered if it actually was, if they'd secretly arranged with my parents to live with us like this, communally, for ever, and I was the last to know.

Over time my resentment towards them blossomed into something more specific and personal: a loathing, fuelled by fear, low-lying, but pernicious all the same.

The summer holidays had begun, and we sat waiting on the climbing frame, my sister and I, on the lookout for Phillip to appear.

'Wotcha!' I shouted when I saw him, panicky eyes peeping over the hedge in search of us.

'Do you want to come over and play House?' my sister called, and he nodded without smiling and solemnly clambered over the back gate to his fate as we slid down the wooden poles to the ground.

We were in our aprons already, which were white nylon frilly ones, like a waitress would wear, given to us last Christmas by Nana. My mother had sighed and held her head in her hands when she saw them, and when we'd opened the joint present – a miniature dustpan and brush – she'd said, 'Good God, no! What kind of message is that?' and Nana had looked at her nonplussed, as did we. We loved that dustpan and brush.

'Take your shoes off, for goodness' sake, you'll ruin my floor!' said my sister, as Phillip dutifully followed orders and unbuckled his sandals, but left his socks defiantly on, pulling them firmly up one by one to the knee. He squatted on the groundsheet under the slide, and he waited then, silent and resigned, for us to begin. He knew the drill. When we wore our aprons we became Tina and Sally-Anne: two grown-up sisters who lived in a brand-new red-brick house (very much as I imagined John Craven's to be) who were house-proud and finicky and scarily quick to anger. We started at once, and shouted at him for being late back from work, screamed at him to tell us where he'd been, what sort of time do you call this?

'I've just been at work, honest!' he said, recoiling from the attack, even though it was familiar enough: that's how it went every time. The name House, with the solid, safe, domesticity it implied, was a misnomer as it happened; there was nothing safe about Tina and Sally-Anne's house, nothing harmonious either. We moved on to some other imagined misdemeanour – *you said you'd walk the dog!* Dredged up another reason – *you forgot to clean the car!* Anything at all to tell him off, as he cowered with shock, fresh and new each time: pleasingly, *addictively* undiminished by repetition.

Mid-shout, just as I was really letting rip – spit flying as I hurled out the abuse – I caught sight of Joe, lying in the hammock at the end of the orchard.

'Oh, don't mind me,' he called, with a wave of a hand, as we sat there frozen and red-faced. 'It's okay, kids, I'm not listening, honest!' he said with a grin. But how could he not be? 'Carry on!' he said, holding up his *Freak Brothers* comic over his face. I never wanted to look him in the eye again. It was as if he'd caught us with our knickers down.

We packed up our house and left. My sister picked up the groundsheet, as Phillip pulled on his shoes, and I took my family in search of a new home; tramping in a fury, huffing through the long grass and the bent metal gate towards the lawn at the front. We could carry on in private there, I said, loudly, so he could see what he had done.

The big lawn, though, was occupied, otherwise engaged, with Deirdre and her new friends from Commerce House. She was sitting on the swing seat, holding forth with Maya and some men that I didn't recognize, who were scattered over the lawn, all of them interchangeable to me: long-haired and pasty-looking, and gazing at her, rapt.

'I want to go home, I do,' Phillip said when he saw them, cupping his groin with both hands. 'I've got to go, haven't I?'

We'd play inside instead, I said, and I pulled him on, along the path above them, my sister trotting beside us, towards the back porch door.

'Hi there, kids!' Deirdre shouted out. 'Isn't it *glorious*? Can you smell it?'

Deirdre liked to marvel. The sights, smells and sounds of the countryside all affected her acutely. 'The bracken!' she said. 'It's so *earthy*, isn't it? Come on, breathe in deep,' and Maya and the men made a show of breathing in: sucking the air in through their nostrils, eyes closed tight with concentration. I ignored her, appalled, as she made an awful moan of pleasure, and flung her head back, shaking out her long black hair so it shimmied and shone in the sunshine.

'Remind me, why exactly am I going to India again, Julian?' she said to a bare-chested man, who was handsome, despite the long hair.

'I don't know.' He stretched out to accept a rolly from

Maya. 'You tell me,' he said, blowing out, smoke streaming through his sizeable lips, which he'd pursed into the shape of an 'oh'.

'Nor me,' she said, and she held her arms up to the mountains, silver bangles clattering. 'Look at them! How can I leave a place like this?' she said, turning then to look at him. 'And how can I leave you?'

'You'll have hubby to keep you company,' he replied. 'I'm sure you'll be just fine.'

'I think I'll be lonely,' she said, in a babyish voice, directing a little pout towards him.

'Don't go then,' said Julian with a shrug. 'Stay here,' and he leant forward to put a hand on her knee.

'Oh, you're so sweet. Aren't you sweet?' she said, putting her hand over his, which he liked very much, you could tell; and he put his hand on top of hers.

Maya grinned. 'How lovely!' she said, adding her hand to the top of the pile, as if they were playing 'One potato, two potato'. 'Feel the love, Julian! Feel that love!'

'Fine with us if you want to stay on, you know,' shouted my father, who was moving chairs out to the terrace by the pond, setting up for the party they were having that evening. He came and sat down and took a rolly from Julian. 'Seriously, Deirdre, are you still really stuck on the Rajneesh ashram?'

'I want to go and check it out, I think, yes!' she said.

'Rajneesh thinks that marriage is bondage,' said Julian.

'So what? I'm not averse to the idea of free love. Nor is Joe,' declared Deirdre, holding a steady gaze on Julian.

'That way madness lies,' said my father, flicking the end of the rolly into an empty mug. 'Come on, give me a hand, someone, will you? I need help shifting tables.'

'Did you mean it? That we could stay a bit longer?' asked Deirdre.

Yes, my father said, he did.

'I might just take you up on that,' she said, and the men and Maya clapped and gave weedy laid-back cheers, as I stood with my hand on the back-porch door, burning with anger, beset with that particular stinging kind of rage that comes from being disregarded by an adult. It was my house. I lived there too. *How dare she? How dare she presume she could stay?*

It was late at night at my parents' party, and I was up still, in my nightie, holding a bowl of olives my mother had said I could hand round as a treat.

'Ooh, look at those! Don't they look nice?' Maya said, in a syrupy-sounding voice. 'I'll take two if that's okay,' and I stared at her big silver and stone rings, one on every finger, even her thumb, as she dipped her hand in the bowl, while I held it up towards her, my arms shaking with the weight of it.

I left her and wound my way across our sitting room, people-lined pathways magically opening up before me as I held the bowl up over my head, through the tie-dye and the cheesecloth and the sweet fug of smoke.

'Off to bed now, Abs,' called my mother as I passed her.

'Yes, come on now, time to go,' said my father, bending down over the record player, a Captain Beefheart album in one hand. I said goodnight to them, accepted their enthusiastic, wine-tinged kisses, and a warm-bosomed squeeze of a hug from Olive, but I didn't go to bed; I couldn't bear to. I stayed put and watched, transfixed, from behind the internal glass window in the hall. It was the biggest party they'd had, though there were only a handful of people that I knew. Deirdre had lured all the commune dwellers in, attracted them with her heightened senses and her love of freedom, and, as I found out years later, the promise of her top-grade London weed.

The slow, buzzing hum of conversation had made way now for shouts of laughter, and I watched, with a horrified kind of elation, as the adults began to dance. Olive started it off by running on the spot, white trainers flashing, not quite in time with the music, as Mike looked on with his weary smile, awkwardly propped against the bookshelves. She held her hands up and gave a fast flurry of claps as if they were maracas and urged everyone to join her, and Joe bounced forward and whirled her around by one hand, to whistles and whoops of encouragement. Maya, languishing Ophelia-like on a velvet cushion in a floor-length dark green dress, rose up and began gyrating, slinky-hipped, around my delighted-looking father, shaking out her waist-length hair, which she wore with a red ribbon tied, karate-style, around her forehead.

I thought of Lisa Evans' mother's birthday party. She'd had a finger buffet in the front room with her relatives on a Sunday afternoon. There were sausage rolls and scotch eggs and pale pink wafer biscuits, and an actual industrial silver urn of tea. Couldn't we have a finger buffet? I wondered, as I watched Maya hugging herself, then raising her arms up high before shimmying reckless and wild across the sitting room.

My mother's favourite Boz Scaggs song came on next, and I heard her delighted screech of recognition, and saw her cutting through the crowd, cigarette aloft, beautiful in a bright blue dress. She grabbed my father and they hugged one another. I had to leave, before they started dancing cheek to cheek; I couldn't bear to witness that.

There was no one else in the kitchen. The candlelit table was crowded with wine bottles, filled-up ashtrays and the last remains of the food. I stood on tiptoe, upending bowls and plates, and found a few olives and pistachio nuts and some hard-boiled eggs, halved and topped with mayonnaise that had gone all crispy around the edges. There was a pause in the music, between the 'Lido Shuffle' and the track that was to follow next, and as I stuffed an egg into my mouth I heard a shriek, particular and familiar: the sound of Deirdre marvelling, unmistakable, from the terrace outside.

'Oh my God,' she said. 'Oh my *God*!'

There was a hedgehog that sometimes visited – 'our hedgehog', we called it, our pet, even though we'd only seen it once or twice, shuffling out from under the laburnum tree outside the sunroom door. My sister and I left out a saucer of milk for it every night, just in case it came back again. Deirdre was obsessed with seeing that hedgehog; she went outside every evening, calling to it, and so far, to my great satisfaction, it had never made an appearance for her.

I took a chair to the sink, scraping its wooden legs across the floor, and climbed up and on to the draining board, where I knelt, bare knees on the damp, cold metal. The window was open, and I leant out into the warm night air, and saw the slate slabs of the terrace, shiny in the candlelight that spilled out from the kitchen window. They were criss-crossed all over with sparkling snail trails. My eyes adjusted and the outlines of trees and bushes emerged, their tops standing proud over our garden wall, silhouetted by the last dregs of daylight in the dusky purple sky.

I could see Deirdre now. She was standing with her back to me, under the laburnum, in the shadows of the garden wall, her long, patterned Indian dress just visible: red and yellow flowers on cream. She shrieked again, so I knew it had to be the hedgehog, and I craned further forward, edged out on to the windowsill, keen to catch a glimpse. It sounded like an echo at first: another shout like hers, but it was deeper, more of a moan.

There was someone with her, I could see him too now, his foot at least: big white toes poking out of a sandal, in between her legs, revealed as her dress slid inexplicably, shockingly upwards. They moved back, and Deirdre trod on the saucer of milk, which rattled on the flagstone and spilt the milk, which looked black on the slate, like water. One of them said 'Shit!' and they vanished then, panting into the darkness, obscured by branches and leaves.

I sat there and waited for something to happen: anything that might explain it.

The noises that I heard now didn't fit with any image that made sense to me. They sounded like some kind of terrible animal keening, like an animal in pain: a fox caught in a trap. The sight of Deirdre's bare white legs stayed with me, and I thought of Sianny Wyn Wyn, lifting up her dress behind the bins for Timothy Jones and Rhys Prichard. She was odd sometimes, Sianny, and young for her age as well, so I'd considered it some kind of babyish aberration, particular only to her. She'd grow out of it in time, that's what I'd thought.

I'd witnessed something private: that hideous, rude word, practically a swear word to me then. I was *party* to something private. The longer I stayed and listened in, the guiltier, the more complicit I would be. I slid down from the sink quickly – nightie ruching up, knees thudding against the kitchen cupboards – and I stepped back on to the floor, and into Joe standing behind me at the kitchen table.

'Hello there!' he said, in his loud, smiley voice, which jarred in the quiet of the kitchen. 'You're still up.' He picked up a bottle of wine to check if there was anything in it. 'Aren't you supposed to be in bed by now?' he asked, wagging a finger at me and pretending to look cross. He looked too ridiculous for me to take him seriously. From the waist up he looked like a businessman in his stripy work shirt with its stiff collar sticking out, but he was wearing it with a sarong. Deirdre had really changed her look since she came to stay; she'd abandoned all her fitted clothes – her lovely clothes – and embraced tassels and ribbons and flowing full-length skirts like Stevie Nicks. Joe, though, couldn't quite fully commit. He even wore cufflinks at the weekends. 'Well, look at you,' Olive had said when she saw him this evening. 'Quite the executive hippy!'

I stared at him and said nothing.

'Tell you what, I won't tell if you won't,' he said, and I thought he must be drunk. That didn't make sense – why would I tell on myself? I watched as he poured red wine into a glass, sloshing half of it on to the table. 'Don't you worry,' he added, 'your secret's safe with me,' and I thought of the secret happening right now, outside the window, and blood rushed round my head in a low-level, ominous hum.

I headed for the door. 'Wait,' he said, pausing to light his cigarette, 'you haven't seen Deirdre anywhere, have you?'

Had I given it away? Was the noise in my head that loud?

'She might be outside,' I said, and I couldn't look him in the eye so I addressed his mouth instead, which had set straight and tight, and was stained – each lip – with a dark red ridge of wine.

'*That's* where she's got to, is it? Thanks,' he said, quietly, as if he was speaking to himself.

I watched him walk through the open back door, bending down as he stepped outside. Even though I wanted to leave, even though I imagined myself thudding up the rust-brown carpet to my room, I didn't. I stayed right there, my bare feet glued to the sticky, wine-spilled floor, the hum in my head now a roar, like fast-moving traffic.

His shout came seconds later, so loud it seemed physical, as though he'd punched the night air with his voice.

'*What the fuck?*'

'Man, just chill, will you?' came back the voice of the man, answered by a splintering crack.

With no warning they were in the kitchen – stumbling in through the door – three of them right in front of me, and I shrank back against the wall, flattened myself up against it, so I could fade right into the background. Not that they were looking: no one was looking at me.

'Fucking *freedom* – is that the fuck what you meant?' said Joe, speaking with his teeth clenched tight together like a ventriloquist, his mouth shiny and slick with spit.

Julian – it had to be him – had blood streaming down from his nose. It was dark and treacly, not bright red like it was in the films, and he was trying to stem the flow with a shirt sleeve, but it bloomed on to his pale blue shirt even so, and splatted in fat drips on to the floor. The front of Deirdre's dress was all undone – gaping wide open – but she didn't seem to notice, as she pulled on Joe's shirt sleeve, implored him – *darling, darling, listen, just listen, please!* He shook her off, but she clung on, so he shoved her off, pushed her up against the sink, and wine glasses juddered and clinked together and smashed then on to the floor.

In the sitting room the music was turned down, and there was a torrent of murmuring, a hum of concerned voices, as I watched on in the kitchen, invisible to them all – plain white nightie against plain white wall – as Deirdre told Joe he'd got it wrong. Her voice was slurry-sounding through her sobs, as she made excuses that made no sense.

And they left the room then, Joe leading the way, with Deirdre pulling at his sleeve, and Julian somewhere in the middle as they poured through the kitchen door, flaring out in opposite directions across the hall at exactly the same time, perfectly co-ordinated, like a Red Arrows display. Deirdre went left, Joe right and Julian straight ahead.

There were raised voices now from the hallway, my mother's rising higher than the rest: '*Deirdre! What were you thinking?*'

And I was mortified, because my mother didn't shout like this, not in front of everyone: not at someone who wasn't me, or my sister or my dad, even when there was no one else to listen. Rhys Prichard's mum did that kind of shouting. She'd let rip outside the pub at her husband and his friends and she didn't care who heard her, who saw her with spit flying out of her mouth. I'd seen her do it once: it was all down to them, she'd yelled, they were leading him astray – bastards, the lot of them; and everyone just stood there not knowing where to look and *I* was embarrassed, even if she wasn't. It was like she'd come out and forgotten to get dressed.

Deirdre was crying even more now, and her words were still sludgy so I couldn't hear what she was saying, but you could tell from her voice, which was high and sorry-sounding, that she was trying to stop my mother from hating her.

'*I can't believe this, Deirdre, I can't believe you'd do such a thing!*'

'Come on now, leave it, Anna. Enough,' my father intervened, in a voice that was low and calm, like a presenter on Radio Four.

'Enough?' my mother shrieked. 'Barry, stop it! Why? Do you think it's okay?'

I knew how serious it was right then: it was the first time I'd ever heard her use my father's full name.

19

'Summer Lovin''

My sister and I read a lot of books. My parents loved to read, and they passed on that love to us, like a baton in a relay, feeding our passion with a constant stream of literature. Life made a reassuring kind of sense in the stories I read: the good were rewarded, the bad were punished and justice was always done. Fiction and fact merged pleasingly together, and at nine I had faith still, an absolute assurance, carried straight from the pages of those books, that, ultimately, fairness would rule, and all would come good in the end.

All had come good with Deirdre and Joe. I'd willed them to go, and the day after the party they did. I'd watched them hastily packing up, filling up their car with their belongings, both of their heads hung shamefully low. India and ashrams were not necessarily on the cards any more, said Joe, through grimly gritted teeth. 'Wouldn't you say, Deirdre?' he added, butting his head towards her like a billy goat. Deirdre shrugged and said nothing, and climbed then into the car. Optimism had bubbled back up in my chest as I'd waved them goodbye through the window. My faith had been restored – temporarily at least – in a framework of sorts – a scaffold – upon which life would unfold the right way . . .

*

A week or so passed and I was sitting cross-legged on the kitchen sideboard, staring out of the window as I waited to be picked up. No one came. Over the road, in Colwyn's field, two black-faced sheep with fat, matted bodies stared back at me. They had shoved their heads through the bottom rung of the gate, in a futile attempt to reach the clover that thrived, tantalizingly out of reach, around its edges. The sheep looked sad and spent, as if they might stay like that for ever. I wondered if they noticed the lack of Deirdre and Joe. If they'd been here still, the little kitchen's window would be open, and there would be some folksy kind of music echoing out into the fields. I'd be watching them right now, most likely, centring themselves in the middle of the verge as the sheep watched on.

The deep hum of a big engine woke the pair from their torpor, and they tried to prise their faces out, swinging them this way and that, bashing them against the wood until they broke free and could join the giant, dirty cloud of sheep that had appeared from nowhere, to sweep them up and take them off towards the mountains.

Deirdre had called my mother up last night to say she was back in Wales. My mother's high-pitched 'What?' had alerted me, drawn me down from my bedroom to the stairs. She'd lasted a week back in London, but she missed the mountains: that's what my mother repeated back, incredulous-sounding, with a question at the end of her voice. She was in Big Town now, staying in Commerce House.

'What about Joe?' I'd wanted to know, when my mother hung up the phone. She wasn't sure about Joe, she said, in the vague voice that meant please don't pry.

'What about India?' I asked. Well remembered, but no, she said; Deirdre wanted to live in town for a while instead.

'Without Joe?'

'Possibly . . . yes . . .' said my mother. 'Now then, what shall I make for supper?'

My lift was here. Evans the Butcher's white meat van pulled up outside our house, a glorious, stomach-lurching sight. I knew it was him because his name and occupation were painted on the side in beautiful, swirly red writing. He was famous, and I was about to ride in his van, for at least twenty-five minutes each way.

Lisa Evans and I were going to the cinema to see the film *Grease*. Mr Evans was taking us there, but he was going to drop us off outside, while he went to watch the rugby in the pub. This was my first unaccompanied-by-an-adult trip to the cinema, though not for Lisa, who'd been allowed to go to the cinema without her parents for the last year or so now, at least. Today she was a professional solo cinema-goer, chaperoning a novice – a position that she'd revel in, but in the most low-key and grown-up way possible. Outright bragging – irritating but familiar – would have been easier by far for me to deal with, but Lisa was never outright about anything. Somehow, at nine years old, she had mastered the art of subtlety.

She already had the *Grease* album. I knew this because she had brought it into school one day and propped it up against the legs of her front-row desk, casually, as if it was just a place to store it. On the cover was a photograph of John Travolta's and Olivia Newton-John's faces, impossibly good-looking in all their blue-eyed, brown-skinned American glory.

'Hey. What's that down by there, Lise?' said Sara, crouching down to scrutinize it, hands on scabby knees.

'Just the *Grease* album, that's all,' said Lisa, making her voice go super-soft, forcing Sara to crane forward, eyes scrunched comedy-tight in concentration as she tried to catch what she was saying.

'Oh yeah, I know it, it's a good one, that,' she said, swirling a string of chewing gum around and around the end of a grubby finger. 'I might go and see the film of that, it's on at the cinema now, it is. I bet you didn't know that, did you?'

'We do! Me and Lisa are going to see it this Saturday!' I said, unable to stop my voice going high-pitched with excitement.

'Go on then, give us a lift – I'll come too,' said Sara.

'Sorry, no room,' Lisa said, staring out of the window at a pigeon pecking on the ledge.

'What? No room in your dad's massive van? Are you having me on or what?' asked Sara, rolling the gum up into a ball and prodding it on to the underside of Lisa's desk. No one did that. Your gum, your desk: that was the rule.

'Yeah, that's right,' said Lisa, 'he's got a meat delivery that day, hasn't he? So just enough room for me and Ab. Sorry about that,' she said, sounding not one bit.

'Like I'd want to sit in your stinky old van! The film's going to be a big bag of cach anyway,' said Sara, turning on her heel and kicking the album over as she went.

Mr Evans beeped his horn, but there was no need: I was already out the door. My mum came hurrying after me, holding up my rust-coloured duffel coat, which I'd carefully hidden, or so I'd thought, at the bottom of the fancy-dress box.

'Don't forget this!'

'But it's sunny, look!'

'But there's a nip,' she said, shoving each arm in, and buttoning me up with its stupidly big Stone Age-looking bone toggles. You couldn't miss me now.

There was a slam of a door, and Mr Evans appeared above us,

blocking out the sun. Next to him my mum looked like an Oompa Loompa, her feet just half the size of his greasy, steel-capped boots.

'Hello, Geraint. Now, you *do* think the film will be okay for them, don't you? I just hope it's not too "grown up".' She said the words 'grown up' in a different kind of voice, which was code. I wasn't stupid. She meant sexy. All of me, even the tips of my ears, prickled with embarrassment.

'Listen, Anna, I've seen it. It's just harmless fun, that's all, don't you go worrying about it,' he assured her, as he slid back the side door of the van. It rumbled open to reveal Lisa, resplendent in purple nylon and patent leather, perched on a white plastic meat box.

'Hiya!' she said, waving at me even though I was only a foot away from her.

'Hello,' I said, feeling both over- and under-dressed in my duffel coat and practical lace-up shoes.

'Here you go, Ab, cooch up next to me by there – I put that box out for you.'

I grabbed her hand and clambered in.

'Mind, though, Ab – no, not by there, step round the blood by there. Mind now. That's it. Lovely,' she said.

Mr Evans gave a heave of the door. 'Duw, I tell you what, it needs some WD-40, this bugger!' And with a grunt and slam we were in the dark.

Sara was right about one thing: it was a stinky van. It smelt of animal fat and coppery blood; and somewhere in amongst it all – mingling unpleasantly in – was Lisa's perfume, which was sickly sweet and soapy-smelling, like Parma violets.

'Girls, have a look down behind my seat, will you? Should be some pork scratchings somewhere down by there to get your teeth into,' said Mr Evans, as he lurched into reverse. 'And chuck us some over by me and all while you're at it.'

We sat side by side in the gloomy half-light, crunching our way through an industrial-sized bag of hairy pigskin, plastic boxes lurching as the van hurtled down the narrow lanes. Branches from the hedgerows whipped at the sides as Mr Evans sped around the bends, his rich baritone rendition of 'Summer Lovin'' accompanying us all the way.

Outside the cinema there was already a queue twisting down the High Street: Big Town teenagers with flicked hair and donkey jackets, slouching, smoking and kicking their feet. We were the youngest by far – not that Lisa looked it in her make-up: lilac eyeshadow right up to her eyebrows and lipstick, pearly pink with a twinkling pale blue sheen, like bacon when it had been left out of the fridge.

I saw Wiggy up ahead of us then, standing a little back from the crowd. He stood out with his long hair and his beige floppy shirt, leaning with one foot up against the chip-shop window. He was smoking a roll-up and chatting to Daffyd Davies, a boy of about sixteen or so I vaguely recognized who lived up the road from Sianny Wyn Wyn's. Wiggy looked straight at me, and I gave him a nod of acknowledgement and mouthed 'Hi' to him, but he didn't seem to register me at all.

I watched as he leant into Daffyd and whispered in his ear. There was something about that gesture that made me stare even more: it looked too intimate and too babyish somehow too; whispering was for little kids, I thought, like my sister. Both of them put their hands in their pockets at exactly the same time, and drew them out at the same time too, like a couple of duelling cowboys. Wiggy placed his hand on top of Daffyd's, and an exchange was made. Something in a small clear bag was passed from hand to hand: a private swapsie of some kind. Then the cinema doors opened and the queue began to shuffle forward and Daffyd left him and hurried to his place at the front.

'Okay, Ab, here we go,' said Lisa. 'Keep to the right. You get through that booth quicker, trust me on that, okay?'

As we moved forward, Rhys Prichard appeared from behind us. 'All right, Lise?' he said. 'I got something for you,' and he shoved a small plastic-bag-wrapped parcel into her hand. 'It's my best one – I found it the other day. You can have it,' he said, grinning, his face brimming with pride.

She looked down at the package and back at him.

'Open it!' he said.

'I will, later,' and she pushed forward and left him standing there at the side of the queue.

The woman in the booth had hair cut scarily short and gold rings on every finger. She was smoking a cigarette and looking the other way.

'Yeah? What film you want, then?' she asked, addressing the question to her fingernails.

Unperturbed, Lisa replied in a clear, strong voice and then strode towards the number two cinema door, holding out our tickets to the spotty-faced ticket man with a bum-fluff moustache.

'All right, Lise, you all right then? Say hiya to your dad, will you?' he said, blushing right down to his dirty white shirt collar.

'Fine, yeah, will do,' she said, turning towards me, eyes rolling upwards to signal 'as if', as she pushed her bottom lip out with her tongue.

'You've got to open Rhys's present,' I said, desperate now to see what it was.

'Can't, can I?'

'Why?'

'Just binned it.'

'Why would you do that?'

'I know what it is – he told me already, didn't he?' she said, catching her reflection in the foyer mirror. 'It's a bloody brake light from a car, isn't it? He found it on the way to school. He said there's just a small crack in one corner.' She dabbed at her lipstick. 'Nutter if he thinks I want that.'

Lisa had our tickets in one hand and the rest of the pork scratchings in the other, so she put her back to the door of Studio Two and pushed in, twirling around to face the right way as the door opened in. This made her look amazing, as if she was someone who could dance really well and blow smoke rings.

We were hit, full in the face, by a wave of heat. Studio Two was a small room, heaving with people, and it smelt of popcorn and sweat and farts. The shiny-faced usherette shone a torch in our eyes, momentarily blinding us.

'What number, cariads?' she asked, tugging away at her toosmall navy uniform, leaf-shaped pockets of white flesh bulging out in between the buttons on her blouse. Lisa held our tickets out for inspection. 'Yep, there we go. Back row down by there,' she said, pointing her torch towards the exit sign and then flicking it down to the seats below. 'Oi! What did I just tell you? Neil Jones, get your feet off of that seat or I'll be having words with your mam!'

Neil, a cocky-looking boy in a leather jacket with the collar turned up, rolled his eyes and took his feet down, deliberately slow, to sniggers and slow claps.

Lisa grabbed my hand and led me down the row, everyone shrinking up in their flip-up seats to let us past as we crunched our way over a sea of already-spilt popcorn to our place.

'All right there, Lise,' said Neil Jones. 'Sit by here, why don't you? Come sit by me,' he said, patting the empty seat next to him.

I waited for her to blank him, but I saw a glimmer of a smile instead.

'Might do,' she said, cocking her head to one side.

'Lise! Lise, by here!' came from the back of the cinema. It was Rhys Prichard, with his older brother Wayne, jumping up and down and waving to her with both hands.

'I've got a place here, haven't I?' she called, sitting next to Neil as he whispered 'Yes!' and turned around to grin triumphantly at a sunken-looking Rhys.

I sat down on the far side of Lisa and she rustled about in her pockets for the giant packet of pick-and-mix her dad had given her as we got out of the van. I thought about it, but decided against getting out my offering: two packets of sesame snaps that my mum had slipped into my pocket as I left – a wholly inappropriate cinema snack; they could wait until the journey home, when I could furtively nibble on them in the darkness of the van.

A couple came and stood directly in front of us, two or three rows down, blocking out the middle of the screen. The girl looked about twelve, but her hair looked much older. It was blonde and rigid and flicked all over, with a perfect duck's tail at the back.

'Lush flicks,' said Lisa. 'I want some like that.'

The girl turned to take her coat off, revealing alarmingly obvious bosoms poking through her fluffy jumper. Lisa didn't say anything, but I was sure that she would want some of those as well.

The boy with his back to me, I was pleased to see, was wearing a duffel coat, like mine but beige, its oversized toggles clacking against each other as he flung it over the back of his seat.

When they sat down their heads were still in the way.

'Oh duw, Ab, would you look at that,' said Lisa, through a mouthful of midget gems.

'Right in the middle of our view,' I complained.

'No!' She swallowed her mouthful in one large, uncomfortable gulp. 'Look what's on, I mean!'

Filling the screen was her dad's van, shiny white and gleaming. Mr Evans himself was leaning against it, with one hand on his hip, rosy-faced and smiling broadly in a brand-new, stain-free apron. *Evans Butcher's, quality cuts guaranteed*, it said in red writing just above him, as giant hairs and scratches leapt about all over the picture.

Mr Evans, who knew my name, and his van, which I had only just been sitting in, were on in the cinema. The enormity of it was too much to take on board all in one go. I was overcome with pride, and then a jealousy so intense that it made my eyes sting. Lisa's dad had just graduated to universal superstar. Every person in the world would know who he was. Why couldn't my dad be shown in a cinema? Or be a policeman at least?

The curtains swung shut on Mr Evans to murmurs of anticipation from Studio Two. 'Shush now, it's starting.' 'Put your fag out.' 'Shut your gob, will you?'

Within seconds the curtains jerked open again, and the credits began to roll. As this happened the boy who was blocking my view yawned loudly and stretched out his arms, letting his right arm drop down on to the shoulder of the girl in front of Lisa. They stayed like that for a moment, until, without warning, he lunged towards her with his mouth open, as if he were about to bite her. She didn't flinch. I expected her to run for the exit sign, screaming. Instead she stayed right where she was, and opened her mouth in return. Their heads locked together, swivelling violently, back and forth, making the same noises a dog might make when it drank thirstily from a water bowl.

'That's frenching, Ab – didn't you know that?' whispered Lisa. 'Stop gawping at them, will you? Just watch the film,' she hissed, shoving the pick-and-mix bag on my lap with one hand and then Neil's hand off her knee with the other. I tried my best to ignore the frenching – what was French about it? – and focused as hard as I could on the screen.

The film hijacked me. I didn't touch the bag; not one sweet passed my lips. I forgot about them, and the couple in front, and Lisa's famous dad. I even forgot that I was a nine-year-old girl with a badly cut pudding basin and home-embroidered dungarees. I was Olivia Newton-John, otherwise known as Sandy, the most beautiful woman in the world. I had lovely, blonde, flippy-up hair and wore sticky-out pastel-coloured skirts, and balanced teeny cardigans on my shoulders without them ever falling off. I looked good in anything pastel, but better still in a black, shiny, spray-on catsuit with really high heels, which didn't in any way hinder my dance moves. I could sing, beautifully, catchy songs that rhymed, just off the top of my head. Everything about me was fabulous, but most fabulous of all, I was hopelessly devoted to John Travolta, or Danny, a man on a par with – or perhaps even more handsome than – John Craven.

Danny tried his best to hide it, and countless obstacles were put in our way, but eventually he had no choice but to admit that we went together like rama lama lama, ke ding a de dinga dong, which was his roundabout way of saying that he loved me.

The lights went up, and no one in the cinema moved. We sat, collectively stunned, staring at the credits. The couple in front of us were the first to stand up. The girl's side-flicks were long gone, and her hair now looked as if it had been backcombed all over. Her eye make-up was smudged down her cheeks, which were flushed in perfect pink circles. She stretched out, revealing her neck, peppered with red welts, and she turned her head towards the back. *I knew her!*

'That's Nell!' I whispered to Lisa. 'Nell from Commerce House!'

'Never!'

'She's got different hair, she's got different . . . everything,' I said, 'but it's her.'

'Don't think she saw much of the film, do you?' said Lisa.

The boy stood up and ran his hand through his sticky-up hair, and straightened up his shirt. It was checked and fitted with piping around the edges, the kind of shirt a cowboy would wear, and I knew, before he even turned to face me, that it was Matthew Martin.

He stared at me, straight in the eye, I was sure of that, but just as I opened my mouth to say hello he turned his head away and whispered something to Nell in her ear. She turned and looked at me, and grinned.

'Top film!' she mouthed and gave me the thumbs-up.

I watched them filing out in front of us, Rhys Prichard ahead of them with his head hung determinedly low. When Matthew was under the exit sign he paused to put his duffel coat on and looked back at me again. This time he gave me a sheepish smile, just briefly, fingers fumbling at his toggles, transforming himself, just like that, from a French-kissing teenager into Paddington Bear.

Part Three

20

Bunking off

The river Dee ran past our school. It bubbled under the blackened humpbacked bridge, in and out of slippery boulders, and
along the edge of the village green in front of us. I could see it
from my desk, a continual, distracting streak of motion running
past my eye-line, as Mrs Bevan murmured on and on. It was
summer, and the windows were wide open, so its distant commotion, the hurried, urgent rush of it, became the backdrop to
our lessons, a constant reminder that life was carrying on –
moving on – without me.

My knees and the top of my legs now pressed uncomfortably tight against the child-sized desk, buffing up the nuggets of
ancient, long-discarded chewing gum stuck there, hidden away
underneath. I felt hemmed in. I *was* hemmed in. I wanted to be
outside and off and away.

Mrs Bevan was usually the teacher on playground duty. I
doubt anyone offered to do it but her. Who can blame them?
Faced with shouting at children and breaking up fights, they
probably preferred the alternative: feet up in the staff room with
a packet of fags, then a quick pop down the pub for a swift one.
Mrs Bevan, though, was dutiful by nature, and she didn't smoke
or drink, so the task fell mainly to her; though she was the least
suited out of all of them, not being physically strong, or loud,

and with a nature that was predominantly kind. She knew her limitations, I think, and stayed mainly inside and left us all to get on with it. If we needed her – which we never did – we knew we could find her hiding out in the classroom, at work on one of her craft projects: knitting a loo-roll cover, or crocheting a tea cosy, while she whispered a running commentary of her progress to a mainly silent Brangwen, who sat, a mountainous presence, on the windowsill behind.

Brangwen was eleven years old, but looked more womanly, oddly, than Mrs Bevan, who had the build of a small child and favoured homemade clothes which were big and mainly rectangular, cut straight up and down, as if she'd made them for her husband and then changed her mind at the last minute. Brangwen dressed in old-fashioned tea dresses, nipped in at the waist, and she wore her hair long, and set in curls like a 1950s starlet. Her legs were ladylike: big but shapely, and finished off with surprisingly small, delicate-looking feet that she pointed like a ballet dancer whenever she was seated, which was most of the time. If you caught sight of them from the far end of the playground, Brangwen sitting self-consciously straight at the window, smoothing down her dress, and Mrs Bevan hunched over the table with her short hair and sensible jumper, Brangwen looked like a middle-aged woman and Mrs Bevan a little old man.

Once in a while Mrs Bevan would check on us, popping her head halfway outside, always with one hand on the door.

'You all all right there, my cariads?' she'd say through a mouthful of pins, eyebrows raised in hopeful anticipation. She was met usually with screams that suggested not. Blood was shed almost every playtime, sometimes by accident but mainly by Sara Fiddick.

'Sara scratched me in my good eye and now look at me! I'm

blind!' shrieked Sianny Wyn Wyn, arms outstretched in front of her, fingers splayed as she shuffled slowly forwards.

'I never did! She's a lying bitch, she is, Mrs Bevan, I'm telling you that now. What would I want to touch her for when she stinks of milk?' shouted Sara from across the playground, hanging half upside down from the bars.

Mrs Bevan's response was a vague, low humming sound, just like our fridge; a sound that we came to understand meant that all facts had been registered, but none would be addressed.

'Yaahmm. Not too bad, though, is it? Just a little scratch, I reckon. Couple of blinks and you'll be fine – that's it – lovely bit of blinking there, Sian. Well done you, keep it up. All all right then now?' she said, backing through the door. 'Ooh, that metal piping doesn't look too clever; I'd put that down if I were you, Rhys – mind yourself now, cariad. Anyway, come and find me then if anyone needs a cooch, will you?' and she pulled the door to, and pattered off along the parquet corridor to the safety of the classroom and her desk, crammed high with wool and snippets of fabrics and half-made bits of lace, to continue her craft tutorial to a wholly unenthusiastic Brangwen, who didn't like exercise in any form, and that included fingers.

There was a lot less to be getting on with at playtime these days. The games we used to play, like House, and Charlie's Angels and Welsh Nash, they'd kept us busy, tidying up and solving crimes and razing houses to the ground, but they were too babyish for us in our last year of school, too stupid altogether. We were left with lounging and lolling around the playground, trading Top Trumps and insults, until Sara, as it usually was, picked a fight.

'Oi, Eleanor, why's your hair all flicky like that? Are you trying to look like Diana Spencer, is that it?'

'Might be. What's it to you?'

'Are you tarting yourself up because you fancy Rhys Prichard? Don't bother, he thinks you're a dog, he said, he told me he did.'

'He never. *Take it back.*'

'Shan't. No, hang on, I got it wrong, I did: it was your *mam* he said was a dog.'

'*Take it back I said, or else.*'

'Or else what? No, no, I got *that* wrong and all, now I remember: it was *dog shit* he said she was.'

'What are you after? A smack in the gob?'

'Go on then, give it a go, right there, you silly bitch, hit me right there, go on.'

Rhys Prichard had started the lunchtime bunk-off. It was the kitchen's fault, he said: mushy peas two days in a row was nothing less than criminal. He was off, he said, off home to see his mam to get some proper food inside him, and none of it would be green or stink like shite: a chip butty would do it, with crisps and Daddies Sauce on the side. He grabbed his trusty white plastic bag – home to his precious collection of car-accident relics: bits of rubber tyre, broken pieces of brake lights, shards of red and orange plastic, all of it lovingly gathered on his journeys to school – flung it over his shoulder and pushed his way through the double doors.

We watched him, all of us, as he headed through the gate, whistling extra loud, one hand in his pocket, to show us he was relaxed. I expected him to turn around – surely any second now? But he carried on, with an exaggerated swagger, across the green and on to the bridge, where he paused in the middle, to bow, and followed it with a regal-looking wave, and marched off then, until he dipped down the other side of the hump and was gone.

'Cocky little shit,' muttered Sara.

'You're just jealous,' said Eleanor, 'that's all.'

Brangwen watched him, gasping at his effrontery, one hand slipping down the window glass, squeaking through the condensation, with Mrs Bevan, bent double on the floor behind her, fiddling with a knee-length skirt pattern.

'Brangwen, cariad, pass us another pin, will you?'

Brangwen wouldn't snitch on Rhys; you could rely on her, always, to keep quiet. She kept her secrets safe, just a hint revealed when she felt the need: her little flash of power.

'Don't you know about Mrs Roberts then, Ab? Ah well, not to worry. It was the pills – that's what they reckon – they made her go funny in the head. That's why she did it; well, that's what she told Mr Roberts anyway.' Just enough, a snippet let out to prick your interest, and then she'd stop and say no more.

Rhys left school the next day too, and still Mrs Bevan didn't notice. Where Rhys led, the rest of us followed, and we all started doing it then: sneaking out on to the green, towards the cool, long grass behind the playing fields, where we revelled in the change of scene, and that heady, uncomfortable pleasure of doing wrong. We sat hidden there and gave each other Chinese burns while Sianny Wyn Wyn set up her tattoo parlour, and we watched then, as she wonkily carved initials on to arms with a compass, tongue sticking out in concentration, good eye extra wide with effort. There was a thrill to be had from watching self-imposed agony at close range. I watched Timothy Jones, transfixed, as Sianny tried to brand him with an anchor on his freckle-dashed upper arm. He sweated, face scrunched up through the pain, teeth biting down on his lip, as she dotted the compass up and down his shoulder like a sewing machine. When she rubbed the biro ink into his bloody arm, he panted like a thirsty dog as he tried to hold back a scream.

'Nearly done now,' said Sianny. 'Be brave, it's going to be worth it, you wait. You're going to have this anchor for ever, think of that, and it's free!'

'Have you ever seen an anchor before, then, Sianny?' asked Sara. 'Because that doesn't look nothing like one,' which made everyone laugh but Timothy.

It was a sweaty-hot lunchtime, a day when the air was still, without the slightest breeze to interrupt it, and Wendy and I left school together, and headed straight down to the river to cool down.

'I can't be doing with heat,' said Wendy, swiping her towelling wristband across her forehead, which had turned bright, shiny gammon pink, like the rest of her. Her white sundress clung to her legs in see-through patches as we scuttled, heads bent, across the green. When we reached the river's edge we pulled our sandals off and clambered down the cracked, orange-brown earth, and slipped our feet into the ripples to find shocking cold relief.

A blur of midges hovered above, following us in a cartoon cloud, and so we waded under the arch of the bridge, into its cool, echoey darkness, where stalactites dripped water in time to a rhythm, like the comforting tick tick of a clock. Without Sara, without Eleanor and Lisa, with their make-up and trainer bras and constant, knee-jerk put-downs, it was easy to slip back, revert to an easy, unselfconscious way of being. We searched for trout to tickle; and finding none, made do instead with sticklebacks and tiddlers, chasing them in and out of the shadows as they darted from rock to rock for cover.

'Let's carry on up the river,' said Wendy, paddling out into the daylight on the far side of the bridge.

'Just quickly,' I said, 'to Ty'n y Wern and back.'

So we waded upriver, dresses hitched up high through the village, singing Bucks Fizz 'Making Your Mind Up', speeding it up then slowing it down all the way, sandals in hands, as we pushed against the water, towards the hill where Matthew Martin lived.

When our feet turned numb with cold, we got out and carried on along the riverbank, and sang Shakin' Stevens then, yelping out 'Green Door', until the houses thinned out and the path grew thick with Indian balsam, and we fought our way along the path, through its tangle of pink flowers, bashing them down, sending seedpods popping open and black seeds shooting out like tiny cannon balls into the water.

'Hey! Girls!' a familiar voice called out behind us, and we turned back to see a girl – Nell from Commerce House – running super-fast towards us down our newly tramped-down path. 'Wait there!' She was running like an athlete, elbows powering at her sides, and she had the look of an athlete too – head bent, lips set thin with determination. We watched as she ducked down under the last bit of straggling foliage, and she jumped up next to us then on to the moss-covered rock we were standing on, and grabbed my wrist. She said nothing for a second, bent down, hands on knees, while she caught her breath.

'Shit,' she said, straightening up, 'I'm knackered now.'

Her hair was blonder again – white almost, as if she were Scandinavian – and it grew upwards now, with record-breaking flicks: they looked like birds' wings spanning out either side of her ears.

Wendy let out a defeated, hissing sigh, like the sound a balloon makes when you're struggling to tie the knot. She gave Nell the once-over, scanned her from top to toe the way my nana liked to do, as she absently tried to flatten down one of her curls – a giveaway – but it sprang back into its tight coil the second she let go.

'Have you seen Wiggy?' asked Nell. 'He's gone AWOL,' she said. 'Maya's going spare.'

I didn't know what AWOL meant – a place perhaps? Near Bala? Wendy can't have known either because we just stood there, the two of us, and said nothing and stared. I tried to picture Nell before her transformation, when she looked just like her parents, as if she actually lived in Commerce House: all flowing hair and flaring fabric. She looked like someone from the city now in her tight, stone-washed jeans, which were dappled with white specks all over like a TV screen when you haven't found the channel.

Wendy recovered a bit of herself then, just enough to put her hands on her hips and pretend to chew gum: her trick to make herself look cool and grown up.

'Not seen him anywhere,' she said.

'I'm going to The Mill,' said Nell. 'I bet you anything that's where he is,' and I found myself grinning, inappropriately, with relief. I'd been sure she'd been heading to Matthew's house.

'He's nicked a tenner from Maya,' she said, 'so he'd have gone there to get his fix.'

'Ahh . . . get you,' said Wendy, still pretend chewing, nodding as if she was a wise old sage, when I knew she had no more of a clue what she was talking about than I did.

Daffyd Davies, who lived up past Sianny Wyn Wyn, was walking our way now on the other side of the river. He was grinning to himself, smoothing one hand over his shaved head as he weaved along the bank as though he was dribbling an imaginary football.

'Oi! Daffyd! Have you seen Wiggy?' Nell shouted, which made me sick with awe and lowliness: I'd never dare shout out to an older boy, especially one dressed all in black with an actual moustache that wasn't bum fluff.

Daffyd didn't say anything, just carried on rubbing his head and nodded and pointed behind him, then carried on weaving towards the village.

'See,' she said, 'didn't I tell you? He's at The Mill getting off his face again,' and she gave a growl of frustration. 'He's such a waste of space!' she shouted.

'You can't say that about your dad, that's not on,' said Wendy. 'My dad would thrash me, he would, if I talked about him like that.'

'Your dad isn't Wiggy, though, is he?' snapped Nell. 'Just leave it, will you? You don't have the first clue.'

'That's a bit off,' Wendy said, her cheeks pink with humiliation, and for a second Nell looked less sure of herself and her eyes looked shiny as if she might start to cry, but she didn't. She turned away and started running again, ahead of us now, and she thundered across the metal footbridge upstream, her footsteps booming down the river, and then she was gone, disappeared up the hill towards The Mill.

Out of the canopy of greenery, we were baking hot from the sun.

'Sod this,' said Wendy, sweat now rolling in fat drips, like tears, down her cheeks. 'I need to get my feet in the water.' And we clambered back down to the river and jumped on to the bridge, its custard-yellow paint peeling off in shiny curls.

We sat down side by side on the warm metal, rough with rust, and plopped our feet back into the water, swishing them forwards and then backwards in time with each other, and picked off pieces of paint, throwing them into the river to confuse the curious ducks that bobbed, heads cocked, towards us.

'We've got ages still, half an hour I reckon, at least,' said Wendy. She was brave, that was why I liked her: bold and fearless like Sabrina, the feistiest Charlie's Angel.

'Bit less,' I said. 'Let's give it ten. Just in case.'

And she raised her eyebrows and called me chicken, but kindly, with a smile, not like Sara Fiddick would've said it.

We had started singing again, 'Brown Girl in the Ring', voices echoing downstream – *she looks like a sugar in a plum. Plum, plum!* – when we were shocked into silence by a noise. The ducks veered off, dispersed in a fan away from us as the sound got louder, more distinctive – the hurried tap tap of shoes on tarmac. A policeman – I was sure of that – sent by our school to arrest us.

The footsteps stopped, and for a second there was silence, followed by the grinding click of a cigarette lighter and a deep breath in and out.

'Just keep your head down and stay quiet,' said Wendy, from the side of her mouth, her beady moustache of sweat sparkling in the sunshine. 'Let me do the talking, okay?' she said, just like Sabrina would have done.

And I bent my head and fixed my stare on a fallen-down tree, half in the river, half out, with duckweed clinging to its underside: bright green fronds in the water flaring out like mermaid's hair.

'Hello there, girls. What are you up to then? Bunking school?' came a man's voice, deep and gurgling with a caught-up cough; and we sat with our backs to him and said nothing, as water frothed over our peeking-out toes.

A tremor signalled he was up on the bridge, and then a

hacking noise, loud and productive-sounding, juddered us up and down, forcing an acknowledgement as the footsteps crunched over rust towards us.

I looked up to see a man in a black leather jacket – not a baton or a whistle in sight – bending over the railing as he spat a gobbet of phlegm into the river, and the shiver of distaste I would have felt was cancelled out, entirely, by relief.

'Well?' he said, wiping his mouth. 'Aren't you going to answer then?' He slicked a hand through his hair, greasy with Brylcreem, teased into a quiff like Elvis's. He winked at us and clicked his tongue, and when his face relaxed the wrinkles around his eyes sprang out white like a sunburst. Sideburns like lightning struck across each cheek.

'Why don't you mind your own business?' said Wendy, frowning at him straight in the eye.

'Cheeky mare! Easy, okay? I'm just asking, that's all,' he said, and he stepped backwards and held his hands above his head, surrendering, as if she was pointing a gun.

'Well, don't,' retorted Wendy. 'Keep your nose out where it's not wanted,' she said, two red blotches blooming on her cheeks.

'Bit of a one, aren't you now? Feisty. I like that,' he said, smiling now, as he lifted up his trouser legs a notch and squatted down between us, his taut, round ball of a belly sticking out proud from his jacket.

'Want a fag?' he offered, holding out a packet of Embassy, with one cigarette sticking out longer than the others, ready to be taken, and I shook my head, expecting Wendy to do the same, but she leant forward and took it, and said, 'Ta.'

'Thought I could tempt you,' he said. 'There you go – I'll do it, look, you've got wet hands,' and he was lighting it and then placing it in her mouth. Wendy gave him a thumbs-up, then breathed in deep and flung her head back, covering up a cough with a swallow.

'So then, girls, want to guess where I'm off to tonight?' said the man, leaning forward to flick his ash into the river. His hands were a faded scrawl of homemade tattoos: shakily rendered letters rippling on every knuckle. There was an L and an O, I could see them, on the fingers that held his cigarette.

'How should we know?' said Wendy.

'Thought you might like to guess, you look like clever sorts,' he said, cocking his head in my direction. 'What about you? Cat got your tongue? Go on then, ask me,' he insisted, bending down to shove me on the shoulder.

'What are you doing?' I said, quieter than I'd have liked.

'I've got tickets for the *wrestling*,' and he gave a crackly whoop. 'It's *special* wrestling,' he said, doing the wink and click again.

'Is it Giant Haystacks?' I asked, staring at the steady stream of smoke that Wendy was now blowing, like a seasoned smoker – like my nana – from the side of her mouth.

'Better than him,' he said. 'Try again.'

'Big Daddy?' guessed Wendy, leaning back on one hand now, tossing her hair back, taking another drag.

'Better than him and all,' he said, crouching lower down again, knees splayed out in uncomfortably tight-looking trousers. 'Give up?' he said.

'Go on then,' said Wendy, tapping the cigarette before the ash was ready to drop.

'It's *mud* wrestling!' he said, grinning wide to show a tumbled-down row of rusty-looking teeth.

'What's the point in that?' said Wendy.

'What's the point?' he repeated, and he laughed so hard he

started coughing: spluttered between his hands, raised up to his mouth, as if he were praying.

'You've got a lot to learn, girl,' he said. 'What's the point in sexy ladies with no tops on, wrestling in mud? Brilliant – I love that. Ask your dad, go on, he'll tell you.'

'My dad wouldn't like that, I know,' she said.

'Come and see for yourself,' he said. 'I've got a ticket spare,' and he went digging around in the inside of his jacket, finally pulling it out to prove it.

'No, you're all right,' said Wendy, crushing the end of her half-smoked cigarette. 'Well,' she said, standing up and dusting off her hands, 'I hope you enjoy yourself,' polite now, as she bent down to pick up her sandals.

'Stay!' he said, rising on his haunches. 'Sit here with me a bit; come on, keep me company,' his signet ring chinking as he patted the metal floor, sending a low boom reverberating down the river.

'The bell's going to go,' she said, jumping down the steps to the road.

'Cap off! Go on, you look like a rule-breaker to me,' he said, but she was off already, running down the narrow pavement away from him.

'Come on, Abs,' she shouted, elbows powering out at either side, in her strange, wiggling, duck-like run.

'Wait!' I called, shoving my squeaking wet feet into my sandals, struggling to prise them on, but she didn't hear me, or didn't want to; either way, she carried on. I cleared the steps in a clumsy jump and chased after her, undone sandals flapping like flip-flops on the tarmac.

'Come back and see me again tomorrow – I'll be waiting for you right here,' he shouted after us. 'Don't forget, now.'

'Okay!' I said, giving him a back-handed wave over my shoulder.

I caught up with Wendy – easy when I was the one in shoes – and we ran side by side down the pavement.

'We can slow down,' I said. 'There's no rush, remember?'

Wendy said nothing, just silently powered on, damp ringlets bouncing, lips pursed tight as she steadfastly chose to ignore me. Who was the chicken now? That's what I thought, as we pattered past Eleanor Williams' house, past Idris' house, the Gwalia shop, up towards the bridge and back over the river to school.

21

'Waltzing Matilda'

I was sprawled out on the shiny cork floor of the playroom, drawing pictures with my sister. My mother was in the kitchen, boiling up a chicken carcass. The familiar, comforting concoction of kitchen sounds carried through the house and told me all was well. Pots and pans bashed, hot liquid bubbled and Tom Waits' voice wailed gravelly and defiant above it all, accompanied as always by my mother's enthusiastic, slightly tuneless hum.

From outside, a distant screeching rose above the din, and through the window I saw the top of Olive's head, bobbing above our wall, shiny and smooth like a cannon ball, hurtling towards us.

'Muuuum!' called my sister. 'Olive's coming,' as she carefully shaded in the crown of her portrait of the Queen: straight pencil lines, one after the other, all in the same direction. The neatness of it made me want to grab a pencil and scribble all over it.

Olive came panting in through the front door. 'Hiya girls,' she said, pausing for a moment to steady herself, one hand on the doorframe, the other under her now prominent pregnant belly, bosoms heaving as she caught her breath. 'Now then. Well. Where can I find your mum?' We pointed our pencils in the direction of the kitchen, and she nodded and powered on, squealing out my mother's name. My sister shook her head, and went back to her particular shading.

'The Queen doesn't look like that,' I said, 'she isn't supposed to be sexy. She doesn't wear all that blue eye-shadow or have giant lips.'

'Anna!' Olive was at the kitchen doorway now. 'There you are! Well. You are never going to believe this,' she said, her voice fading as she was enveloped into the steam-filled room. 'Guess what happened in The Miner's last night?' she said. 'Just wait. *Wait* until I tell you!'

'Actually the Queen can be sexy if she wants to be,' said my sister with a sigh, applying heavy blusher now – streaks of bright pink – to the Queen's cheeks so she looked as if she'd been stung by a triffid.

My father poked his head round the front door from outside. He was bare-chested and in his baggy yoga shorts, with a towel slung over one shoulder.

'Wiggy hasn't come this way, has he?'

We shook our heads.

'If you see him, tell him I'm waiting for him in the garden, at the front. Usual place.'

'He's not coming, Dad,' my sister said. 'He didn't come last week either, remember?'

In the kitchen the furious boiling had stopped, and Tom Waits was reduced to a whisper. There was the sound of chair legs scraping across the floor and I heard a match striking, and then a lull as they both inhaled; which meant that it was a cigarette-worthy piece of news. Curious, I put my pencil down and skated, sock-clad, across the slippery floor towards the kitchen.

Olive was leaning in next to my mother, and when she saw me she sat up straight and looked at me with her mouth shut tight. I'd never been in a room with a silent Olive before, and it felt odd and wrong and magnified the silence somehow. I poured water into my glass and it sounded like Niagara Falls.

'Come through to the sitting room, Olive, I've got something to show you,' said my mother, loud and clonky-sounding, like my sister when she was trying to act.

'Ooh, I'd love to!' said Olive, and she jumped to her feet and bounced after her. I left it a couple of seconds then followed them out into the hallway as they disappeared into the sitting room.

'They don't want you around, Abbie, can't you tell?' said my sister from the playroom. 'Just leave them to it, I would.'

I stood by the internal glass window and looked into the sitting room at Olive and my mother sitting side by side on the sofa with their backs to me, cigarettes aloft and perfectly parallel. Olive's head was only just visible over the top of the sofa, and she leant in towards my mother again.

'. . . And then Bryn Prichard goes and punches him square in the face, just like that! And next thing you know they're both down on the floor and Evans has pinned him down, and he's yelling at Bryn – spit flying all over the place – "You stupid drunken bastard!"'

'No!' said my mother.

'Yes!' said Olive. 'You should have seen Bryn, he looked so ridiculous – arms and legs flailing about all over the place like a dying fly!' And she started laughing and I heard her slap her leg, or my mother's, I couldn't tell.

I wanted more. Why had Rhys's dad hit Evans the Butcher? What had he done? But Olive did one of her wind-down happy-sounding sighs; the kind that signalled she was rounding a conversation off, as if she was reminiscing about it already.

'Aww,' she sighed, 'ahh,' and she took a long hard drag of

her cigarette. 'That's nice. Lovely,' she said. 'I tell you, it's been all go this morning: two haircuts in a row. Eirian's fringe needed sorting, and then Colwyn, bless him, he popped in for his short back and sides.'

Colwyn Parry had kept himself even more to himself since Olwenna died. He and his wife had retreated yet further into the gloom of their farm, only venturing out on market days. It was good, I thought, that he was still dropping in to see Olive.

'I think I managed to put a smile back on his face,' she confided. 'Poor love, it's just affection really, that's what he's after,' she went on. 'He's not getting any at home by the sounds of it.'

'Oh Olive,' said my mother, sounding, for some reason, disappointed. 'What are you saying?'

'*It was him,*' she said, 'not me! I was doing his sideburns, and all I said was "I'll set about those eyebrows in a minute, Colwyn, I'm surprised you can see out".' She paused as she bent down to pick up her cup of tea. 'And then he said, "Olive, I'll set about *those* in a minute if you're not careful," and next thing I know he was grabbing me *boobs* and giving them a GREAT BIG SQUEEZE!'

My mother sighed out her cigarette smoke and shook her head.

I sat with my cheek now squished hard against the glass, thinking of how I might have misheard, but nothing that made sense rhymed with boobs.

'What did you do?' asked my mother.

'Well, I let him have a bit of a go on them, didn't I?' Olive said. 'Come on, Anna, you've got to feel for him – he's been through enough, hasn't he? That's all he wanted really, just a bit of fun. How could I deny him that?' she said, as if he'd asked her for a ticket to a fairground ride; and she sighed again – the finishing-off sigh – which meant that was the end of that. 'What say you?' she said. 'Shall we have one last ciggie?'

'It's always your last one,' said my mother, and Olive actually laughed.

I sat there, sick to the bottom of my stomach, watching her merrily chuckling away, when there was nothing to laugh about, and she looked like someone else now, like a stranger to me entirely.

I got up and ran through the playroom – fast – so my sister couldn't see my face.

'Wait! What do you think of my picture, Abs?' she called. 'I've put the royal crest on her bikini!'

I took the back stairs two at a time towards my bedroom. I didn't ever want to be an adult. Sara Fiddick would thump me in the face for saying it, but if it was possible, if I could find some way to make it happen, then I'd stay a child for ever.

I sat on the window seat in my bedroom, and stayed there waiting for something to happen. *Something was going to have to happen.* Dusk fell as I looked out across the now hateful Colwyn's fields, and watched them slowly turn from green to soft lilac-grey. A rabbit bounded across, its tail the only sign: a bright, round, flash of white illuminating the gloom.

The punishment would have to be big. My mother must have called the police. Both Colwyn and Olive would be arrested. I imagined a tear-streaked Phillip standing with Mike in their yard, watching a handcuffed Olive being shoved into the back of a police van. 'Mam, don't go! When will I see you? Mam!'

I listened out for the sound of a siren, but there was nothing. There were bats now, swooping down from the eaves, and the outline of the mountains had disappeared, merged in with the lead-coloured sky.

From below, there was the familiar creak of our front door, and it opened wide, light spilling out on to the flagstones of the courtyard. Olive was outside now, murmuring her farewells to my mother, telling her she'd see her tomorrow; 'Take care,' she said. 'And you,' murmured my mother back. Moths flitted around the porch light as it shone down on their heads. My mother said a cheery goodbye, and I watched as Olive skipped off down the road. The front door shut, and then Tom Waits was back, wailing for Matilda to come waltzing with him, and my mother was singing along.

22

Sitting tight

New motherhood hadn't altered Olive much; the most noticeable change was her hair. Before baby Kerry only perfectly straight and shiny would do, but now it stuck up in all directions in kinky-looking clumps and it didn't seem to bother her at all. She still dressed the same, in her favourite navy sweatshirts, but this one was blotchy now at the front with damp patches. The sitting room looked as it always did, but with the addition of a small, moon-faced baby lying on a blanket by the gas fire, and an absence of Phillip sitting pantless on the windowsill.

'Bless Phil, he's not taken it very well,' said Olive, handing Kerry to my mother in reverential slow motion, her hands still splaying out like starfish. 'He's never been keen on change.'

My mother smiled down at the bundle on her knee. 'He'll come round,' she said, as she stroked Kerry's peachy little cheek. 'How can he not? Look,' she said, 'just look at this.'

'Has Phillip run away?' my sister asked. 'I said that, didn't I, Abbie? That he might.'

'Not yet, love, no,' said Olive. 'He's outside in the swimming pool – look, there he is, having a little think, God love him. Look at his little face.' She leant forward to bury her nose in the wisps of Kerry's hair, and breathed in deep. 'It's the smell of their little heads . . . delicious,' she said with a sigh.

Colwyn and boob-fondling blurred from a shaky kind of fact into fiction for me then. I'd not *seen* it happen, so it hadn't: this was the real Olive right here, the Olive that I knew, and she was maternal and domestic and soft.

My sister and I leant on the windowsill and stared out at Phillip, sitting cross-legged in the grown-over dent of our swimming pool, a vast oblong in the middle of the lawn, like the relic of a long-forgotten UFO landing. One side of it was shaded by the corrugated-iron roof of their garage, jaggedy and orange with rust around its edges, and on the other side a mass of fruit bushes – redcurrants, gooseberries and raspberries. Phillip's face was paler than ever, set still and smooth like a milk pudding. I gave him a double thumbs-up, pressing my thumbs against the window pane, but he didn't notice. He just sat there, with his mouth gaping open, as if his batteries had run out.

'He doesn't look like he's thinking to me,' said my sister.

'He's in shock,' explained my mother. 'It's a lot to take in.'

'I'm trying to tempt him back in with cheese,' Olive said. 'Nice bit of Red Leicester on a Tuc biscuit, that might do the trick.' She cocked her head towards a smoke-coloured glass plate on the windowsill.

Olive was at sixes and sevens with her bowels since the baby, she told my mother. She was bunged up still and there'd been no success toilet-wise for days.

'God. Sick. I'm never going to get pregnant, are you?' whispered my sister, mock vomiting behind Olive's sofa.

'I think some roughage would help,' said my mother, one of her own mother's favourite words. Roughage sounded unpleasantly unappetizing to me, whatever it was: brown and scratchy and difficult to swallow, like the sisal carpet in our bedroom.

*

An hour later, and we were sitting outside Roughage Central –
The Happy Pear – Katherine and me, with Phillip sandwiched in
between us. Refreshers had turned him around in the end; it was
the sweets always that did it. We crunched our way through them
– chalkily fizzy – on the steps by the shop, while inside our
mothers discussed the merits of figs versus linseed with Anthony.

We were under strict instructions from Olive to hold on tight
to Phillip. 'Just give us a shout, will you,' she said, 'if he looks
like he's going to go off on one.' I was honoured that she trusted
me, but it was daunting all the same, the responsibility of sitting
with a gently hyperventilating Phillip Brown by a busy main road.
Traffic roared past our feet, bathing us all in soft, warm clouds of
fumes. I pictured Phillip breaking free, skedaddling across the
road in and out of the juggernauts, and panting off and away
towards the fire station: his failsafe destination of choice whenever he had a panic in Big Town. He wanted to be a fireman when
he grew up, he told us – something exciting and heroic like that
– successfully re-imagining his personality in one statement.

'I don't like it here, I don't,' he said, with the quiet, flat under-
statement that I'd come to recognize concealed a rising, soon to
be uncontrollable panic. In his head I knew he would be
shouting, 'I hate it here! I'm going to wet my pants! I'm going to
stop breathing! Help me!'

'They won't be long now,' I said, taking one of his sweaty
palms in mine. It was slippery and slick like an eel. He tried to
wriggle it free, and I clutched it as tight as I was able, as I caught
my sister's eye over his head. She gave me a stretchy-mouthed
'Don't ask me' look, shrugged her shoulders, and glanced
towards The Happy Pear, where our mothers were fully
ensconced. I could see Olive waving her hands about delightedly
in the window, Kerry strapped to her chest, throwing her head

back with laughter; she was only getting started, you could tell.

Progress had been made with Phillip, of sorts. He didn't mind coming to Big Town these days; the sound of cars no longer frightened him, for one thing, which was good. Still, he wasn't immune to the odd flip-out once in a while; and if he was going to turn, it would be right here, I knew, in this particular part of the street, with the doctor's surgery and the chemist's shop opposite. Anything medical made Phillip agitated.

My sister and I thought a visit to the chemist's was a treat; it sold sugar-free whistle lollies and hair clips and bobbles that hung from a spinning display. Phillip, though, noticed only the packets of pills, the ointments and plasters: reminders of illness and pain. You could get ill at any time, he said, any one of us could, and there was nothing you could do to stop it. He'd bolted from every medical appointment he'd had: doctors and dentists alike, emboldened by the horror of an impending injection, convinced as he was that any treatment would involve a needle. His terror lent him uncharacteristic speed and strength, enough to propel him out of the surgery and send him wailing down the High Street, out of town, towards the refuge of the fire station, with Olive in furious, steaming pursuit. If Olive blamed my sister and her past life as a nurse, she never mentioned it, as far as I knew. Phillip had got used to being told he was sick and the diagnosis had never been good – 'Look at you, *you're so ill!*' my sister would say before mending him with some spit or a spud gun.

The uniform and games were long gone; even so, Phillip still viewed my sister with a reverence that really grated with me. He was six months older than she was, and I had a full year and a half on him, so it disrupted the natural order of things, that's what I thought: he should be looking up, not down. Definitely not down.

Olive had bribed Phillip to stay put with a promise of a visit to the General Stores, a shop of wonder and delight, further on up the High Street next to Evans the Butcher's.

'Sit tight with the girls and I'll get you a toy, a little something when we're done, okay?' she'd said, patting the stone step as if it was a comfy treat to sit on, and then pressing a white paper bag of sherbet pips into Phillip's hand. To hear that – the easy, casual promise of a toy to a child who wasn't me – always used to make me sick with envy, but nothing happened now. I didn't want a toy. I didn't want any toys. How could that be? I was eleven now, so it was as it should be, but the suddenness of the change made sweat prick my palms.

A man called Bryn Williams ran the General Stores. He was a solitary, shy man in his forties who still lived with his mother and his sister, which we weren't to think was right, was loosely the general consensus. Even though he'd owned a shop on the High Street for the last ten years – and a useful, heavily frequented one at that – he'd managed nonetheless to remain determinedly apart from everyone, separate from local society, which, given the way he mumbled and stuttered and blushed his way through every transaction, was probably just the way he wanted it. It didn't sit right in general, though, a shopkeeper not being a friend to all: it made people feel ill at ease, and so the failing, if that's what it was – the failure to connect – must be his, not anyone else's. He was an oddball, not right in the head, and there were murkier mutterings still; and if proof were needed of his outsider status, his name alone was the glaring reminder. Had he been held in any affection at all, he'd have been known as 'Williams the Stores' by now, or something like it, but he was only ever known formally, as Bryn Williams, first name and surname never parted.

From a distance, or in the dim, shadowy depths of his shop,

he looked a little like Clark Kent. Close up, sadly, he was nothing like him. He was pallid and a bit doughy-looking, with not even the faintest promise of a superhero about him; but he had the glasses – thick and black-rimmed – which magnified his eyes to comedy, cartoon proportions, making him look perky and surprisingly wide-eyed for the brief second that he looked at you before fixing his stare to the floor.

Inside his shop, the ceiling-to-floor shelves were filled to bursting, and secreted here and there, in among the egg cups and the scouring pads and every size of battery you could ever need, was a huge selection of plastic toys, all the more precious and desirable-looking against the backdrop of all that perfunctory, workaday hardware.

The only clue to Bryn Williams' character could be found in his shop window: it was an ongoing work of art, which changed every week. No one ever saw him do it, so we all assumed he must work through the dead of night. This week he'd dressed mops and brushes in floral swimming hats, with light bulbs for eyes and lace curtains for dresses, and lined them up like models in the window.

'Look by there, will you?' Phillip was edging up on to the step above and gesturing towards Commerce House. 'Is that Wiggy, is it?' he asked, straining his head above the upper pavement to get a better look.

It was too. There he was, leaning on the paint-flaked windowsill of Commerce House, blinking in the bright sunshine. We watched as he tucked his stringy hair behind his ears and shuffled around in his tiny little Indian mirrored bag for cigarette papers, holding each one up to the sky to check for the strip of glue.

'Oi! Wiggy!' shouted Phillip, making me bow my head with

shame. For the most part Phillip was painfully shy with adults, but with the odd person he was unexpectedly, overtly confident. Wiggy, inexplicably, was one of them.

I didn't want Wiggy to see me. My father had had a row with him the other night; I knew because I'd heard it from the top of the stairs. My father said 'bullshit' a lot when he was angry, and I couldn't hear if Wiggy was swearing too, because he kept his voice level and calm. My father was asking him questions – I could just about make that out, as I hung over the banisters – I could hear the lilt, the word rising higher at the end of the sentence, and whatever Wiggy murmured in reply, no matter what, my father just shouted 'Bullshit!'

Wiggy looked up from sticking his papers together and grinned and waved at an empty street.

'I'm here, aren't I?' shouted Phillip, through his cupped-hand megaphone. 'It's Phil, isn't it! Down here, look!'

Wiggy looked around again, but still he didn't see him. He took a step forward, and swayed gently above us. 'Who is that then? Have you got a light?' he said, and his voice sounded sticky, like treacle. He took another unsteady step forward, and he wavered as if he was being buffeted by non-existent wind.

Then his knees buckled beneath him. And he fell face down on to the pavement.

In my memory he fell in slow motion, floated to the ground, like a slowed-down sequence in an action film, which made the crunch – the sickening sound of flesh and bone hitting tarmac – come from nowhere, and made me leap up in the air with the shock of it.

All three of us shouted out, but it was Phillip who jumped to his feet, ran up the steps and was bending down over Wiggy as my sister and I sat there, rooted to the steps.

'You all right there, Wig?' he said. 'Come on now, there, there.' He'd turned him over by the time we got to him, and pulled his head on to his knee. We watched Wiggy's eyes flutter open and shut.

'You got any tissue, Kath?' asked Phillip. My sister nodded and handed over a scrumpled length of loo roll, streaked with dirt, from her dungaree bib pocket.

'Go on then, spit on it, will you?' ordered Phillip. She did, and he took it back and laid it over the cut on Wiggy's forehead. 'There, there now, mate,' he said, 'don't worry, will you? All okay now – we'll sort you out in no time.'

Wiggy didn't look worried. He was grinning, a super-wide, teeth-revealing grin, which didn't make sense when he had a huge, grit-covered gash pumping blood out all over his forehead. Froth had gathered around his mouth, bubbling white as if he had a mouthful of toothpaste, and he carried on grinning, even when he started twitching, convulsing on the pavement as if he was holding on to an electric fence.

'Go and get Mam now, will you, Ab?' said Phillip. It was the first thing he'd ever asked me to do, and it was in a voice that didn't sound like his, so it felt odd, but I did it straight away. I picked my way up the narrow steps, past Wiggy, into The Happy Pear and shouted as loud as I could.

23

Big school

I was going to go to the same secondary school as Lisa Evans.

'That's brilliant, Ab!' she said, when I told her in the back of the 2CV. '*Just me and you*,' she said, as my mother reversed out of the school car park. 'Thank God we're not going to Bala. I'd hate that, wouldn't you?' she asked, as the car stalled and my mother said, 'Shit! Shit! Shit!'

Mr Roberts leant out of the staff-room window and started beckoning her out. 'Oh shit,' she said, 'here we go. I'm okay!' she shouted out of the window. 'It's all right – I can do this, I'm fine!'

'Poor buggers, the rest of them,' Lisa went on. 'I feel sorry for them, don't you? Bala's cach, that's what my mam says, and she should know, she went there and all.'

We drove on to the main road from the green. The car tipped right, and my face was pressed up against the window by Lisa's voluminous padded coat. It was brand-new, bought especially for big school; white, with fur around the hood which honest to God came from a real-life rabbit, she said, and she swore on her brother's life, crossed her heart and hoped to die, as we swung along the winding roads towards my house, glimpses of glittering blue river flashing through holes in the hedge.

'I know tons of people at the school already, I do,' said Lisa, leaning down to buff up her already shiny, grown-up-looking shoes with a tissue from her very own packet in her pocket. 'Do you?' she asked, scrunching the tissue up and – before I could stop her – shoving it through the jaggedy hole in the floor of the car, out on to the streaking tarmac below. I watched it in the wing mirror, tumbling away, unfurling and lifting off up over the hedgerows: dazzling white against the cloudless sky, a ball of fear knotting in my stomach.

'You know Nell from Commerce House, don't you, Abs?' said my mother, turning round to face us, sending the car veering to the middle of the road. 'She goes there now.'

Nell had finally got her own way. She'd been nagging Wiggy and Maya for ages to let her go to school. She'd beaten them down – she was good at beating down: she'd cajoled and debated and laid out pros and cons on a chart, she said – until they'd said yes just to shut her up. She'd gone in then a whole year above. 'There you go! I can't have done such a bad job, can I now?' Maya said. 'That's the proof!'

'I know her a bit,' I said. 'Not very well.'

'So you know about her dad then, do you?' asked Lisa.

And I thought of Wiggy lying there frothing and jerking about on the pavement of the High Street. I'd had nightmares about that afternoon. In my dream Wiggy died right there in front of us, with his head in Phillip's arms. I'd sat bolt upright when it came to that, and screamed out for my mum. 'There there,' she'd said, 'just calm,' and she'd stroke my hair. 'He didn't die, he's better now,' she said.

'Wiggy's gone to prison,' said Lisa. 'Did you know that?' and she smiled when I shook my head, because she knew something that I didn't, and that always made her happy. 'He got three years for dealing.'

'Dealing what?' I asked.

'Don't ask me,' she said, with a shrug, 'but that's what my dad said, all right?'

'Thank you, Lisa,' said my mother, with a flat, warning edge to her voice.

'Is that true?' I said.

'He did a very silly thing,' said my mother. 'I'll talk about it with you later, when your father's home.' I could hear my heart beating in my chest, thudding like a giant's footsteps. *People only went to prison in films.*

'And do you know Daffyd Davies?' said Lisa. 'My dad says he's a junkie, and that's down to Wiggy and all.'

'What's a junkie?' I asked.

'Idiot, I think,' said Lisa, and my mother let out a long, strangulated-sounding noise, and gripped the steering wheel so tight you could see her knucklebones poking white through her skin.

'Lisa,' she said in a brand-new, bright, wide-awake voice, 'you know lots of people at your new secondary school, don't you? Why don't you tell us about them?'

'Yeah. Tons. You can meet some of them, Ab, if you like,' she offered, huffing out her breath on to the window and squeaking the outline of a heart with an arrow through it in the ready-made condensation.

We were friends with a criminal. That was all I could think. We could be arrested too, just for knowing him.

'I've got my cousins there, haven't I?' Lisa continued. 'Kerys in second year, and Bryn and Stefan in third. They said they'll look out for me.' We were climbing the hill towards our house now, wheels skidding on the disintegrating tarmac, past Colwyn's house, past the monkey-puzzle tree in his front garden.

'That's good,' I said. *Wiggy was locked up in a cell.*

'Look, girls – curlews!' said my mother, pointing towards one of Colwyn's fields, swerving the car towards the hedge and then back again on to the other side of the road. In the far distance I could see their hunched silhouettes, hooked beaks down, as they picked their long legs through the marshland at the back of the field, and I watched them weaving in and out of the marsh marigolds – bright yellow and super-sized like giant buttercups.

On the first day of big school my mother drove me to town where the bus would come. The bus stop was outside The Old Mill, a big, damp-looking centre dedicated to the crafts. She stalled to a bouncing halt on the other side of the road, opposite the empty forecourt, where the tea shop was. Inside, the strip-lights were on already, casting their pale blue glow on to the plastic-covered counter, where there would be stale, raisin-dotted scones and icing-coated slices filled with custard that had gone crusty round the edges. On the pavement in front of the tea shop was a small crowd of children, all of them older-looking than me, watching me without expression from under their fringes; heads bent to one side as though they'd cricked their necks, as they leant, slumped, against the railings.

I stayed put for a second, searching for Lisa in amongst the sea of black. Matthew was right: it was Harringtons and donkey jackets all the way when you got to secondary school; it didn't matter, it was all the same – pretty much everyone was mad about Harringtons, he'd said. I asked if I could see his, but he didn't actually have one; they weren't his thing at all, he'd said. He only wore a denim jacket, but not one with rock bands' logos stitched all over: his was plain and fitted – Western style. So I had a Harrington now too, thanks to Matthew, and I was grateful to him – my first piece of black clothing – and he'd even shown me how to wear it: only half zipped up so that you could still see the tartan lining.

On the seat next to me was my nana and poppa's present. 'Something special,' Nana had said, 'to make you feel a bit grown up.'

'I can't see anyone else with briefcases, can you?' I asked.

'No,' said my mother, 'you're right.'

I'd leave it here for today, I said, as I returned my mother's kiss with a covert tip of my head, and shoved the car door, once and then a second time, with my elbow, until it burst open and I tipped out on to the road. As I waited to cross, I caught sight of Lisa at the back of the crowd, standing straight and stiff and glaringly white, with her hood pulled up, the fluff around the collar blowing in the breeze.

Nell was standing next to her, almost unrecognizable now, with bosoms and make-up, and earrings: she looked about sixteen at least. Her hair was shorter and blonder too, and was flicked like Princess Diana's.

'Hiya, Ab! All right?' said Lisa, and she broke into a smile – a proper smile that revealed all her teeth, white and straight and perfectly even.

'Go on then, Abbie, smell my mouth, will you?' said Nell, puckering up her lips, which were coated in a glassy sheen, as if she'd just eaten a giant saveloy sausage and forgotten to wipe her mouth. 'It's Coca-Cola flavour, can you tell?' she said. I caught a waft of it and it smelled sweet and artificially delicious.

'Sorry about your dad,' I said.

'What about him?' she said, and her arms were crossed and she was looking at me, challenging me for more.

'Prison,' was all I could say.

'Shut up about it, okay?' she said. 'It doesn't matter. Forget it.'

'Here it is!' someone shouted from the back, and we were pushed from all sides then, squeezed up in the middle of a swell and carried forward in a scuffle of feet right to the edge of the pavement, as the bus appeared, colossally white, lurching around the corner.

The doors fizzed back to reveal the driver. 'Hiya all,' he said, swiping a hand through his white nicotine-tinged hair. 'Easy now. Come on, steady as you go – watch yourself, will you?' He lit up a cigarette as the crowd poured up the steps, grunting and shoving forwards in the desperate, unspoken battle to be the first to the back of the bus.

I looked at Lisa, and waited for her to lead the way, but she stayed put on the edge of the pavement until it was just the two of us outside the bus, with an audience: a row of teenagers, all looking down at us from their seats. I took her by her padded white sleeve and pulled her up the steps, and we took the only double seat left, right behind the driver.

'Good!' I said, and I looked at Lisa; her eyes looked especially shiny and I wondered if she was trying not to cry. Neither of us spoke as we watched the craft centre retreating in the wing mirror, until we swung left round a bend and it was gone.

All around us, the strangers settled in. Behind us jokes were shared as coats were flung carelessly on to the backs of seats; bags were unzipped and packed lunches set on knees.

'What you got in there then?'

'Let's have a look. Two Mars Bars, packet of crisps – plain ones, rubbish – orange Panda pop and cheese sandwich, disgusting.'

'I'll do swapsies if you like: a Mars Bar for my Topic. I can't stand nuts, I keep saying to my mam, but she won't believe me, will she?'

Crisps packets were popped undone and their contents crunched through conversations; wrappers were ripped apart and chocolate bars pushed into mouths like blenders, disposed of, magically, in seconds. Cans hissed open and pop glugged down in one, and burped back up again, as the bus weaved along the valley, along the precipitous road sliced into the edge of a mountain, towards the big new school.

We reached the outskirts of the big town and drove alongside a canal edged with bright-coloured barges, and then on to the High Street: a line of white houses with black-painted windows and fudge shops with signs saying Wall's ice-cream. I thought of Sara, and Eleanor Williams, on their bus journey to Bala. Wendy had gone back to Manchester now, and I pictured her too, in her burgundy uniform and her newly bobbed hair, walking to her school for girls.

The bus strained around a corner and the school rose into view. Another corner then, and the whole sprawling mass of it was revealed: vast, flat-roofed concrete buildings scattered all over the side of a hill. I thought of my old school, with its swings and its pointy, old-fashioned roof. It was too babyish for me now, and too small for someone almost teenaged like me.

Bags were repacked as the bus climbed the hill. The sandwiches, the worst bit, examined: white sliced bread peeled back to check the filling and then shoved back in for later. We jerked to a stop outside the main gates, and children kicked their way along the aisle, through the mass of discarded packaging – chocolate wrappers and panda pop cartons, cling film and foil – and streamed towards the open doors. I grabbed Lisa's hand and pulled her up, and we trailed after them, the last ones on and off.

Teachers led us along walkways, and we crossed through

yard after yard, to where our classrooms were: a row of three identical Portacabins, mine at one end and Lisa's right at the other.

'See you at breaktime then – meet me right here, won't you?' said Lisa, her first words since we'd got on the bus, and briefly, clumsily, she grabbed at my hand and gave it a hurried squeeze. 'Take care,' she said, and she rushed to catch up with the back of her crowd, filing away without her.

I was in my new classroom: me and thirty other children, whose names I didn't know.

'My name is Mr Williams,' said the teacher, pointing to the blackboard where his name was written to prove it. '*Croeso.* Welcome,' he said, the flatness of his voice making me feel not one bit. He wiped a hand across his jumper, which had geometric lines in shades of grey with a V neck and a tie underneath: sort of John Craven clothes, but nowhere near as good.

'Well. There we are,' he continued. 'Let's introduce ourselves, shall we? I want each of you to tell me your name and your date of birth,' and he pointed to a girl in the front.

'Joanne Davies, fifteenth of the sixth, nineteen seventy,' she said.

I could hear my breath going in and out: extra loud and fast. I knew when my birthday was, but my date of birth said in numbers meant nothing to me at all. I thought about bolting before he got to me: running out of the door, through the endless concrete playgrounds, to the canal; and I was just wondering how I'd get home from there when silence brought me back, and Mr Williams was looking at me, chins pulled into his neck.

'Well?'

I told him my name.

'And?' he said, turning his palms upwards. 'Your date of birth?'

I stared down at the floor, at the khaki-coloured carpet tiles. They were worn threadbare in patches and covered all over in stains.

'What. Month. Were. You. Born?' he asked, pronouncing his words laboriously slowly, as if he were pushing each one through a sieve.

'May,' I said.

'So. Where does May come in the months of the year?'

I didn't know, I said.

He let out a half-hearted-sounding laugh, and started chanting the months of the year, expecting me to join him, and when I didn't he slowed to a stop and shook his head, before looking over my head and pointing to the person behind.

'Gaynor Jones, third of the fourth, nineteen seventy,' she said, as fast as possible to highlight the straightforward ease of it, and she turned round then and gave me a wink.

At home time I walked down the hill with Gaynor. She was funny and she liked Kim Wilde: 'Kids in America' was the best song ever, she said. She thought I was funny too. 'That was brilliant,' she said, 'when you took the piss out of Mr Williams with your date of birth. Classic! I reckon he believed you and all, don't you?'

The tall wall above the canal was where everyone waited for their buses to come. I pulled myself up and gave Gaynor a hitch, and we sat there looking down at the road curving up the hillside, and the town spreading out beyond it. More children swarmed down the hill towards us, spilling out from the gates; and Lisa appeared amongst them, head bobbing in the crowd, zigzagging in and out of everyone as she ran down to where I was sitting.

'Hiya, Ab,' she said. 'Phew! Knackered, I am!' She was breathless and pink-cheeked from running, and she leant on the wall and stared down into the water. She had a Co-op plastic bag in one hand, and her coat was in it, crammed in, one padded sleeve bursting out at a right angle, as if it was trying to break free and clamber out.

'What happened to your coat?'

'Nothing,' she said, shooting me a narrow-eyed stare. 'I got too hot, didn't I?', the goosebumps on her arms betraying her.

Directly underneath us the canal ran alongside the wall, discreet and silent and oddly still. The water was dotted with pools of petrol, shimmering islands of green and purple decorating the surface of the sludge-brown water. A red-and-blue chocolate wrapper hung suspended, rotating in the breeze, and I watched as a moorhen picked its way towards the water's edge on bandy knock-kneed legs. Our bus was arriving now, the ground vibrating as it climbed the hill, and the moorhen gave a nervous glance upwards and slipped gracefully into the water, navigating its way stiffly around the litter before disappearing off into the distance.

24

I'll be there now in a min

It was nearly suppertime. Katherine and I were sitting at the kitchen table pretending to finish our homework, and my parents were going to tell us something we wouldn't like, I could tell. My father was just loitering, leaning against the fridge, trying to look casual, with his arms and his legs crossed; but he didn't look casual at all. He looked awkward, like if he stayed that way much longer he might just tip over and fall flat on the floor. That's how he stood, though, chatting to my mother, and they had a squished-up, weedy kind of conversation, as if there was a much bigger, heavier one inside their heads, pressing down on everything they said. Their voices were sing-song high and pretend jovial, like children's television presenters, and this made me feel uncomfortable, because Sara Fiddick had told me once in front of Rhys Prichard that my dad looked like he should be a presenter on *Magpie*. She'd tried to make it sound like a compliment, but you only had to watch it to see that it wasn't. The men on *Magpie* had wild, sticky-up, curly hair just like his, and wore huge flappy flares, so he'd fit right in, I know that's what she meant. I'd gone bright red, and she'd laughed, and worse still Rhys Prichard had put his arm round me and said, 'Hey, look at you! Don't look so upset there, Ab, will you?' and that had made me go even redder, because I didn't want him to think that I had emotions. I wanted him to think of me as someone who wasn't touched by anything, least of all the state of their dad's hair.

'It's the *television*,' my sister whispered. 'They're getting rid of it, I reckon.'

'They can't!'

'They're grown-ups, they can do what they like,' she said, scribbling out a sum.

'But . . . what about *Dynasty*?'

'I know,' she said with a shrug, 'we won't find out now if Krystle really does leave Blake.'

I drew a fingernail across the soft wooden surface of the kitchen table, up and down, back and forth, marking line after line: a crosshatched memento of my fury.

'Right! It's ready,' said my mother, still shrill, as she flapped across the kitchen in her culottes. She put the plates down in front of us. 'A treat supper for you today!'

And it was – our dream meal, in fact, made entirely from packets and jars. Frozen scampi with chips and chopped-up gherkins on the side – tartare without the sauce. Pudding was going to be Arctic Roll, she said. Our favourite food, all in one go, and it wasn't even anyone's birthday.

We crunched our way through the scorching-hot scampi, and I was finessing the speech in my head, about the worth of Noel's *Swap Shop*, when my father cleared his throat and leant forward and put both his hands on the table as if he was the president of the United States, or JR Ewing or someone big and important like that. He made a growling noise and said, 'Girls,' and then he stopped, and my mother gave him a little nod and he started up again and just said, 'Girls.'

We stopped crunching. It was a noisy meal, all of it crunchy, even the chips, which were the oven kind and slightly overcooked.

He cleared his throat. 'Girls. We're going to move house.'

I don't know what my sister was thinking, but I thought that he *still* looked awkward, even more so. He was leaning too far forward, and his hands had gone all red with the pressure of it, and I wondered how he would right himself without the help of my mother pulling him up, which would be embarrassing for all of us.

'Will we be taking the telly?' asked my sister.

'What?' he said. '*Yes*, but what I'm saying is: we're going to be *moving*. We're going to leave North Wales.'

I looked down at my plate. One of my gherkins hadn't been chopped up, and I put it in whole and chomped, as he cleared his throat again.

'I'm so sorry,' he said. 'You don't know how hard it's been to make this decision,' and his voice cracked, and I had to look down at the floor, just in case; I'd never want to see him upset. 'I just need to be nearer London,' he went on, 'that's all,' and his voice ran out altogether then and trailed off into a whisper.

The tartness of the vinegar hit the back of my throat, and the weight of his words slammed like a fist into my chest, and I started to cry – both of us did – great, heaving, shoulder-juddering sobs. *Everything was going to be lost.*

My mother crouched down between us and gave us soft assurances and hugged us, as we wailed and carried on eating, noses running into the bright orange breadcrumbs, and the whole meal, all that extra-special food, was wasted then.

It wouldn't happen, that's what I said; they'd never find a house. They couldn't find a place that was better than this; it didn't exist. They should go and check themselves into Denbigh nuthouse – I said that, and they didn't even tell me off, they just nodded and said nothing, making everything – the whole world – feel off kilter.

Later, when I should have been asleep, my mother juddered open my bedroom door, forcing it over the carpet with a vigorous shove of her shoulder, holding a glass of wine up high, as if to steady it somehow against spillage.

'We should have got that fixed – we never did, did we?' she said, and she smiled and gave a little sigh of a laugh, and I felt sick because she'd said it past tense.

'We still could,' I said, 'take a bit off the bottom of the door, I mean,' as she sat down by the window on the little nursing chair that we'd had since I was born.

Even with the curtains drawn and just the bedside light on, I could see her eyes looked pink and puffed up. I thought of Sara's grey rabbit, Misty. His eyes had gone like that just before he died of myxomatosis. We made him a little gravestone out of a slate roof tile, and scraped on RIP with a nail. Sara loved that rabbit more than her whole family and everyone she knew put together, she said – which offended me a bit: even for a rabbit he was boring – but she still didn't cry when we buried him.

My mother leant forward and pulled back a curtain, and I watched her light a cigarette: inhale, and then exhale a pinky-lilac flume of smoke into the dusk. She sat back and took a sip of her wine. She looked beautiful, even with puffed-up eyes. My mother didn't smoke like everyone else; she stuck to two a day at the most: early evening usually, when she was on the phone. I'd sit on the stairs sometimes and listen in on her, laughing, relaying stories, exchanging confidences with friends, and I'd feel a pang of jealousy. *I wanted to be let in.* Now, she'd brought the wine and the cigarettes to my bedroom, and more than anything I felt absurdly flattered. She thought I was someone to talk to as an equal now – that's how I took it – and she was right: I *was* grown up. I had a poster of The Police above my bed and would have my ears pierced tomorrow – double studs in each – if I could.

'I'm so sorry, Abs,' she said. 'I don't want to leave any more than you do, I really don't.' She was blinking extra fast and I could see her eyes were shiny with held-back tears.

'Well, don't then,' I said, rolling over towards the spare bed – my sister's old bed when we used to share – and I heard her padding barefoot across the carpet then towards me, and she sat down on my bed.

'All things must pass,' she murmured, stroking my hair. 'Nothing can stay the same for ever, you know that, don't you?' and it felt like my heart shrank: squeezed tight with shock when she said it. 'Do you remember how Commerce House used to be, years ago?' she asked, tucking a stray strand of hair behind her ear. 'It was such a happy, creative place, do you remember that? How lovely it was?'

I tried to, but no, nothing lovely sprang to mind; still, I nodded because she looked so sad.

'Well . . . it's *different* there now,' she said. 'No one makes things there these days, not really.'

I thought of the psychedelic planet painting hanging in our hall, and my father's brown open-toed sandals made by Wiggy, the basket Maya had woven for my mother that rolled over to one side, and thought maybe that wasn't such a bad thing.

'Can I ask you something?' she said. Yes, I said, yes! Delighted that she'd asked me like that, like she'd ask a friend, not me, her eleven-year-old daughter. 'Do you know why Wiggy went to prison?' She smoothed down my patchwork quilt.

I didn't. I'd asked her, often, but she'd brushed me off each time, just shoved that one to the back of the drawer: he'd been bad, she'd said, he'd done a silly thing; which was a stupid thing to say – clowns did silly things, I said, not people who went to prison – but she'd change the subject, she'd do something to distract me, and it was always so cringingly obvious what she was doing that I'd go red and I'd shut up then, embarrassed for her as much as me. I never stopped wondering why he was there, though.

'Budge up,' she said, and I moved over and she propped herself up on my pillow.

She told me about heroin then.

I pretended that I'd heard of it. I nodded slowly, and tried not to look surprised, *sickened*, that anyone, *an adult*, would do that to themselves.

'Do you remember Daffyd Davies?' she asked.

Yes, I said, I did.

'It's so awful,' she said. 'I met his mother in Gwalia and she's just devastated. He's only seventeen.'

'What?' I asked.

'He's going to prison,' she explained, 'for dealing – can you believe it? He's clever! He should have been going to university,' and she got up and opened my bedroom window. 'We need some fresh air – you should always sleep with the windows open,' she said.

I looked up at her, waiting for her to say more, but she was looking down at my quilt now, not me, as if she were ashamed, or embarrassed, or it was in some way all her fault.

'We thought, with Wiggy at least, that he was just dabbling,' she said. 'We thought it would just be a phase. We're optimists, Dad and I; we're similar in that way, which makes me wonder if we've been quite naïve,' and the way she said it made it almost sound like a question, as if she wanted my opinion, and I loved her for that, even though I didn't have one: I just loved that she thought that I did.

'I think we're fairly open-minded,' she went on, 'but there were some choices friends were making that I suppose we just couldn't reconcile ourselves with. Do you understand what I mean?' And the absurdity of that question, *aimed at me*, took me by surprise and I laughed. Years of yearning for a conventional life, and I didn't want it now: not if it meant leaving North Wales. *All things didn't have to pass.* I could stay here, in my peachy-orange bedroom, just like this, with my mother hugging me, and smelling of fresh grass and honeysuckle: like summer.

'It's hard to understand, when you know how much we love it here, but everything just feels a little tainted now, can you see?' she said, addressing the poster of John Travolta above my dressing table, and he looked back at her, all wide blue eyes, as if he understood her absolutely, not like me. She shook her head, as though she was arguing with herself: 'We just think it's time to move on.'

We were left with Olive then, once a week or so, as my mother drove to Gloucestershire, or Worcestershire, or Hampshire, to view a rival house, just a little nearer London, with a disappointing garden, or a too dark, poky kitchen, or a view that included a sewerage.

My nana rang up all the time, hungrily taking in every detail, like a detective, as if she was Cagney from *Cagney & Lacey*. Every shortfall of every house confirmed to her that there was nowhere as lovely to live as Liverpool.

'Well, that's Worcester for you, Anna, I'm not sure what you expected. Poky place and small-minded people as well. Didn't I say, Les? Aren't they, Les? The people? That tournament, do you remember?'

She wanted to keep us close: that was the driving force behind all her hard work.

'I've signed up with the agents, Anna. I'm sending you through details about a fabulous house in Kirkby. It's got electric gates and a swimming pool, if you can believe it, in the basement.'

My sister and I would watch my mother's orange 2CV disappearing off down the hill from Olive's kitchen window, baby Kerry waving her off, smiling a wet, gummy smile of encouragement.

'Is it me?' said Olive. 'Everyone's upping sticks! There'll be no one left before I know it.'

Maya and Nell were leaving too. They were going to London. We heard Maya telling Olive when we were in Phillip's dining room: Phillip, my sister and me. Maya and Nell were in the room next door, in Olive's kitchen, waiting to have their hair cut, and the serving-hatch doors were wide open so we could hear every word, and peek in too if we wanted.

'It's the right thing to do, Maya, definitely,' said Olive. 'There, there now, come on. Hang on a sec. Oh dear, let me get you a little tissue,' and there was silence, then a trumpeting blow.

'Do you think?' asked Maya. 'Oh God, Olive, I just don't know,' and we could hear her crying then – really sobbing now – and my sister and Phillip and I all looked at each other and froze, mortified: for her, as well as us. An adult crying was only ever embarrassing and wrong; it turned everything upside down.

'It's terrible for you, my love, just terrible,' said Olive, and her voice was soft and cooing and it made me want to sidle on in there and have a cuddle. 'I don't know what I'd do – *God* knows what I'd do – if it was Mike,' she said, and Maya started giggling then.

'Can you imagine?' she said. 'Mike, dealing drugs! I can't quite see it, can you?'

Olive hooted. 'No! Nettle wine, maybe. Not illegal, but so blimmin' strong it might as well be,' and they both started laughing then.

'Do you know what's going to cheer you up?' said Olive. 'A nice new haircut. It works every time. Trust me.'

Olive cut hair for a living now. She'd put an advert up in the Gwalia shop: 'Semi-professional mobile hairdresser', it read; which wasn't strictly true. What was the point in all that training, she said, when you could teach yourself for free? She put the mobile bit in so clients would think she was a flexible and adaptable person, she said; though really she preferred it if people came to her kitchen, where she knew the tea would always be spot on, and the biscuits would never run out.

The Browns' dining room was a games room really. There was a pool table in the middle, and a dartboard on the back of the door, and that was it. Phillip tried to tell us he was a champion pool player – the trophies in the cabinet in the sitting room were all his, he said, honest to God – but you only had to watch him sprawled inelegantly half on, half off the table, thwacking the balls everywhere but the pockets, to know it was all rubbish: he didn't really have the first clue.

'Hats off to you, Maya, I say,' said Olive, as my sister handed me the cue. 'How can you stay here? Why would you want to, after that? Stupid man, honestly, what a stupid man,' and I craned in towards the hatch so I could see what Maya thought of that. She was actually nodding and smiling – a half smile though – which made her look sad, rather than happy: sad and tired and spent.

'I still love him, though,' she said, as Olive unwrapped the towel on her head. 'Isn't that mad? I still love the bastard. Bet I always will too.'

'Of course you do,' said Olive. 'That's Wiggy. We all love him, don't we?'

And Maya just nodded, and her mouth had turned downwards like a camel's, and it wobbled as she tried to keep the crying inside.

'Now then, come on,' said Olive. 'How much do you want off? I was thinking of a little light feathering around the fringe, just to give it a lift, you know.'

'Chop it all off!' said Maya, as Nell passed her a ready-lit roll-up. 'Seriously, just go for it.' Her cigarette wiggled up and down in her mouth as Olive scrubbed her scalp dry. 'Go on!' said Maya. 'Wiggy liked it long, so it's two fingers up to him!'

'Are you sure about that?' asked Olive. 'You just might regret it, that's what I'm saying. Perhaps have a little think about it first?'

'I've thought about it. Done. New life: new haircut. Go for it.'

I could catch a glimpse of Nell if I pressed my cheek tight against the wall. She was perched on the sideboard, reading a book by the looks of it, but half listening in: nodding along, murmuring once in a while in agreement.

'Goal!' Phillip shouted, as a ball rolled into the pocket.

London had been Nell's idea, Maya said, beaming proudly across at her when she said it. She'd heard about a school, and she'd looked into it all by herself. She'd sent off for the scholarship forms, sorted it all out, she said, as Olive snip-snipped below her ears. Wiggy's parents were going to help them out. She hadn't asked them, they'd insisted; they were going to let them live rent-free in their London pied-à-terre.

'I'm going to be an entrepreneur now, what do you think of that?' Maya said, and I smiled and thought of my nana and poppa, as she talked about the shop she was going to open in

Carnaby Street. No communes now, she said, no dilly-dallying about.

'Your turn, Nell, come on,' said Olive, brushing off the cut bits of hair from Maya's shoulders.

'God, now would you take a look at that!' said Olive, and even Phillip crowded to the hatch then and we stood poking our heads through the shiny, peach-coloured doors. 'I've done a lovely job, if I do say so myself,' she sighed, leaning back to admire Maya's new bob. 'It's taken years off you, just like that.'

'Is it meant to be like that?' asked Nell. 'Longer on one side than the other?'

'Definitely,' said Olive, hands clasped under her bosoms, 'absolutely, Nell, that's à la mode, I'd thought you'd know. You need to know these things if you're moving to a fancy-pants pied-à-terre in Kensington, don't you know.'

'Well, you can keep mine straight, if that's okay,' she said.

My sister decided she wanted her hair cut when Olive had finished with Nell; and Nell and I waited together outside, leaning against the railings at the front.

'I miss Wiggy,' Nell said, smoothing down her new hair in the reflection of the kitchen window. 'Is it wonky, do you think?'

'Maybe, just a bit,' I said.

'He's not bad, you know, I don't want you to think he was bad.'

'I don't,' I said, which was a bit of a lie: bad people in prison made sense.

'He's just a big, soft kid really; he needs looking after, that's all,' she said, head tipped to one side. 'Does it look more even if I do that?' and I watched as she walked down the path to the gate, swinging her hips like a model.

'This is how they walk down the King's Road,' she said, and

she turned back and did it again; and she looked about eighteen years old to me then: like a young woman who knew all the answers.

When they'd gone we went to sit in the sitting room. Phillip, Katherine and I pushed past each other to be the first ones in, and clambered up over the chair where Mike was sitting, slumped behind his paper, and squeezed ourselves up behind him on to the windowsill. We sat like that for the rest of the afternoon, slipping and sliding around on the gloss-painted wood, where we'd eat a free-form meal, grazing our way through never-ending nibbles brought to us on saucers: tiny cubes of orange cheese and then crackers, and then perhaps some cheese again, cut up this time in sticks, delivered to us by Olive with a 'yoo hoo!' and a wave.

We had sweets for pudding, and we took them upstairs – Olive didn't mind, she was nice like that – so we moved window-sills to the glossy pale blue one in Phillip's bedroom, where we crunched for a while in companionable silence, splintering the sweets between our teeth, as we looked out over Colwyn's fields, at the river glinting through the alders, and past it, down the valley, the slate roofs of the houses in the village – our village.

'See that land there? All that there in front, that's mine, that is,' Phillip announced.

'I don't think it is,' said my sister, glancing at me for reassurance.

'Yep. Mine,' he said. 'My dad bought it. All them fields there that you can see. He's going to build a water park there in that field. A massive one. Next year, though. You won't see it, you'll be gone, won't you?'

'We might not be, you never know,' said my sister, casting a hopeful glance towards the fields.

'But you are, though, I know you are,' Phillip said. 'What about me then? What will I do?' he asked, spit flying from his mouth.

'You could come with us?' I said, a ridiculous suggestion, met with a glare.

'You could finish off the swimming pool,' my sister told him. 'If you dug just a couple more inches down you'd be ready to lay the tiles.'

'Why? What's the point? *I can't swim, can I?*' he said, stabbing a finger in her direction, as if it was her fault he was scared of water. He clambered down to the floor and stood up square to us, bare-legged, two big pressure marks from the windowsill on his knees, round and red and big as apples.

'I don't need a swimming pool now, do I? Not with a water park over the road,' he said. His socks were inside out and trailing in points way beyond his toes, doubling the size of his feet.

Phillip needed his time without his trousers on – it did him good to come out of his shell, that's what Olive said, as if he were a cripplingly shy tortoise. I had a sudden sick-making thought of Phillip standing just like this, here in his bedroom, fully himself, hand on hip, in his dearly beloved red Y-fronts with the contrasting royal blue trim, but with the new children – the imaginary future next-door neighbours – happily coming out of his shell with them as well.

'*I'll fill it in,*' he said, jutting his chin towards my sister.

'But you can't,' she said, whipping her hand over her open mouth. 'What about all that work we put in?' Instant tears rolled down her cheeks.

He'd intended to hurt her; he wanted to try it out at least, but when he saw that he'd done it, and easily too, he looked like

Phillip again, and his eyes bulged with panic as he clambered over his Superman duvet to squeeze her shoulders just slightly uncomfortably too tight. 'Make your mam change her mind. You could if you tried, you know,' he said.

It took months for my parents to find the house – a great stretch of limbo-filled time – the power of prayer, or my mother being impossible to please, depending on whether you believed my sister or my father.

We were moving to England, they told us, hundreds of miles away to Gloucestershire, which sounded like a miserable place to me: damp and mouldering, somewhere where it rained night and day, with Doctor Foster-sized puddles to drown in.

Matthew Martin told me that his new girlfriend had been to Gloucestershire on a camping holiday and she reckoned it was a 'stonking' place, and I had no idea what that meant, whether it was a good or a bad thing, so I'd just nodded and hoped that was enough, and wondered why he couldn't tell that I didn't care what his girlfriend thought about anything. We'd been sitting on the bottom step of our stairs playing Pac-Man together, while our parents enjoyed a raucous-sounding farewell supper in the kitchen. Matthew couldn't get the hang of the controls and didn't seem to care too much for it either, so I was happily thrashing him, while we listened in through the beeps. Anthony made toast after toast to us, and my mother cried and laughed at the same time to every one of them. Changes were afoot for the Martins too; Anthony announced then that he was opening up a factory on the outskirts of town. He had big plans. Before too long he'd be a manufacturer and nationwide supplier of health food. Wales first, he said, then England, and world domination after that.

*

Lisa cried when I told her we were leaving; her face crumpled up like a paper bag and it didn't look like her face at all. In eight years I'd never seen her upset, and I struggled to know what to say. I patted her hand, and handed her some loo roll for her nose. I'd come back and see her, I said, and she betted I wouldn't. I'd not bother, she said, in between hiccups; why would I bother? I'd forget her, that's what I'd do. She *hated* school, she said, pausing to let out a sob. If I was leaving, then she would too, she'd go to Bala instead.

'But I thought you said it was cach!'

'I never did,' she said. 'I said *Gloucestershire's* cach: not Bala.'

We left in the boot of my father's white Volvo, my sister and I, squeezed in between the cardboard boxes filled with my parents' record collection. I lay down and curled up – deliberately with my back to the house – facing my silent sister and the box with the Rolling Stones albums. The top half of Mick Jagger's face stared back at me, and he looked insolent, and entirely unmoved.

I dug my hand into my jeans pocket and pulled out the loo-roll-wrapped lump that jutted into my hip – Sara Fiddick's parting gift, shoved into my hand yesterday, when my mother had driven us over there to say our goodbyes.

'Right. There you go – this is for you, this is,' she'd said. 'See you then.' Like she'd be seeing me tomorrow instead of maybe never again, and then she'd run off down the path, through the grass towards the orchard, without even a backward glance. She paused for a second, which made me think she was going to turn around and run back and hug me, but she just shouted out hoarsely, 'Nev, Aled? Where are you then?'

'By here!' yelled Nev.

'Wait for us, will you?' she shouted. 'I'll be there now in a min.'

And she was gone. She'd slipped off between the trees, and I'd not even thanked her, or unwrapped it – though I knew exactly what it was; I could tell from the weight and the size of it, I could feel its knobbly eye through the loo roll. It was Eirian's glass baby deer.

I shut my eyes tight as the car made its stately departure, stones crackling under the wheels. We heaved right for the last time, around the corner, bouncing in and out of potholes, the familiar pitted landscape of our road. I could tell where we were, always, even with my eyes closed. We dipped into the biggest one – crater-like – just before Phillip's house, and the wheels skidded, whirred around without purchase, spitting out gravel. Phillip told us once that a meteor had landed there in the middle of the night, that's what made the hole, he said; he'd seen it landing from his bedroom window, crashing into the tarmac, glowing green and full of tiny aliens. They'd all jumped out, and when they'd seen him looking they'd run into the rhododendrons at the bottom of our garden. Listen out for them, he'd said, they're still there, I reckon. I squeezed my eyes tighter shut again when I heard Olive whooping out her goodbyes, higher and higher until her 'ta-taas' became one long, excitable squeal over my father's pip-pipping of the horn.

The car tipped down the last steep part, brakes gently squeaking as we entered the dark canopy of trees, and there was the obligatory pause – the check for non-existent traffic – before we swung a sharp right into daylight, and my mother turned to look at me and smiled. I unwound the loo roll until the glass deer tumbled out, landing upright on its spindly legs on my palm. In Eirian's mahogany display cabinet it had looked brown, the colour of an actual baby deer; but it was pale pink now – the colour of the skin on my hand, the lines of my palm magnified through its clear glass body.

Outside, I could see the river Dee glittering in the distance. There was a river where we were going – that's what my mother said – just a few minutes' walk from the front door. She'd shown me the photograph, and I'd turned the other way. I leant my head against the window now, and tried to cement that half a second glimpse of our new house – lock it into my mind – as my father went up a gear, and then another; and then we were travelling fast, driving down the empty road, straight on, and out of Wales.

Acknowledgements

I'm hugely indebted to Julia Gregson; without all her encouragement and advice over the years on our riverside walks I'm not sure I would have started writing in the first place.

Thank you to my parents. My mother's feedback in particular was invaluable: 'Celery! In the summer! Don't be ridiculous, it wasn't in season then!' Thank you also to my sister for her enthusiasm and good grace; I'm sure she remembers it all entirely differently. I'm mightily grateful to my husband Dickie for reading and re-reading and for all his stellar, unfluffy feedback. To my children, Louis and Alice, whose constant refrain was '*When are you going to be finished?*' There we are, it's done! I promised Louis that I would tell everyone that he wrote most of the book while I sat on the sofa eating cake, and you are most welcome to believe that.

Extra-special couldn't-have-done-it-without-you thanks to Gilly Macmillan, my trusted writing partner and friend; to Caroline Sutton, who is family to me; and to Chris Wakling, my clever, funny friend over the road.

Thanks to all my early readers: Emily Heard, Jules Macmillan, Vix Milne, John Miller, Catherine Naughton, Diane Pitt and Matthew Turner; and to everyone in my writing group.

Writing is a solitary pursuit and I'm pretty bad at solitary, so thank you to my remarkable, funny, life-enhancing girlfriends for all the nonsense and the coffee and the laughs.

I'm very lucky to have found my agent, the extraordinary Kate Hordern, and my editor too: the one-woman human dynamo that is Susanna Wadeson – thank you. To the enthusiastic team at Transworld, including Brenda Updegraff, Katrina Whone, Kate Samano, Bella Whittington, Lizzy Goudsmit, Phil Lord, Claire Ward, Geraldine Ellison and Alison Barrow: I'm very grateful to you all, it's been proper lovely.

Finally to all my friends who I grew up with in North Wales: thank you for making my childhood such a rich and happy one; and to 'Matthew Martin', of course, the original Hippy Dinners.

Abbie Ross moved from London to North Wales when she was two years old and lived there until she was twelve, when her family moved to West Gloucestershire. She has a degree in psychology from Cardiff University and worked for Aardman Animations as a senior commercial producer. She lives in Bristol with her husband and children and is working on a novel.